Gay Men
and Anal Eroticism
Tops, Bottoms, and Versatiles

Gay Men
and Anal Eroticism
Tops, Bottoms, and Versatiles

Steven G. Underwood

Harrington Park Press®
An Imprint of The Haworth Press, Inc.
New York • London • Oxford

Published by

Harrington Park Press®, an imprint of The Haworth Press, Inc., 10 Alice Street, Binghamton, NY 13904-1580.

PUBLISHER'S NOTE
Identities and circumstances of individuals discussed in this book have been changed to protect confidentiality.

Section illustrations by John Andert, an artist and illustrator who lives in Provincetown, Massachusetts.

Cover design by Marylouise E. Doyle.

Cover photo by Mark Lynch.

Library of Congress Cataloging-in-Publication Data

Underwood, Steven G. (Steven Gregory), 1958-
    Gay men and anal eroticism : tops, bottoms, and versatiles / Steven G. Underwood.
       p. cm.
    Includes bibliographical references.
    ISBN 1-56023-374-5 (hard : alk. paper)—ISBN 1-56023-375-3 (soft : alk. paper)
    1. Gay men—Sexual behavior. 2. Anal sex. 3. Anus (Psychology) 4. Dominance (Psychology).
5. Gay men—Identity. 6. Gay men—United States—Interviews. I. Title.

HQ76 .U53 2003
306.77'3—dc21

                                                                              2002068851

My thanks go to
John Andert, Nilüfer Isvan, Eric Rofes, and Susan Seligson
for their help and generous support.

ABOUT THE AUTHOR

Steven G. Underwood is a freelance writer who lives in Province-town, Massachusetts.

CONTENTS

Introduction

Is it a Natural Thing?

Introduction: Is It a Natural Thing?

I was twenty-one years old when I came out to my parents. The following night my father, who seemed to have taken the news surprisingly well, came home late and dead drunk. Reeking of alcohol and cigarettes, he staggered up to me and blurted out the most appalling question imaginable: "So, do you take it up the ass? Is that what you *faggots* do?"

I stood there baffled and unable to utter a single word in my defense. If I'd said no, he'd have known it was a lie. And if I'd said yes? . . . Well, that was unthinkable. A moment later, his eyes bulging with rage, he was advancing toward me with the sharpest kitchen knife in the house.

I honestly don't remember how I got myself out of that mess. Either I got lucky or I did something brilliant to save my ass. I remember lying awake most of the night and getting up early the next morning to catch a bus out of town. Distance and time settled things down and my father and I eventually became better friends. He left me with a slew of memories to contend with when he died of lung cancer a couple of years ago. The memory of that night is the one that haunts me the most.

Like many other gay men, I avoided talking or even thinking about anal sex most of my life. I engaged in it occasionally but always felt that there was something shameful and embarrassing about it. As an adolescent I pitied men who got fucked as I speculated that their real desire was to be women.

I started experimenting with a boy in the neighborhood when I reached puberty. After we'd done the usual feeling each other up, licking and jacking each other's cocks, we decided it was time to see what fucking would feel like. We made a peculiar deal. One of us would lie face down on the bed, allowing the other to mount him; the bottom boy would be under no obligation to comply or to facilitate penetration. In fact, he was expected to squeeze his butt as hard as possible to resist it. He'd also keep an eye on his watch to make sure that the fucker got his business done in under two minutes. I was the first one to top. There was no lube involved and try as I might, I couldn't even begin to invade that tight butt hole of his. Soon my time was up; I relinquished and handed him the reins. Smart boy that he was, he got off the bed, marched to the bathroom, and lathered his cock with soap. He returned and aimed at my virgin hole while I tried, as best I could, to conceal how aroused I truly was. He started to push, not gently, and a moment later I was in the throes of the most intense pain I'd ever experienced in my twelve years. I pushed him off of me and, as one of the guys interviewed for this book says about his own first anal sex experience, "that was that." I wouldn't let a dick get that close to my asshole again for eight years.

Thankfully, gay men don't abide by the general (and boring) heterosexual assumption that sex is not sex unless it involves some form of genital fucking. We take pride in our sexual creativity. Sucking, licking, frottage, and mutual masturbation—a mere fraction of the rich repertoire gay men habitually indulge in—have been the highlights of many a sexual encounter in my life. Although butt-fucking is not as commonly practiced as sucking or jacking off, it's still very popular. Roughly three-fourths of gay men have anal sex at one time or another in their lives, with an equal percentage participating as tops and bottoms.[1] A survey published in *The Advocate* in 1994 indicates that 46 percent of gay men "love" to fuck, while 43 percent "love" taking it up the ass.[2] This, in spite of the fact that anal sexuality is one of the most persistent social taboos we must contend with every day.

In the only book currently on the market that deals with anal sex in an unflinching manner, *Anal Pleasure and Health: A Guide for Men and Women,* Jack Morin, PhD, examines why anal sex (both homosexual and heterosexual) is such a taboo all over the world. First, negative attitudes toward the anal area have to do with concerns of cleanliness.[3] We're fascinated by our asshole and feces as infants. Not surprisingly, our parents and other responsible adults discourage us from fingering our asshole in public, spreading fecal matter all over the living room, or confusing it with an afternoon snack. No matter how gentle this chiding may be, however, it still creates in us an estrangement from the anal area and a general discomfort with our bodies. Physically and psychologically remote and unacknowledged, our asshole becomes a symbol of all that is dirty and revolting. These opposing dynamics of attraction versus revulsion send us into that thorny but all too familiar place where we deny ourselves pleasure and feel guilty when we experience it.

Just as insidious a role in making anal sex such a powerful taboo is its relation to homophobia. Byrne Fone writes that homophobia stems from the assumption that homosexuality disrupts the gender roles supposedly established by the Bible or "natural law." [4] That version of heterosexuality exists on the narrow assumption that women are penetrable and men are definitely not. The idea of a man getting fucked is so threatening to the homophobic male's masculine identity that it can send him reeling into pure disgust or murderous rage. It denotes that the male body, of which he too is in possession, is capable of getting fucked. He'd just rather not know about that, thank you very much. In an attempt at uncompromising manliness, he's banished one of his most sensitive erogenous zones to where, sadly, no one will ever touch or acknowledge it.

The idea of a man getting fucked generates a universally strong emotional response. Not surprisingly, bottoms are judged on an entirely separate scale than tops. They're more severely stigmatized because getting ass-fucked, similar to a woman having vaginal intercourse, is considered feminizing and shameful.[5] The consequences of such stigma vary from culture to culture: a guy who's found out to have been fucked may lose his job in Boston or merely be ridiculed in Paris. But there are still areas in the world where he might have his genitals or head lopped off.

The anal taboo lurks everywhere. Twenty-five states still have sodomy laws on the books, with five of them specifically banning only homosexual acts.[6] Although attitudes are steadily shifting, some medical practitioners are still under the influence of anal phobia. Even some proctologists (the doctors who specialize in anal and rectal health) are reluctant to acknowledge that the anus has an erotic potential.[7] When I set out to gather information for this book I was frustrated by how difficult it was to find any research material on male anal sex. The only statistics I came across exclusively concerned HIV safety. It appears that as far as the medical establishment is concerned, male fucking didn't even exist before the onset of AIDS. Homosexuality may be more visible nowadays, but most people, including some in the helping professions, would still rather not know what gay men actually do when they have sex.

The message that anal sex is repulsive, unnatural, and unlawful is deliberately and subliminally hammered into us all of our lives. Every time we fuck the message that we're doing something illegal and perverse echoes in our consciousness. The chilling effect this kind of bombast has on our self-esteem and behavior is all but inevitable. In spite of that, we still continue to fuck. In fact, this unrelenting admonition often makes anal intercourse an even more irresistible activity. It certainly contributes to the formation of the rich variety of meanings we attach to butt-fucking.

My interest in writing about male fucking evolved over several years. One distinct experience—during an evening at the theatre—triggered a series of thoughts that would eventually prod me toward accumulating a complete manuscript. I was attending the performance of a rather mediocre play in New York City about the lifelong relationship of two gay men, spanning from their first meeting in a park right before World War II until the present, when they're in their seventies. In a rather inventive device, the playwright had decided to have two sets of actors portray the younger and older men. The title of the play and the names of the characters escape me, but I remember the story line very well.

After the performance ended, an older gentleman, Bob, began to chat with me. He said he was puzzled by the suggestion that one of the men was the bottom early on in the relationship, but seemed to take the top role when the men got older.

The earlier story did not spell out the characters' preferences in sex. One of the guys was older than the other, sexually more experienced, and came from a wealthier family. He was also more assertive, independent, and remote. He was reluctant to commit to a homosexual relationship while his partner, more innocent and deeply infatuated, was pressing for them to live together as a couple. Bob had concluded from all of this that the older guy was the top and the younger one the bottom.

In later life, however, in an explicit scene between the older men, the younger of the two clearly fucks the other guy. This did not strike me as odd while I was watching the play. To me it seemed perfectly natural that the men should fuck or get fucked according to their mood or the circumstances. I didn't feel that one man or the other should be exclusively the top or the bottom. The power discrepancy, apparent when the guys were younger, did not define the sexual relationship in my mind. "Do you think men can switch those roles over the years?" Bob asked. I was taken aback by the question and had no good answer. I made a smart-ass remark to the effect that gay men "had, by now, left those archaic, hetero-based roles behind." He smiled graciously, moved on to talk to people who were presumably more balanced, and I felt like an idiot. I knew I couldn't entirely dismiss the question. Days later, I was still thinking about it.

Had I been naïve to think that men were generally versatile; that the top and bottom roles were interchangeable? I knew from personal experience that this was not true for many. I realized I was resisting the notion that many men identified themselves according to those preferences and that they held fast to these roles for one reason or another. So was my own assertion about being versatile an honest one or did I in fact have a heavier inclination toward one role or the other? The narrator in Andrew Holleran's short story "The Stain on the Other Man's Pants" says that when he was a young man he thought that all gay men were bottoms.[8] I wanted to know what other men thought about these questions.

I posted my first notice to recruit "tops, bottoms, and versatiles" at the local grocery store in Provincetown, where I live. When I got back home the phone was already ringing. My first interview, also my most awkward, was with James, the following day at noon. My desire to appear professional and his overt wish to turn our meeting into a sexual encounter posed considerable obstacles for us at first. But once we overcame them, we had what ultimately turned out to be one of the most revealing conversations printed in this book.

Encouraged by the success of my first interview, I posted more notices: on the Internet and at a couple of gay bookstores in Boston. Men immediately began to contact me over e-mail and the phone. I was delighted by the interest the mere idea of a book about male anal sex was generating. It quickly became obvious that gay men had a definite need to discuss this issue.

Male fucking is an endlessly complex issue. It's impossible to address all the psychological, philosophical, and medical dimensions of the subject here. I hope, however, to at least touch on some central issues and to pose some relevant questions. I must give credit to two studies and one book about male fucking that helped me to sort out my thoughts. The first study was done in 1998 with seventy-one Dutch gay and bisexual men. It analyzes the structure and meaning of anal sex among men in the era of AIDS.[9] The second study, published in 2000, explores the top/bottom self-label, anal sex, and HIV risk in gay men in New York City.[10] In his book *Practicing Desire: Homosexual Sex in the Era of AIDS,* Australian social scientist Gary W. Dowsett explores the meaning of anal sex as the symbolic center of gay male identity.[11] His work yields valuable insights. All three writings set out to analyze how the meanings of anal sex affect safe-sex practices.

The Dutch study explores the complex set of meanings gay men assign to fucking, using a frame of scenarios. Four specific scenarios—the physical, the intimate, the power, and the reciprocal—all consistent with what interviews in this book also suggest, emerge from the study.

The physical scenario is the one we engage in most commonly. Most of us, at one time or another, like to screw purely for the sake of sensual pleasure. The asshole is loaded with nerve endings and is extremely sensitive to erotic stimulation. The initial moment of penetration when the cock head breaks through the sphincter; the rubbing of the penis against the bottom's prostate during the actual fucking; the contraction of the rectum around the penis; these are the highlights of a memorable fuck session for both partners. The internal stimulation can be so intense that some bottoms, like Lenny, are able to cum without even touching their dicks. Many men agree that fucking is physically more fulfilling than any other sexual activity. The decision to top or bottom sometimes depends on pure sensory preference. Whether that preference is genetically based or socially formed is an endless source of discussion among scientists and social thinkers.

The intimate scenario is about the emotional satisfaction gay men derive from anal intercourse. Many consider fucking a deeply personal and exhilarating experience—way more intimate than sucking and jerking off. Some even talk about it in mystical terms: Lito says it's a "higher level of communication." Trust plays a crucial role in the intimate scenario. Bottoms who consider getting fucked a vulnerable act are reluctant to engage in anal sex unless they've established a level of trust with their partners. If trust is not present, Kevin has trouble relaxing and being penetrated becomes difficult and painful. Earning Kevin's trust becomes, in a sense, a test the top must pass.

Tops, on the other hand, value the exchange of trust because it gives them a sense of gaining physical and psychological entry into a sacred place. The biggest turn-on for Tom is the trust a man invests in him to allow getting fucked. His partner's vulnerability becomes a symbol of Tom's own benevolence.

Whether it's a lifelong commitment or a quick one behind the bush, we all assert or withhold power in relationships. Every decision (will you suck me first or will I suck you?) brings about a negotiation. The power scenario involves the complex interplay of dominance and submission where the opposing roles are emphasized, even magnified. Fucking and getting fucked traditionally symbolize opposite poles of the power spectrum: getting fucked is considered the ultimate act of submission while fucking someone is viewed as taking control and dominating them. In S&M and B&D one partner takes the submissive role while the other (or others) takes the dominant role. The power scenario evolves around specific boundaries the men set for themselves at the outset; the permission of the submissive guy is essential.[12] It plays out as a ritualized test of trust, submission, and power.

The reciprocal scenario, where both men take turns fucking each other, is often exercised as a celebration of equality. What sets this scenario apart from the others is the versatility of the men involved. Versatility is a unique and important feature of male anal sex.[13] Some men consider it liberating; they enjoy the freedom the male body offers to alternately fuck and get fucked. Versatility to them is akin to speaking two different languages. It requires a special kind of playfulness, creativity, curiosity, and coordination. Not all men are comfortable with versatility, however. Those who prefer to stick to one role or the other regard it as an annoying, sometimes even frustrating, complication.

History tell us that versatility in male fucking has always been, at least until recently, a rare, if at all, notable phenomenon. Starting with the ancient Greeks, from whom we get our first accounts of male anal sex, men fucked men according to status and age stratification. The Greeks thought that the love between an older man and a younger one was honorable and pure as long as the older man was the top. In fact, such a relationship was considered essential to a young man's growth and education. It was also acceptable for a guy from a higher class to fuck a slave or a man with lower status, but if a wealthy and powerful adult male was found out to have been fucked, he'd be the subject of scandal and be in danger of losing his social position. What made a sexual act acceptable for the Greeks was not the sex of the partners involved, but rather whether they performed the roles determined by the power balance between them.[14]

The Greeks were intolerant of effeminacy and passivity in men. Boys who behaved effeminately or who continued to get fucked as they aged were suspected and shunned. "Most discussion of appropriate sexual conduct in ancient texts," writes Byrne Fone, "had as its subtext the seemingly unbridgeable distance between masculinity and effeminacy, between being sexually active and sexually passive, not the difference between homosexuality or heterosexuality."[15]

The notion that tops and bottoms are socially and morally unequal creatures has been the overriding assumption about male fucking throughout history. That version of homosexuality was accepted in ancient Greece, Rome, and Egypt. It was condemned, but still prevalent in Europe through the Middle Ages, the Renaissance, and the Age of Enlightenment. Even as late as early twentieth-century New York, gay men operated underground as either the limp-wristed fairies or the masculine "trade" that the fairies pursued.[16] Today, in a predominantly Islamic but westernized country such as Turkey, men who are "active" in homosexual encounters are often not considered homosexual at all. Instead, their domination of passive men is considered evidence of their hyper-masculinity.[17] In El Salvador, as Lito reports, being fucked is considered a "kind of degeneration," while the top is "just being a man." Bottoms are still stigmatized all over the world, including isolated pockets in the West (such as prisons), while tops are viewed as exercising their male prerogative.

The Western view about role separation in male fucking began to shift in the middle of the last century, in the 1960s and 1970s. The seeds of that change were planted several decades earlier, by a few turn-of-the-century authors—Karl Ulrichs, John Addington Symonds, Edward Carpenter, and Havelock Ellis—who were the first to launch a movement toward the "normalization" of homosexuality. These writers portrayed gay men as ordinary, normal citizens (not prisoners or inmates in an asylum), no different from everyone else except for their attraction to their own sex. Havelock Ellis's *Sexual Inversion* began the first heated discussion over sexuality in a society that was just emerging from the morally oppressive Victorian era.[18]

This effort was thwarted by the followers of Freud who, by emphasizing early childhood traumas as its explanation, categorized homosexuality as a clinical abnormality.[19] Normalization was brought to the forefront once again in 1948 by Alfred Kinsey and his *Sexual Behavior in the Human Male*.[20] Kinsey's assertion that homosexuality was common and that it should not be considered a crime against nature was met with great resistance in the scientific community.[21] Thirty more years would pass before the American Psychiatric Association would finally remove homosexuality from its list of mental disorders.

By this time a gay liberation movement was under way and the existence of homosexuals was taken for granted. Gay men began to regard the separation of top and bottom roles as a mimicry of heterosexual functions and a form of self-oppression.[22] In his essay, published in 1970, "Refugees from Amerika: A Gay Manifesto," Carl Wittman listed four statements he considers antigay perversions:

- I like to make it with straight guys.
- I'm not gay but I like to be "done."
- I like to fuck but I don't want to be fucked.
- I don't like to be touched above the neck.

"This," wrote Wittman, "is role playing at its worst; we must transcend these roles. We strive for *democratic, mutual, reciprocal sex*."[23] In a radical reinvention of their own image, large numbers of gay men abandoned the stereotype of the limp-wristed fairy as a relic of an oppressive past. They began to have sex with each other instead of trade. They effectively transformed themselves to become the masculine men they'd always desired to have sex with.

More than three decades after Wittman's declaration, the effort to understand the meaning of "democratic, mutual, reciprocal sex" continues. All of the men in this book, including myself, are engaged in that quest. The overriding theme that emerges from these interviews is that equality in man-to-man sex is as varied as the number of individuals who strive for it.

Are versatility and normalization intrinsic to each other? It certainly appears so. An acceptance of homosexuality as normal also means an acceptance of bottoming under the same terms. Fourteen of the twenty-three men represented here identify themselves as versatile. The remaining nine who say they're strictly tops (four) or strictly bottoms (five) have only reached that certainty after trying, or at least considering, the alternative. In a sense the notion of versatility expands beyond the perfunctory act of fucking; it resides in the mind. Whether they engage in both or not, gay men today consider both fucking and getting fucked as normal possibilities for sexual enjoyment in a way most heterosexual guys never do. The existence of that choice is at the core of the definition of versatility.

Once they've decided to have anal sex, gay men must decide who will top and who will bottom (or who will top and who will bottom *first*). Some guys eliminate this negotiation altogether by letting it be known that they're inflexible. Some are flexible enough to go along with their partners' preferences. Others, like Richard, view the question as a mystery or an adventure. They enjoy it as an aspect of seduction and sex play and prefer to let things evolve as they will. Some people think of this choice as liberating while others consider it a burden and inconvenience. Sometimes, it's easier to let outside circumstances or the physical characteristics of the partners determine the outcome of this negotiation.

The balance of power is an undeniable aspect of any relationship. Many personal characteristics—physical attractiveness, wealth, social dexterity, sexual confidence, penis size, age, and race, to name a few—often symbolize power positions. In anal sex, these symbols often serve as the deciding factor in which partner will bottom and which will top. Penis size often plays a role in whether a man will be perceived as a top or a bottom. I was curious to find out if the stereotype of the size queen held up. I asked the guys I interviewed if dick size in a partner mattered to them. Most replied that it did not. Many said that they avoided getting fucked by a big dick because it caused them physical pain. Still, it's generally believed that men are stimulated to get fucked when they encounter a partner with a large dick. In porn flicks, the guy with the bigger cock is almost inevitably the one who does the fucking.

Although some of us consider them outdated, many of us still use these power symbols to conjecture a man's sexual preference. When one of the waiters I worked with several years ago met my partner John for the first time, he pulled me aside and said: "I bet he throws you across the bed and fucks you silly." It's no surprise that people assume John's the top and I'm the bottom. He's taller than me, physically much stronger, and has a very built, hot body. But his physical appearance is no indication of what we do in sex. In fact, I was first drawn to him nineteen years ago (I'm forty-three, he's forty-two) partially because of his contrasting characteristics: a manly guy who's also the most gentle, sensitive, and mild-mannered person I'd met.

Although Andy says that the stereotype of the effeminate bottom is "bogus, bogus, bogus," he insists that men still display telltale signs (which he claims he can decode through his fascinating, if not convoluted, system) that give away their preferences.

Being penetrated still symbolizes a lack of power. For some men, emphasizing their vulnerability can be freeing. It liberates them from bearing responsibility for what happens and allows them to enjoy the forbidden pleasures without the guilt. But for others being dominated is difficult. Payne says getting fucked compromises his masculinity and makes it difficult for him to reconcile his view of himself. For Sam, being a bottom is a demeaning, all encompassing state of mind. He says it transforms him into something "all the way from my feet to the top of my head." Helpless against his urge to service men, he's constantly on the lookout for sex. He knows all too well that it will only leave him with near suicidal feelings of guilt and self-contempt.

We've been conditioned to think that tops and bottoms fit into opposing roles: controlling versus controlled; active versus passive; pursuer versus pursued; older versus younger; masculine versus feminine; rich versus poor—well, you get the picture. These dichotomies are the products of a misogynistic tradition. They all imply a gender gap: the female is weak and passive; she's needy and subservient; male is superior to female. Even the terms top and bottom (everything on top is superior to everything on the bottom), active and passive (obviously), insertive and receptive (one is active, the other is not), all imply a status discrepancy. Nowadays, many men don't consider getting fucked a passive act. "The desiring anus is not passive," writes Dowsett. "A man's desiring anus knows something remarkable about pleasure. Any man who has taken another man's cock up his ass knows all too well that sex will never be the same again."[24] There's no active language to describe the act of getting fucked. One writer, Mitch Walker, charmingly, but inadequately, terms the partners in anal sex as the "ass person" and the "penis person."[25] Our perception of male fucking is muddled by stereotypes, preconceived notions, exaggerated scenarios (which we get from porn flicks, books, and magazines), and the inadequacy of the language we use to address this issue.

Nevertheless, words are just words and can easily be replaced, just as concepts and notions can be twisted and redefined. Eric Rofes writes about his own realization that "erotic desires and practices are not inbred genetic qualities, but are constantly reinvented and turned on their heads through complex social and cultural processes."[26] We're increasingly coming to understand that power symbols are not carved in stone. Flipping them around can be as much a part of the joy of anal sex as conforming to them. For Aaron, getting a top to submit to his desires is empowering. He defies the stereotype of the passive bottom by challenging tops "who can handle it" to meet him as an equal. When porn star Cole Tucker bottoms on screen, everything he does or says ("Yeah boy, shove that cock up my ass!") projects the attitude of an aggressive top. He says his audience, who is heavily invested in him as a cigar-chomping leather top, is not even cognizant of the fact that he's actually getting fucked.

Equality in sex or in a relationship is never static. Power roles shift, dominance and submission are twisted around. The bottom can be butch and aggressive, the top can be passive and submissive. Dominance in certain areas in the relationship, including the sexual, are counterbalanced by dominance elsewhere. Equality is a dynamic and symmetrical exchange of power roles and is only achieved through mutual acceptance and respect, which are, in a global sense, the central principles of democracy. According to Jay Mohr, "Equality is the ideal, male homosexuality its model, and democracy the realization of the ideal in practice."[27]

Normalization means coming to terms with our feminine aspects. As children, many of us are taunted by peers for being nonathletic, feminine, too weak, or too thin. It takes us years to get over the constant torment of being chided for who we are. Accepting our feminine side can be a long and arduous process. As we grow increasingly comfortable with the notion that we can be masculine as well as feminine, that male and female are not necessarily opposites but can coexist in playful harmony, we come to see ourselves as healthy, well-adjusted, creative, normal men. Some of us use versatility as an expression of the male and female aspects of our personalities.

Normalization means getting over feeling guilty for having sex, especially anal sex. "We're being held prisoners for fucking," announces Eddie. "If we admitted to the cardinal, 'Sure we fuck each other,' if we got organized and said, 'Yes, Mommy, we fuck, yes, Daddy, we fuck,' if we can get past that, we can take on anyone and we'll be fine."

One of the questions I asked each of the men was whether they thought anal sex was natural; whether the creative force, were it God or nature, made the male body to get fucked. Most men were taken aback by the question. They'd never thought about it before. Some said it was comparable to oral sex: it wasn't really natural, but "everyone does it anyway." Others considered the question for a while and concluded that, yes, anal sex is natural. "God would not have given us the ability to fuck if he didn't want us to experience it," said Jackson. "Anything that feels so good and is such a higher level of sharing," said Lito, "is definitely natural." The more we accept getting butt-fucked as a natural function of the body and the more openly and unashamedly we're able to talk about it, the closer we come to normalization, to equality, to self-respect, and to higher self-esteem.

A discussion of the normalization of homosexuality inevitably brings about the age-old question of nature versus nurture: Do you think you were born gay? Although I agree that the question itself is irrelevant (why don't we ask people why they're heterosexual?), I was curious to know whether top guys had a different take on the subject than bottoms. Almost all of the men I interviewed said that they had homosexual feelings very early in life and that they were definitely born gay. One guy, Andy, didn't have any sexual feelings until he was nineteen, but even he thought that his homosexuality was genetic. Some men agreed that the environment may have had some effect on their sexuality, but that they were already genetically inclined to be homosexual.

It's impossible to avoid addressing the AIDS epidemic and its repercussions in any discussion about sexuality. I got a variety of answers to my question about safe-sex practices. Although most have adopted safer sex ("No matter how safe you are," says Cole Tucker, "there is always an element of risk") as an intrinsic aspect of their sexualities, there's no doubt that it represents a significant loss for gay men.[28] Condoms are regarded as a hindrance to bodily pleasure and to emotional closeness. AIDS has altered the negotiations around anal sex (or any sex) and has brought on additional layers of meaning. Caution and distrust around sex and potential partners have become a daily routine. We live in a state of tension between a desire to remain healthy and a genuine need to experience intimacy and physical pleasure. Men react to this tension in different ways: some have adopted safety as an unquestionable aspect of their sexuality while others compromise safety for a variety of reasons.

Some studies suggest that closeted behavior linked with guilt and shame may be negatively associated with safer-sex practices.[29] Men who are not open with themselves and with others about being bottoms are often less prepared to have safer sex. They may put themselves at risk of infection more frequently than men who are comfortable about getting fucked. Aaron and Sam are good examples of these two extremes. Aaron is young, optimistic, and completely at peace with bottoming. Safety is not even an issue for him; he doesn't even think about it. At twenty-six, he's never been fucked without a condom. Sam, on the other hand, is depressed and conflicted about bottoming. He says he doesn't like to be fucked with a condom because condoms hurt. He's often inclined to forgo safety, especially if he's been drinking. When a man wants to fuck him raw, Sam finds it hard to say no. Studies suggest that normalizing and validating receptive anal intercourse may facilitate safer sex. The only way to achieve this is to reduce the guilt and shame connected to getting ass-fucked by countering the negative stereotypes associated with it.

The need for safer-sex education to take into account the symbolic meanings of anal sex seems all too obvious. As the AIDS epidemic evolves from a state of panic to become a routine aspect of our lives, we must keep the tension between safer sex and the urge for intimacy and pleasure under consideration.

These interviews were conducted in a relaxed, informal environment. Most of the men who contacted me were either from Provincetown or the Boston area; I didn't have to travel far to meet them. Some of the guys were trusting, ready, and able to meet right away. Others were more cautious. They asked me to explain the project in more detail and to clarify my motivations. Some of them, like James, were probably hoping for a sexual encounter, a possibility that often occurred to me as well. The ones that sounded like the regular Joe, "Aw shucks" kind of guys on the phone would get me going every time. I soon found out, however, that nothing kills a hot fantasy faster than serious talk about sex. As soon as we met and got into the nitty-gritty of the subject, the fantasy rapidly faded away.

Many of these guys had never told anyone how they felt about fucking or getting fucked. They hadn't thought about why they labeled themselves as a top, bottom, or versatile, nor about the effect such labeling had on their self-esteem and the way they relate to their friends, lovers, and tricks. Some, if they had a definite preference, were extremely open about it. Others, although out as gay men, were closeted about being a top or a bottom. They all had strong feelings about the issue and welcomed the opportunity to explore it. They told me about their fears, doubts, joys, and pleasures. They talked about childhood traumas, first-time sexual encounters, loves, desires, and obsessions. They allowed me into the most private regions of their spirits as they unraveled the complex mosaic of their sexualities. At the end, I didn't regret that these meetings didn't turn sexual. They were some of the most intimate moments I've ever spent with other men in my life.

NOTES

1. McWherter, D.P. and Mattison, A.M. (1984). *The Male Couple: How Relationships Develop.* Englewood Cliffs, NJ: Prentice-Hall.

2. Lever, J. (1994). Sex Survey. *The Advocate,* August 23.

3. Morin, J. (1998). *Anal Pleasure and Health: A Guide for Men and Women.* San Francisco, CA: Down There Press.

4. Fone, B. (2000). *Homophobia.* New York: Metropolitan Books, p. 5.

5. Morin, *Anal Pleasure and Health,* p. 18.

6. Ibid., p. 18.

7. Ibid., p. 23.

8. Published in Lowenthal, M. (ed.) (1999). *Obsessed: A Flesh and the Word Collection of Gay Erotic Memoirs.* New York: Plume.

9. de Zwart, O., van Kerkhoff, M.P.N., and Sandfort, T.G.M. (1998). Anal Sex and Gay Men: The Challenge of HIV and Beyond. *Journal of Psychology and Human Sexuality* 10(3/4): 89-102.

10. Wegesin, M.L., Elwood, W.N., and Bowen, A.M. (2000). Top/Bottom Self-Label, Anal Sex Practices, HIV Risk and Gender Role Identity in Gay Men in New York City. *Journal of Psychology and Human Sexuality* 12(3): 43-62.

11. Dowsett, G.W. (1996). *Practicing Desire: Homosexual Sex in the Era of AIDS.* Stanford, CA: Stanford University Press.

12. de Zwart, van Kerkhoff, and Sandfort, Anal Sex and Gay Men, p. 99.

13. Dowsett, *Practicing Desire,* p. 155.

14. Mondimore, F.M. (1996). *A Natural History of Homosexuality.* Baltimore, MD: The Johns Hopkins University Press, p. 8.

15. Fone, *Homophobia,* p. 60.

16. Chauncey, G. (1994). *Gay New York: Gender, Urban Culture, and the Making of the Gay Male World, 1890-1940.* New York: BasicBooks.

17. Tapinc, H. (1992). Masculinity, Femininity, and Turkish Male Homosexuality. In Kenneth Plummer (ed.), *Modern Homosexualities: Fragments of Lesbian and Gay Experiences.* London: Routledge, p. 46.

18. Mondimore, *A Natural History of Homosexuality,* p. 49.

19. Freud himself did not share this opinion. Ibid., p. 75.

20. Kinsey, A., Pomeroy, W., and Martin, C. (1948). *Sexual Behavior in the Human Male.* Philadelphia, PA: W.B. Saunders.

21. Mondimore, *A Natural History of Homosexuality,* p. 86.

22. Rotello, G. (1997). *Sexual Ecology: AIDS and the Destiny of Gay Men.* New York: Penguin Books Ltd., p. 77.

23. Reprinted in Jay, K. and Young, A. (eds.) (1972). *Out of the Closets: Voices of Gay Liberation.* New York: New York University Press, p. 337.

24. Dowsett, *Practicing Desire,* p. 213.

25. Walker, M. (1994). *Men Loving Men: A Gay Sex Guide and Consciousness Book.* San Francisco, CA: Gay Sunshine Press, p. 96.

26. Rofes, E. (1998). *Dry Bones Breathe: Gay Men Creating Post-AIDS Identities and Cultures.* Binghamton, NY: The Haworth Press.

27. Mohr, R.D. (1992). *Gay Ideas: Outing and Other Controversies.* Boston, MA: Beacon Press, p. 197.

28. Dowsett, *Practicing Desire,* p. 279.

29. Wegesin, Elwood, and Bowen, Top/Bottom Self-Label, p. 59, quoting Mosher, D.L. and Vonderheide, S.G. (1985). Contributions of Sex Guilt and Masturbation Guilt to Women's Contraceptive Attitudes and Use. *The Journal of Sex Research* 21(1): 24-39.

Aaron: Labels Exist for a Reason

Bottom, Age 24

I met Aaron at Boston's South Station, a few minutes past five, shortly after he got off work. He's a twenty-four-year-old dynamic man, about five foot eleven inches, lean and angular, with brown hair and hazel eyes. We walk out of the train station together and enter a big, eerily vacant office building across the street. We find a table and chairs in the lobby and settle down to talk.

Aaron realized he was gay and started to "make noise" in his early teens. His mother, his closest friends, and the people at work all knew about his sexuality by the time he was fifteen. Perhaps it's his relatively young age that affords Aaron such strong opinions and such an impassioned attitude. He considers himself an "intellectual," he says, and his eyes sparkle with enthusiasm when he argues a certain point. I can just picture him sitting up until all hours of the night with his buddies, arguing, banging fists, drinking, and finally falling into bed at sunrise for a few hours of sleep before work. He has an erratic, free-associating pattern of speech, and I have to stop him several times to go back and explain what he's talking about. Often, what he says now is in direct conflict with what he said a few minutes earlier. Oblivious to these contradictions, he charmingly rolls right along, spouting out his beliefs and theories. Overall, it's great fun—if not bewildering—to be around his zestful, young, passionate presence.

* * *

I didn't know any gay people when I was in high school. People in my school were unaware of the fact that there might be gay people running around. I didn't even know what it might be like to be friends with a gay person, much less actually get to date another guy. I sort of missed out.

I had my first sexual experience when I went to college at eighteen. For the next four years I learned the gay language, the gay culture. I remember my freshman year thinking, "My God, I lived my whole life in a foreign land and now I'm finally around people who speak my language." It was weird, but great fun.

I slept around with a few guys in college, but my sexual experience was very limited. Just random little gropings and oral stuff. I had certain standards, some personal and physical ideals that I wanted to hold on to. I also had very conflicted ideas about what it meant to be gay. I thought you didn't do certain things until you were with somebody in a committed relationship, blah, blah, blah, anal sex being the biggest. I wasn't going to do that. I *would not* do it. I got such flack for it. I had a major falling out with the leading queers at school because I was reactionary to a lot of the stuff they were spouting off. Of course now, three years later, looking back, I think, "God, we were young." We were so full of those passionate ideas. I had it all figured out. A lot of the guys were so much more sophisticated, so much more liberated. They wanted to be very cutting edge. They had these romantic notions of being sex radicals. [Laughs] It was kinda funny. I went completely one hundred eighty degrees away from that, to the opposite extreme. I was the token Log Cabin Republican, that sort of thing.

When I graduated from college I'd already been out for like six years and I'd had no relationship or dating experience. I dated one guy for a month which barely made a blip on the radar screen. And then I met somebody else and we got very serious very fast. Jeff and I were the same age, but he was much more experienced than I was. He considered himself a top, and I sometimes wonder in retrospect if I've sort of become a bottom in default. We went out for about three months before I would let him fuck me. He was pretty patient and he didn't put any pressure on me one way or the other, but he wanted to do it and I was resisting. I told him I'm sorry and he said it's okay. So after three months we finally did it and I have to admit, I was amazed. It was like, "Holy shit, I missed out on this all this time? What the hell is wrong with me?" It was sort of a revelation. But even after that, while we were still dating, I still held onto a lot of what I now consider puritanical ideas. It was okay to have anal sex with him only because we were in a long-term relationship. We had an extremely rocky relationship and it ended pretty soon, which was all fine and good.

After that I went on a kind of rampage. I don't know how much of that was in reaction to breaking up with Jeff or how much of it was in reaction to the fact that I'd been holding myself to a certain standard. I said to myself, "Jesus Christ, I'm twenty-four years old now, why am I doing this? Obviously I enjoy doing a lot of this stuff physically, why should I sit around waiting for the next pumping candidate to come along?" Those ideals seemed very antiquated at that point. I knew the physical possibilities of getting fucked by this time. I will give Jeff that. He was very good at what he did. I wasn't about to give that up. So I started going out with three or four guys a week. And all of a sudden I'm all the rage, which definitely contributed to me suddenly expanding what I considered acceptable possibilities. If I met somebody who was really cute and he wanted to go home with me, by God, I was going to do it. Part of that was ego stroking and part of it was my wanting to just get over it and have fun. Live a little. So, basically I was racking up a guy a month and it was getting more and more frequent. If they'd all been just one-night stands, I'd have been racking up a lot more, but a lot of them would continue for a few weeks and then they'd be like, "Gotta go." And then I'd be at the club to meet the next best thing that came along and I'd have my fun. I had anal sex with a lot of them.

I've never actually topped anyone, although I'm entertaining the notion that I should try it and see what it's about. I can't remember once thinking about wanting to be a top. It wasn't so much that I said I'm going to be a bottom, it was more that I never contemplated being a top. And as my personality developed, that's the way it worked out. My next boyfriend after Jeff was also very much a top and it wasn't going to happen with him either. He said, "Okay, sure, we'll do it if you want," but the situation would never arise. It felt silly. It wasn't an image of myself that I could realistically see. All of the guys I'd been with were happy to top.

I sort of fell into this image of myself as being a very aggressive bottom, a guy who knew what he wanted and who didn't want any wimps applying. Next thing I knew, people were calling me a pushy bottom. I prefer the term "power bottom," but hey. So that's just the way it went.

Recently, I got into a whole discussion with this guy about the labeling issue. He was saying that you shouldn't label people, and why do you constrain yourself that way. And I was like, "Well, look. Number one: I'm not constraining myself. I'm going with what makes me happy. Number two: It's something that happens. People by their very nature categorize. It's part of human nature to try to make order out of the world. And in a world like ours, I think it's even more reinforced. There's the whole butch and fem thing, top and bottom thing, and the whole idea that you're one or the other. You can argue that it's tied into the heterosexual gender roles, blah, blah, blah, who's going to play the woman and so on and if you want to argue against categorizing on that basis I can see your point."

You cannot say that somebody should not identify something. A label exists for a reason. Now, if it's unfairly applied, like if it's labeled a good or bad thing, that's a different story. But it's okay to say this is the way I see myself, or this is the way this person is, and that's the way I'm going to identify them. What made the whole discussion funny down the road was that guess what: this guy only tops! And I'm like, "How is somebody supposed to describe you?" It all boils down to semantics. If you want to get into some silly game of, you know, anal receptor, anal insertive, then it would get even more ridiculous. What's the point?

He was basically saying that we shouldn't use these terms, because it denotes a certain thing about people. It limits people. And I was saying you've got to have some sort of terminology to describe how people interact with each other in this world, to describe who they are. And we sort of chafed each other around on it. I was saying, "How do you not have the label? How do you not have the category? They're going to exist!"

I think the whole point is kinda moot. It's a lot of smoke and mirrors. Some people make an issue of it because they get very hung up on what those labels can mean. I mean Jeff was very effeminate. And you know, I probably have my moments, but I'm not fem, especially in comparison to him. I remember sitting there one weekend morning and a friend of ours came into the kitchen and it was funny because everyone knew Jeff was the top. And I'm sitting there reading the paper at the kitchen table and he's cooking breakfast. And Mike comes in and he's like, "Okay, you two have your roles screwed up." And we just laughed. Because it's like, who cares?

In an ideal relationship I would probably be the bottom. If I met a guy who really, really wanted to be a bottom too, we'd have to meet each other half way. I'd definitely try it. I have no idea if I would enjoy it. I honestly don't know. I don't see why I wouldn't, but I'd probably miss what makes being a bottom so great.

One of the things that makes being a bottom great is the prostate. That was the thing with Jeffrey. He swore he didn't have a prostate, so getting fucked didn't do anything for him. I find that hard to believe. He'd bottomed on more than one occasion. He'd tried it on a regular basis, but he still found that it didn't do a damn thing for him.

Did you ever see *JFK,* the movie? There's a scene where Kevin Costner, the attorney, goes to interview the Kevin Bacon character. He's sitting there talking to him and asking questions and Kevin Bacon's being very difficult. And Kevin Costner says, "No, you don't seem to understand." And Kevin Bacon says, "No, sir. You've never been fucked up the ass so *you* don't understand." And this was long before, long, long, long before I became a power, pushy bottom, whatever you want to call it. But that stuck in my head as a kind of clubby mentality. "We know something you don't." Guys who've done this know something.

When I was much younger I used to wonder what sex was like for women. This was long before I even thought about the fact that I could find out. I read some things in *Cosmo* and all those women's magazines and various books, where women were describing what it was like. They described it in this very emotional and psychological way. Way beyond pure sensation. The sensation of being "filled up." When it finally happened, and I remember the very first time distinctly, I remember thinking, "Oh shit, this is what it feels like!" And it was with Jeff, who was somebody I cared about deeply. There was an emotional aspect to having someone inside of me. I mean that was pretty phenomenal. All that stuff I'd read sort of came flooding back and I'm like, "Ah, this is what they meant." I have to admit, it's been a long time since I've been with somebody where I was loved and it was an emotional issue. But that was sort of what I was looking for from that point forward. I had that feeling with Jeff, but I really haven't had it since.

With a lot of guys it's a one-time deal. We're just having fun, whatever. It doesn't amount to much. But the power bottom thing became for me this sort of image which is also part of the emotional aspect of the experience. A self image of letting a guy know that I have control. Some guy once told me, "You know, anybody who has any kind of negative attitude about a bottom should just remember, they come in hard but they leave limp." Basically, it means that they pay their tribute. Obviously, the bottom gets off on the physical stimulation, but there's also this kind of haughty, "Show me what you've got. You think you're this big bad boy, you're gonna rock my world, so let's see how good you really are. All I have to do is lie here." Ultimately, the tops are the ones who are on the spot. It's a position of power.

I was in a chat room a week or two ago and ninety percent of the people in there are looking for a hookup. Their profile usually tells you what they are and what they're looking for. Somebody made some kind of comment like, "Look at all these big bad tops." I was being catty at the time, so I typed in, "Oh, yeah, they're just saying they're all macho so you won't pay attention to the fact that they really aren't any good." That got everybody in there cracking up. I mean all the bottoms were all just like howling. And pretty soon the bottoms started to talk like a bunch of women, like, "Mmm-hmmm, he said he was this and that and whatever," tearing up on these guys. And none of the tops were really able to take back the initiative and tell us to shut up or back off. I found that kind of amusing. And sort of, I guess, validating. I mean they obviously couldn't come to their own defense. We're the ones who are more in control.

I do think that most people are either top or bottom. I'm not going to say that it's because they're genetically predisposed to it. I think there are a host of things involved: personality; your first experience; the way other people view you. I'll be in a club and somebody walks by and I'll go, "Oh, my God, what a bottom!" Just sort of base it on the vibes. One time someone asked me, "Well, how do you know?" And I was like, "Watch him dance." If you watch a guy dance, that'll tell you a whole lot about what they are. It doesn't have anything to do with being effeminate. It has to do with the way they move. I guess it's sort of like gaydar. You notice little subtle clues, things that other people are not looking for. People have a certain image of themselves and what they prefer gets projected out, not necessarily because they want people to know.

For me, being a bottom is very much connected to my self-esteem because I'm highly arrogant about it. I have high self-esteem. I know there are people out there who view being a bottom as some sort of humiliating, invasive, belittling type of thing. I don't see it as a passive, feminine thing. But I'm sure there are some guys who would, and they would enjoy that. That's what they want. Some little queeny boy sees himself as being the submissive bottom. Some people put in their profiles, "Submissive bottom." And I'll put something like, "Power bottom looking for tops who can handle it." You should see the responses I get for that.

In one phrase, power bottom means, "Shut up and lie down. I'll take care of the rest. Don't just assume I'm going to lie on my back and let you go away at it. You're going to lie on your back and you're going to shut up and I'm going to show you what can really be done." It's that whole emotional, psychological thing. "I'm going to engulf you; you are not going to penetrate me. I'm gonna swallow you up whole. You're going to find out who's really in control. Can you take control, can you stop asking me what I want and just do it?" It's a whole power trip to have someone who can meet you as an equal.

I guess my biggest fantasy right now is to find the type of guy who can meet me as an equal. Someone who is smart and sophisticated enough. If I were to be in a serious relationship, it would involve somebody who is as smart or smarter than I am and that reflects into the whole sex thing too. I don't necessarily want to be in control all the time. I think that guy is out there somewhere.

I think there are certain things that gay guys have in common in their childhood and upbringing. People want to pitch Freud out with the bathwater, but I think there is a certain element of truth to it. I grew up with my mother and I had virtually no contact with my father. My parents were divorced before I was two years old. I used to see my father, but it was sporadic and limited. I think that happens a lot. Very strong mother, distant father. I don't think it has anything to do with, you know, my mother making me knit, but it's one of those things that I've seen repeated enough. I don't think that makes anybody gay, but I don't think it would make anybody straight either. I still think that being gay is eighty percent nature, twenty percent nurture. I think the clear majority is from some sort of genetic influence.

My ass and prostate respond wonderfully to being fucked. There are lots of straight guys who like it too. And although the mouth wasn't intended to be wrapped around a dick, and there is no directly pleasurable physical feeling derived from that (at least not for me, I don't know about someone who might have an oral fixation or something), people still have oral sex. Different people enjoy different things. For me, it's not even a question about whether a certain orifice was created for that purpose or not. It's really about, "Well, do you like it?" And if you do, then that's the way it was supposed to happen for you. Knock yourself out.

I've never kicked anyone out of bed for having a big dick, but I have to say there's a limit. Usually the guys with the big ones are of no use because they think, "I'm big and that's what you have." Usually, they don't know what they're doing.

I'm completely opposed to barebacking, like I'm opposed to tobacco law suits. I don't believe you pick up a cigarette and think, "Oh, this is not going to hurt, this is not going to be a problem." You know you're the dumb ass who stuck it in your mouth in the first place.

–2–

Andy: Bottoms Get No Respect

Bottom, Age 34

Andy and his partner John agreed to be interviewed together, but Andy showed up alone. He told me that they left Boston together to drive to Provincetown, but had a fight on the way. Andy took John back to Boston, dropped him off, and drove over by himself. He assured me that John wanted to be interviewed as well, and that he'd come over at another time. John and I never hooked up (I don't think he ever really wanted to), but my talk with Andy was pretty fascinating.

Andy is masculine, a stocky five feet seven inches, with brown hair and brown eyes. He grew up in Springfield, Massachusetts, and moved to Boston when he was twenty-four. His first sexual experience was with a woman when he was nineteen, and he was engaged to be married to another woman at one point. Although he says he sensed he was different in some ways when he was very young, he was not consciously aware of his homosexual feelings until he was twenty-seven.

He seems tense when we first meet. I offer him a comfortable spot on the couch, but he won't sit back and relax. I offer him a pillow, but he refuses, assures me that he's fine, but remains erect and alert throughout our conversation.

*　　*　　*

Thoughts of being gay hit me for the first time when I was walking somewhere with my cousin in Boston. My cousin is very beautiful and men would constantly turn their heads to look at her. I made some comment to that effect and she turned to me and said, "They're not looking at me, they're looking at you." My idea of a gay man was someone like Liberace. These men were young and good-looking and I'd never have pegged them as gay. They shattered all stereotypes I had of gay men. Her whole building was gay, except her, which was weird to me. She also showed me a gay bar in the neighborhood and I went there.

My first encounters with men didn't end up in sex. I was too afraid to even speak so they always picked me up. There was one guy who was very strange. He picked me up and I followed him in his car to a hotel. He had blond hair and blue eyes and I thought he was very attractive. He went through a bunch of side streets and stopped at a convenience store to buy condoms. I was very nervous, I was petrified of sex. I was living with my aunt in Boston at that point so this was a big secret.

We got to the hotel room and all I wanted was to lie next to a man. That's what I was looking for. I didn't even want to have sex. I wouldn't have felt comfortable having sex with someone at that point. So I just got into bed. He told me he was married and had two kids. He started to talk about his kids, which was very strange. Then his clothes came off, he got into bed and he said, "Fuck me, fuck me, fuck me!" That totally turned me off. Now, I was sobering up and all my inhibitions were coming back. I was saying to myself, "What are you doing?" I mean if he had said, "Let's make love" or something, things would've been different.

I'm thirty-four years old now and I've only had sex with four people. The first guy I had sex with was Alex, who was a Hispanic man. It was Sunday night at the Ramrod and you had to either wear leather or take your shirt off. I just wanted to dance. He came in with a cut lip; he'd been beaten by his boyfriend. He was very good looking and talked with an accent. We looked at each other and something happened. We felt compelled. We started kissing each other. We started to dance together and he was touching me while we danced. The whole world seemed to disappear.

We wound up at The Safari Club, which is closed now. We went up the elevator and I had to hand over my ID and I was petrified that someone would know my name. I left my underwear on under the towel, which everyone seemed to think was strange. We went into one of those cubicle things and it was very dark. I had him in a weird position and I told him I didn't know what to do. And he goes, "Oh, you're a virgin!" He got all excited over that and before I knew it he was on his back with his knees almost to his shoulders and I was on top of him. I was really good to go and before I knew it there was some guy, an older guy who came up from wherever in this dark room, came up from behind me. I assumed he wanted to have intercourse with me and that was just really weird. Alex yelled at him and before I knew it there were five guys in this room and I didn't know what was happening and I just left the room. It was very strange. They whole place was very strange for me. They had some porno and I sat and watched gay porno for the first time in my life. I thought it was interesting. Some guys were playing with themselves or whatever. Needless to say, I left the place without Alex.

I was young and got hit on all the time. One night at the Ramrod I refused to take off my shirt, so I took off my pants instead. All of a sudden I was the life of the party and I was dancing on top of the bar and stuff, which was cool. The bartender was giving me free drinks and I was sloshed. As I was getting a drink, all of a sudden this guy started going down on me. I felt like throwing up and I was saying to myself, "This is not happening. You need to control yourself." I kept pushing the guy's head away, but he kept following me like a little troll. I opened the front door and threw myself outside and vomited in front of these straight people. It was very embarrassing. I wouldn't go back to the Ramrod after that.

Another time I met this African-American man who was taller and older than me. He invited me to his house and he was all touchy feely when we walked down Huntington Avenue, which I didn't like. I don't like it when guys are like that, when they hold doors open for me and stuff, things of that nature, like they'd do for a woman. Anyway, this guy took off his clothes and sat on the couch and fed me and showed me his photo albums. All very strange, but I did my first sexual act, so to speak: I went down on him. Two days later I was at UMass and sure enough, he was with a group of teachers and it turns out he's a college professor. We were heading toward the elevator at the same time, but when I saw who it was, I went and took the stairs. After that, I just avoided that building.

I met Wayne a few weeks later and he was the first man to fuck me. We met at a bar. He came over and said hi and just kissed me right off the bat. Before I knew it I was pinned up against the wall and it was very erotic. We went to his house and I was petrified to no end. He was bigger, I guess he was a bear type, with gorgeous blue eyes. He told me he was a bottom, which meant nothing to me. I had no clue what a top or a bottom was. He apologized for having a small penis, which I thought was the strangest thing in the world. I always thought guys were one and the same. He took something out of his nightstand and penetrated me, although he never did that with anyone, ever. He seemed quite satisfied with his accomplishment, but it wasn't a pleasant experience for me. After it was done he fell asleep and I kept feeling like I had to go to the bathroom. He's on me, I push him off, he falls asleep, and I'm in a strange household petrified to death and I have to go to the bathroom. He had four roommates and they were all asleep. The next day I kept feeling like I couldn't clean myself.

I was happy about it, though. I felt it was a successful experience. The next morning we woke up and he seemed very happy that someone like me would want to be with him. I felt very nice around him. I wanted to see him again, but he was going to Provincetown the following week to spend the summer and he said he couldn't guarantee that he would be faithful. I met him in Provincetown one time and we had sex and I was a bottom again and it was much better the second time.

The next guy I had sex with was Todd and I had a relationship with him for a year and a half. He was a drag queen and the first time we had sex was my first experience as a top. After that, I was mostly the bottom. He introduced me to rimming and everything else. The problem with him was that he was extremely effeminate and he was promiscuous. We had sex constantly. He was very quick. He'd stroke himself three times and ejaculate. I used to piss him off because I have the ability to ejaculate without taking my clothes off. Like if I'm in a car or something, if no one's looking at me, I can touch myself and cum. I can do it anywhere, anytime, no problem. That pissed him off.

Everyone assumed he was the bottom and I was the top because he was so flamboyant. And he even told people I was the top, which was even more bizarre because nine out of ten times it was the other way around. One time I caught him having sex with someone in an alley and I picked him up and carried him home on my shoulder. He used to call me an extremely butch bottom.

Todd was very good at being able to tell who was a top and who was a bottom. From him, I learned to observe the behavior of tops and bottoms and now I'm very accurate in predicting too. People think if a guy is taller he's probably the top. Or that the feminine guys are generally the bottoms. Bogus, bogus, bogus. But there are definite telltale signs. Very obvious ones. One example is what I talked about before, prodding the door. When a man treats the other guy as inferior in some way, you're talking about the top. Because most relationships are about control and tops will do very control things to their bottoms. They can be gentle things, but I find them very insulting. I feel if you're a gay man, you like men, so you should act like a man and be with a man. I don't want to be a man trapped in a woman's body and vice versa.

Another telltale sign is that a bottom likes to be *looked at*. They want to make sure someone's looking at them. A top, on the other hand, is the one who's doing the *looking at*. You need to see the two of them together to see how they react. It doesn't matter which one is feminine or not. It's the way they act around each other. If I'm the bottom and you're the top and we go to order drinks in a bar, even if you let me order the drink, the way you grab the drink and hand it to me would suggest that you're a top. It's similar to how straight men act around women. If you're a top and you're having a conversation, you *lean into*. You don't see bottoms leaning into tops. According to *The Joy of Gay Sex,* tops lean against a wall and they look out. No one can explain why.

Watch a gay couple when the bill actually comes. It doesn't matter which one is paying the bill. The bottom will ask, "What are you leaving for a tip?" Or the top might ask the bottom, "What should I leave for a tip?" Why it's the bottom's job to decide what the tip is going to be is beyond me.

The other day I saw this guy was on the subway with his lover. The bottom says, "Oh, this is our stop." And the top says, "Oh, okay." Gets up, literally pauses, and gently prods the bottom toward the door like he's going to protect him somehow from this crowd. See, I'd be bullshit over that. At one point I'd have thought that was a loving gesture, but now I can't stand it. I don't need a man for protection, so to speak.

Maybe tops do those things out of respect or they do it because they want to get in your pants. They're doing it without thinking because it's something they think they should do. And if the top is a feminine guy and he's doing that, it blows my mind. I can only assume that they're trying to be caring and positive.

What defines manhood is to fuck something. That's what makes a man. You go from being a boy to being a man because you need to fuck someone. The opposite of that would obviously be someone on the receiving end, the one who gets fucked. Society has very negative connotations to getting fucked. Barnicle* talks on the radio about what Exxon Mobil is doing and he says, "What that means to the consumer is that they have to bend over." What is he trying to say? When they say "bent over" or "fucked over" it's kind of degrading. That's just society. Top guys practically announce it. You don't see a bottom going around telling people, "Oh, I'm a bottom." I don't understand why that's demeaning at all. It boggles my mind. I think disrespect of bottoms is one of the biggest problems gay society has.

I told you already that I'm petrified of sex. It doesn't mean I don't have sex, it just means I'm petrified of it. I don't know why. Sometimes, I'm good to go and at the point of entry or something the guy says something and that totally turns me off. If you're going to have sex with me, just don't speak and it will be fine. [Laughs] If some guy comes up to me and says something like, "I'd love nothing more that you to sit on me and rotate and I'll show you a good time," or something to that effect, I'm done for. I know it's not logical.

I met my current lover, John, through work. He's extremely flamboyant and everyone knows he's gay so when we moved in together, that was my outing at work. He's the total opposite of me. He was married and at that time he was doing the rest areas, parks, public bathrooms and so on. It's a monogamous relationship, but he has a big problem about cheating. Like I always have to account for my time. I always have to explain why it took me so long to get home from work. He always thinks I'm cheating on him. Constantly. There's no way I could go to a gay bar without him. That's just wrong. You don't do that. When we finally got a computer and we got on the Internet, we weren't allowed to go to certain sites. Very bizarre behavior. He's very controlling and possessive. We're fighting now because he found an ATM receipt that proves I was on Boylston Avenue at one o'clock in the morning. He's totally convinced I was at the Ramrod.

I don't think everyone in relationships are defined as a top and a bottom. Some people, like my friends Mike and Joe, are versatile.

---

*Boston radio talk show host.

They're both skinny and they look roughly like each other and I couldn't figure out which was which. They were a mystery to me. Sure enough they're versatile and they literally take turns, so to speak. Another couple I know are both tops. One's older than the other and they were a mystery to me too. They're very much in love with each other, but they seek out bottoms only for sex purposes, which I think is kind of bizarre.

I don't think being a bottom for me is even a preference. It's just the way it is. It's my history. I would always look for a top because two bottoms make a dull relationship. Tops don't think bottom or top. They don't think, "Gee, that person's a bottom." It's a whole mental thing in your head. If you look at a hot guy, there are two things you want to do to that guy. Either you're thinking, "He can do anything to me that he wants to," or, "Wow, he's really cute. I'd love to possess him or have him." Being a top is definitely more of a possessing thing.

The passive-active element is definitely there. It's just like a hetero relationship. The woman gives the signal to the man before the man comes over and goes up to the woman. Like I said, the bottom wants someone to look at him. It's up to him to tap into the top, get in his line of vision, make eye contact, whatever. Here's a funny thing: tops always looks at a guy's crotch and bottoms always look at asses. I'm more turned on by ass, but John is fascinated with my dick.

John and I have had some incredible sex. He's very insecure about it, but he's actually a very good lover. I tell him that all the time. We tried it with me being a top a few times, but he's very tight and it's very painful for him when I enter him. I'd say he's a bottom, but he doesn't know it.

I'm not into oral sex at all. In fact I hate doing blow jobs. I'll do it to please him or whatever, but I definitely prefer anal. The best sex for me was when I was lying on my stomach and he was on my back, humping on me without entering me. That's sometimes more satisfying than actual penetration. Go figure.

For a bottom, sex is about the relationship. I have more needs than he does. I get off an awful lot, like abnormally a lot compared to other men, for some reason. I can't remember any day that I've gotten off less than twice. It's the first thing I do when I wake up and the last thing I do before bed. If I get a hard-on out of the blue, which is rare because I get off so much, but if I do, for some reason, I have to take care of it as soon as possible. No matter what. If I'm wearing clothes or if I'm somewhere where there are other people, as long as someone is not looking at me, I can do it.

I can't get off in anyone's presence or if someone is looking at me. If John's looking at me, it's not gonna happen. When he's done, he rolls over and goes to sleep and then I can jack off. If he looks at me. I just freeze. In the morning, he gets out of bed and goes to the bathroom, which is when I do it. I never jack off when I'm getting fucked; in fact I hate that. I can't explain why that is. I remember the sensation as soon as he falls asleep and that's what turns me on. Actually, I'm getting better now; now he doesn't even have to fall asleep. [Laughs] Why I'm telling you this, I don't know.

I'm very good at jacking people, off but I hate it. I hate sperm. Ugh! Get that stuff off me. So when I'm jacking him off and he's about to cum, I back off. He wears a condom every single time we have anal sex and sometimes he ejaculates inside of me. That's his preferred thing. Except for the frottage thing, which was gross because I had cum all over my back.

Getting fucked, for me, is a mode. I can't separate the physical feeling from the mental. It's about me being the only one who matters to him at that moment. And me doing anything to please him, to make him happy. And by doing that, I get happy. Do I think my prostate has something to do with it? That's not for me to know. That's for the scientists. When he exits, when he's done, and I recuperate, so to speak, I can still feel him. Just because he's done, doesn't mean the feeling's done for me. Tops don't understand that.

I kinda believe we're born gay. We know it's not a choice. We know that men without male role models wind up straight and some men who grow up in very normal families wind up gay. So we can't say it's the environment. What makes a gay person is what turns them on. We know people who are straight who've done gay acts, but it's not what ultimately turns them on. I mean I would love nothing more than to be married and have kids. That would be heaven for me. But I was definitely born gay.

Anal sex is totally natural for me. My lover is a hyper worrier. He thinks people are going to damage themselves, especially those guys in porno movies who take up huge dildos and fists. Like they're not going to be able to go to the bathroom right. But women have had anal sex since time immemorial and no one flinches. What's the difference? The latest thing in straight porno is the woman sticking her finger up the guy's ass before he cums. Straight people are finding that enjoyable. So it's like you can do all these gay things as long as you're not gay.

The guy who fucked me the first time, Wayne, had a very small dick, but he was the most painful fuck of all of them. Tops are always comparing dick sizes. They don't want to be with a bottom who has a bigger dick than them. It's one of their fears. I don't get that at all.

The best sex I've had was with John, twice in one day. We were in the Berkshires, on top of a mountain. It's all green and beautiful and they've put a bench up there. A lot of artists go up there to paint, so it's very unusual to be alone. We had sex up there, overlooking all these other mountains and rivers and it was wonderful. We had anal sex. Anybody could've shown up at any time. After that we went to a cornfield and did it again.

Sam: The Darkness That Looms Inside

Bottom, Age 36

The courtyard of St. Mary's of the Harbor is one of the most serene spots in Provincetown. It's also one of the few places where the public is allowed to enter and to cross over to the bay from Commercial Street—a wonderful and generous gift, since most of the waterfront houses forbid access to the beach with "No Trespassing" signs.

Sam called me on the phone and most likely gave me a fake name. He'd seen my sign at the grocery store and told me he was glad I was writing about tops and bottoms because, he said, "someone had to."

We meet at St. Mary's of the Harbor and sit on a couple of plastic deck chairs in the church yard, facing the bay. It's a beautiful fall afternoon and sitting in the sun feels nice. We spread our legs and extend our feet over the retaining wall, soaking in the rays. The tide is rather loud so we sit close to each other to make sure the tape picks up our voices. He's a handsome, young-looking, thirty-six-year-old with a sweet, wholesome smile. He has a small, five-eleven frame, narrow shoulders, and short brown hair which he fiddles with the entire time we talk.

Our conversation begins in a relaxed and comfortable tone. He tells me he was in a relationship recently which lasted three months and ended roughly seven weeks ago; but that's not the only thing that weighs heavily on Sam's mind. As we delve into the memories of his childhood, he grows increasingly somber. At a certain point the hurt and confusion he recounts is so overwhelming that we both sit quietly for a while as he stares off at the horizon. The clouds begin to move in and a lone woman attempts to swim in the receding tide.

*　　*　　*

I think the tops and bottoms issue is something that plays into all male-male relationships. There's a lot of casual talk about it, but no one talks about it seriously. People say things like, "Boston is full of bottoms and there aren't enough tops." Or they say things like, "Oh, he's such a big bottom." And there's always a negative undertone in there.

I hate to say it, but I'm a bottom. If someone asked me if I was a bottom in a different kind of situation, like if I told someone I was doing this interview and they asked me, I'd tell them it's none of their business. I guess I'm a little embarrassed to say it. I don't like to be identified like that because I feel like it turns me into something all the way from my feet up to my head. It's like completely encompassing. It means that I'm submissive, that I *need* somebody else, like someone else is gonna have control over me. I feel like it diminishes me in some way. I mean, when I try to guess what people think of me when I tell them that I'm a bottom, the first word that comes to my mind is *pig*. That's the first word that comes to my mind.

On one level, I think both of those things are true: that I'm submissive and that I need somebody. But that's not the whole picture; it's only part of the picture. There's some power element in being a bottom too.

I had my first sexual experience when I was six. It was with a brother who's seven years older than me. I have three brothers and he's the oldest and the only straight one. He had me blowing him and all this stuff. I didn't know what I was doing. Once I asked him what he was doing and he said, "I'm sick and you're helping me get better." When I asked him a second time he went to the dictionary and pointed out the word *homosexual*. I don't even remember seeing the word, I just remember a big H in the corner of the dictionary. Of course, I had no idea what it meant. It was his way of explaining it. He was just repeating what was done to him at summer camp. I don't think he even understood it himself.

I've never suppressed that memory or anything. I've always remembered that as clear as day. I've even referred to it as though I was talking about grocery shopping. It's only in recent times that there's been more of an emotional attachment to it. Fear. Anger. I think there was real fear going on when it happened and I didn't realize it, because at the time I thought I was dying. Like somebody was trying to kill me. I was a little six-year-old boy with a big dick in my mouth and I'm sure it felt like I was suffocating or something. It was traumatic. I've gotten more in touch with that.

He didn't try any of that with my other brothers. One of my other brothers said that he knew something was going on, but he didn't know what it was specifically. His impression was that it went on for a whole summer. I don't remember how long it was. It finally ended because one time my mother walked in on us. There was screaming and yelling and every other thing. She asked me what was going on and I just walked over to the dictionary and pointed to the word. My brother was pissed because he'd told me never to tell anybody. That was the end of that. But at some point, and I don't know what the time frame was, I started to go after him and I tried to reinitiate it. That went on for years. I used to masturbate while he was in the room to try to get his attention. One time I was doing that when he was in the other bed and he raised his arm up and violently slammed it down on my bed. It was a definite, "You'd better stop it!" It never got reinitiated, but I think I developed a pattern of chasing men or something like that.

When I was a freshman or sophomore in high school, I can't remember exactly, I found out that one of my brothers had gone to the Boston Public Library and had sex. I either heard this or I intuitively knew it because we certainly didn't talk about it. I took the bus downtown and went into the public restroom at the library. This guy started to blow me inside a stall. I didn't even know what was going on and I came. The second time I went there another guy took me to the older part of the library. I must've been sixteen or something and I had no idea what anal sex was, but he started to put his dick in my ass and I had no clue what was going on. It didn't happen. On my way home on the bus I told myself I'd never do that again. I never went back there after that.

I went to Boston College and then to UMass Amherst for college, which is when I started to have sex in public bathrooms. I got into that full steam ahead. I used to develop these mad crushes on guys and I'd pursue them. Sometimes I'd try to stand next to a guy on a crowded subway, that kind of stuff. I still don't think I even understood what anal sex was. I'd go to the Art Cinema* to have sex with people, but I actually kind of avoided looking at the movie pretty much.

---

*Cruisy movie theater in Boston where they show porn flicks.

At one point during this period I got a red spot on my hand and I went to a clinic with an alias name because I thought I had AIDS. The doctor asked me what I'd done sexually and I told him about the oral stuff. He asked about the anal stuff and I think I still didn't know anything about it. Maybe that clued me in that the anal stuff was kind of big stuff or something.

When I was twenty-three, a childhood friend of mine died from cystic fibrosis. When I got back from the funeral, I went to the campus center where there was a hotel. I met someone in the lobby. He had blond hair and he was good-looking. He was definitely older than me. He took me to his hotel room and that was the first time I got fucked. I remember liking it. I probably still didn't know what was going on. I remember it being a pleasant experience, but I always associated fucking with a way of coping with loss. I connected that experience with the loss I'd just experienced.

In 1994, I remember going out to a bar in Boston and meeting this couple. They were very good-looking and they invited me back to their house. The guy just started fucking me without a condom, like without asking. I remember enjoying it. I didn't resist it. So I guess that's when I kinda, I don't know, accepted—or thought of myself—as a bottom. 'Cause I did enjoy it. He was attractive and masculine and he looked like he was enjoying it too. Because of the way he did it, I mean without asking, I did feel like a piece of trash. And then another part of me felt almost like he was at my mercy. In a way. I think there's a darkness that looms inside of me. I mean ultimately, of course, I want to be in control 'cause I want to feel like I can protect myself and survive. But I think on some level I've learned that I can play this submissive role to rope people in, like almost as a form of manipulation. I think there's either a lot to it or I've just completely complicated it. I'm not sure. It may be as simple as the fact that I like the sensation of getting fucked.

I feel completely incompetent in fucking anybody else. It's like I can't even do it. I can't stay hard enough. Although one time recently I was at a bathhouse and I was hard and this guy just came up and sat on me. I didn't have a condom on and I didn't even realize what was happening until I was in him. God, the sensation was incredible. I enjoyed it for a brief moment, but I pulled out before I came. I lose my erection a little bit when I'm getting fucked. I jerk off and I can't lie there for hours either. It still hurts. I mean it feels good, but in some ways it still hurts. So I'm a twenty-minute kind of guy. I could probably get off in five minutes, but I usually let it go longer than that.

I got tested for HIV about a year and a half ago and I was negative. I haven't had it checked since. I got fucked without a condom for the first time the other night in well over a year. I encouraged the guy to do it partly because the condoms burn and it hurts more. It feels much better without it.

I'm not sure if I was born gay because I have the whole Freudian archetype recipe for being gay. The domineering mother, the passive, absent father. I mean it's textbook. I always thought that played into it. I mean, as I read this stuff that Freud wrote and I see my situation, I mean it's completely parallel. Sometimes I wonder. Like I can't fuck men, and I know I can't fuck women. I tried to when I was younger and I could never do it. So sometimes I still wonder, is it fear? Like a Freudian fear of castration? I don't know. It's a little bit embarrassing, but I remember like putting a carrot up my ass with Crisco on it and all this stuff when I was a kid. I wasn't even in high school yet. My brother had never tried any of that. So I think something was going on.

When people approach me, I ask them what they like before they get to say it. Sometimes, if the guy is really cute, I don't want to say, "Oh, I'm a bottom," because I think he's probably a bottom too, and that would be the end of it. I usually don't meet people I'm that attracted to. The rejection factor is like unbelievable. Which adds to my sense of feeling like a piece of shit. I'm usually attracted to men who are a little older. Sometimes I worry because I think, "God, I want them to be seven years older than me, that means I'm really looking for my brother again." I mean that starts to play into it. I like them kind of masculine. Heaviness is a real turn off. I like a big, developed chest and I prefer smooth over hairy.

The guy I was going out with told me he was a top when we first met, but I think he lied to me about that because he definitely seemed to be more of a bottom. He wanted me to fuck him, but I couldn't get hard enough to do it. I didn't want to tell him I couldn't fuck him. And then, for the longest time, I didn't want him to fuck me because I thought it would imply some commitment to each other and I wasn't sure if we were gonna go in that direction or not. I was either afraid of the commitment or I thought it meant "Oh, I'm going to be the submissive one in this relationship." I'm not sure what. Something was going on. I liked being in a relationship and cuddling and hugging, but I started to think, "Oh, he's not a top and I want a top." There's a lot of confusion about all of this.

One night he and I were supposed to meet, but I ended up going to the A-House* and drinking. Then I went down to the dick-dock† and met someone and brought him back to my room. I encouraged him to fuck me without a condom. And I remember lying there thinking, "What am I doing?" I mean I wouldn't even let the guy that I was going out with fuck me and here I was letting a perfect stranger do it without a condom. I thought this was the end of my relationship. Again, the fucking took on this value, like I was trying to make a statement or I was trying to act something out. The first time I did it my friend had died so I associated it with that. The second time I did it with those two guys my friend Steven was dying. And then I did it with them again after he died. So I always associated fucking with some major event and here I was associating it with the end of my relationship.

I went to my boyfriend and told him what I'd done and broke up with him. And I thought, "Well, I'm glad he wasn't a top. I don't really want a top because I'd feel completely controlled or something." He went and got another boyfriend right away and then I wanted him back. It was the most extreme emotional pain I've ever had in my life. I was walking down Commercial Street wishing I had a fucking gun. I was so miserable that I'd just as soon wished I was dead. It was unbelievable.

Last time I had anal sex was about a week ago. I did the phone sex thing and invited somebody over to my house. He showed up at three o'clock in the morning and he fucked me with a condom on. And it was okay. I wasn't like totally into it. And then the other night I was just walking around this town like a complete stoned out heroin addict looking for sex. Finally, at three in the morning, I met these two guys and we went to one of the guys' house in town. I wasn't attracted to one of them at all, but I was mildly attracted to the other one. He was cold and distant. He said he was a top and he was gonna try to fuck me without a condom. I told him he had to put a condom on and then he did it just a little bit, but he couldn't stay hard enough or stay in. He turned around and started to fuck this other guy without a con-

---

*The Atlantic House: a gay bar in Provincetown.
†The old boatyard in Provincetown is a popular late-night cruising spot.

dom. A lot of men prefer to do it without a condom. My impression is that there is a lot of barebacking going on.

I'm just going to come out and say it: In some respects, I hate tops. They're fucking aggressive, mean, unkind, and insensitive people. I mean that goes through my mind sometimes. I'm in a therapy group for gay men who are sexually compulsive. There's a guy there who's a top. He found out that somebody he fucked was HIV positive and he was all upset about it. And I was just like totally pissed at him. I said, "What are you talking about? You're not the one that has to worry!" A lot of anger came out. So there's stuff going on underneath the surface and I don't completely understand it.

I think I enjoy talking and fantasizing about sex more than the reality of it. I'm terribly promiscuous. I've been in P-town for three days and every day I've either had sex on the beach or gone to the dick-dock every single night and had sex. So you'd assume that I must like it very much. I guess I should assume that I like it very much, but then, as I said to someone yesterday, I think sex is highly overrated.

I go to Sex and Love Addicts Anonymous and to AA now. Because the drinking inevitably leads to a situation where there's a higher chance of me having unsafe sex. I haven't been drinking this trip, but I've still been having a lot of sex. There's alcoholism in my family. I don't drink the way the alcoholics in my family drank, like throw furniture and end up in detox, but I drink enough. In my head I figure sex is equal to like four tequila shots. So I can drink less than an alcoholic drinks, but I can get just as high when I combine sex with a little booze.

There's no question that I enjoy my sex life up to a point. I met someone last night at dick-dock and I started blowing him. He was a top and extremely handsome. I told him that I'd service him and all this stuff and invited him back to my room. He came over and then he saw me in the light and he goes, "Oh, you're cuter in the light than I thought," or something like that. I didn't feel like getting fucked last night. Again, it was more about the fantasy of it. But we made a date to meet later tonight for me to get fucked. I think he's terribly cute, but now I'm afraid he's going to want to do it without a condom. Part of me would like to do that. I told my AA sponsor that I wouldn't drink, I wouldn't use poppers, and I wouldn't have unsafe sex. But I know the condom is going to burn and hurt. I'll also be doing it without drinking so that will also play into it. If I broke one of those commitments, I feel like I'd break them all. And then I'd end up back where I was seven weeks ago when my relationship ended. We'll see what happens.

Top and bottom concepts are definitely related to male and female roles. I used to have a fantasy about being a woman when I was in my twenties. The power versus submissive concepts are also true. Not too long ago I got slapped and kicked around in the bathhouse a bit. It was hot. I mean I didn't feel great afterward, but at the time it was hot.

I don't usually feel okay about sex. This interview showed me how much confusion there still is. I've been talking about this stuff for too long. This might have helped me clarify things a little bit.

−4−

Kevin: A Certain Honesty

Bottom, Age 41

Kevin is a strikingly handsome man. When he greets me at his bayside studio on a beautiful summer morning, I'm struck by his expressive eyes, his vibrant olive skin, and tall athletic physique. When I complement him on how wonderful he looks, he tells me he had some serious health problems recently, brought upon by a change in his HIV regimen prior to a trip to Paris, his favorite city. He suffered from diarrhea and weight loss and some of his friends stopped him on the street, concerned, to ask him how he was doing. Kevin says he resented them for that. "If I'd looked better they wouldn't have bothered to ask how I was at all," he says.

Kevin's charming studio is steps away from the beach. Large glass doors face a small garden in front, which Kevin says, "keeps me happy." He lounges on the couch, facing the garden, and extends his long, muscular legs. As I turn on the tape recorder, I realize it's going to be hard to stay focused. Kevin's gentle manner, his near-perfect body, and deep thoughtful gaze are all intoxicating. He intermittently looks away as he contemplates a question which is my opportunity to study him. It's clear that he enjoys talking about his erotic past and relishes being the center of attention. He says that the essence of being a bottom, for him, is about being desired and admired.

Kevin works out several hours each week. He takes pride in his body. He loves to go swimming, water skiing, sailing, and gliding on the bay. He has an interest in psychology and philosophy and is a self-taught expert on computers.

A neighbor crosses the garden outside and calls at Kevin: "Good morning, Rasputin!" Kevin smiles at me seductively. "Sometimes I'm Wagner," he says. "Today I'm Rasputin."

*   *   *

When you asked to interview me, I thought it might be disappointing for you because I don't consider my sex life particularly interesting. We, as gay men, talk about our choices as tops and bottoms in a very quick and pejorative way. I hear men talking among themselves, as "queens," saying, "Ah, she's a bottom," like it's a bad thing. I don't know why that is. It could be because historically, in our society, women have had less value than men. Certainly in the patriarchal society that we live in. I think some men carry it on to having shame about themselves. And the shame is so great that they must project it unto others.

I'm a bottom and I enjoy that aspect of myself. I speak of it in celebratory terms almost as an act of defiance. I made a conscious effort to negate the negative connotations, or at least to balance them. I did that by affirming my love in and my desire to be receptive, to be a bottom. And by affirming that it's not a bad thing. It's something to be honored and enjoyed. I want to honor the act.

I just finished spending some time with a man who was a lover, but moved to Utah a year ago. He's a minister. He returned recently and we spent some time together. It was so beautiful. It was a time of sharing. There wasn't this carnal desire. It was beauty. It was about wanting to be next to this person. All along I knew he wanted to be inside me. I've recently had some doubts about my sexuality. I even thought I could be impotent, but being with him made it clear that I wasn't. I didn't even think about it. The emotional bond, being close to him, trusting him, being comfortable with him was all it took. It was a beautiful moment with him. A two day moment. He wants me to move to Utah. But I don't know if I can be a minister's wife. An HIV-positive wife in a Mormon community.

I had my first sexual experience when I was fifteen. It was with an older man. He was a DJ on the radio. I called up for a song and he started to come on to me on the phone. He wanted to meet me. Of course I was very naïve and, you know, easily taken by the excitement of the whole idea. It was brash and therefore it had great appeal, but it didn't turn out to be a very good meeting. We got in his car and went to a parking lot. And for the first time in my life I got to see this . . . this *penis. Big* penis. I was like "Oh my God!" But I don't think he was very attracted to me. I think he wanted a really big dick and he was disappointed. I was like "Oh, well." So that was the first experience. For me, it was mostly about being brash and getting away with it. It was looking at a penis and sucking it. I guess I could pull a Clinton here, like is that the definition of sex?

Around the same time period I went to see a straight porno flick and a guy in the audience sat right next to me, and started to, you know, jerk off. And I thought, "Oh, my God, this is so wild!" I was totally turned on. I always thought of gay people as old and disfigured and all of a sudden I thought, "God this is going to happen." It totally turned me on. We went to a hotel room and made love. It was incredible. When he found out I was fifteen, he totally freaked.

This experience was more akin to sharing and cuddling. I may have been sixteen by then. Although it was a good experience, it probably contributed to the problems I already had with my family. My father had left when I was small and I lived with my mother. This sexual experience didn't help my emotional stability, my self-esteem, or my self-worth. Having a beautiful sharing experience with someone and having them disappear was par for the course. Now as a middle-aged man, I look back on it and I clearly see the dysfunction and how it affected my emotional relationships. Seeing that is an opportunity for healing. Neither one of these early experiences involved anal sex.

In fact, I couldn't get fucked for years. It was always too painful. I had a friend, Martin, and he really wanted to fuck me and I really wanted him to, but it was so painful that we couldn't do it. Finally, we thought we should freeze my asshole with that stuff you use on your teeth! [Laughs] So we put it up my asshole to freeze it. Except his dick got totally numb too! We couldn't do it! I'd been obese as a child and I had hemorrhoids. And being so anal, my sphincter was really tight. [Laughs]

I was nineteen the first time I actually had a penis in me. And I was drugged. It took a lot of drugs. This guy made it really clear that he wanted to fuck me. I knew he had a big dick. I'd always fantasized about having a big dick in me. So sure enough he did. It took him about an hour to get it in. And as soon as he got it in, that was it. I pushed him right off, because it was painful and it didn't feel right. It felt like I had the wrong person in me. I think if it happened today, with the point of view that I have at present, I wouldn't let it happen. I had no connection whatsoever with this human being other than the totally sexual connection. I knew nothing about him. I didn't care to know anything about him. It was just that he had a big dick. So there was no sharing.

But all that changed with my first lover, Donny. He was able to fuck me. He knew how to get it in. Being receptive demands a certain honesty. For me, being receptive has always been about the idea of being desired. That line goes through my life, starting with my relationship with Donny when I was twenty-three. After that, if someone wanted to penetrate me, it was about being desired. Donny and I fucked once or twice a day, every day, for a year and a half. Having him inside me, I can't describe the feeling, it was wonderful. I was able to cum every time. He just knew. I don't know if he knew where my prostate was, but he knew how to massage, how to fuck. I've never had that since. That kind of trust. He used to say that when he fucked me, it was like a sanctuary, a special place. I think of him dearly.

I was very jealous and our relationship became troubled. I took his acts to extreme. I went into fits of rage. He was Portuguese and Latin and we'd have these incredible flare-ups. Finally, I left because I wanted to know more of the world.

I have gotten fucked when the emotional connection wasn't there. It's what I call "hate fuck," by people who were totally insensitive to my asshole. It's not a glory hole that you just poke and put it in. You gotta be tender. You gotta soften me up. If I'm not emotionally relaxed, I'm in a fighting pattern, I'm constricting. I have to let loose at a certain point to allow entry. Because if I don't, it's going to hurt. Part of me is saying no and another part is saying yes and there is this pain. It's probably how I got HIV.

The top/bottom roles are conceptualized in our society as aggressive and passive, but I believe they're much more complex than that. When I'm getting fucked, I want to make sure that my prostate is getting massaged. So I take charge. Unless the other guy really knows what he's doing, I'm not going to just let him do what he will. With certain people, like one of the recent lovers I've had, it can be pretty amazing. Some people have an innate sense, like what they're doing is just, "Oh my God, we're definitely going for a ride here." And maybe that's passive, I don't know. It's obviously passive because you're allowing someone to enter you, but then there's also controlling of the rhythm and controlling how deep it goes. In that sense, there's control in being receptive, but it's still filed under passive. Mmm. Wonderfully so.

A friend from Paris visited me recently and it was so beautiful. He was with me for almost three weeks. Usually, I want my guests to leave, like fresh fish, it gets stale. Three weeks went by and I wanted him to stay longer. It wasn't a sexual relationship, but we share a lot of interests, like graphic arts and psychological issues. There's no limitation to where we can take our conversations, and I realized, "Oh my God, this is what a partnership would be like." I got up in the morning and I didn't feel constricted. Just another beautiful day and whatever develops, develops. Just free flowing. I didn't want him to leave. Maybe I'm made to be celibate. I mean it's almost not worth it. Having that was so beautiful to me that I'm willing to forgo all sex. Unfortunately, I'm not sexually attracted to this person. So a relationship with him would definitely be an effort.

The last guy I was attracted to was bad news because he was married. We saw each other for a year and a half. But it was hopeless. Do I have stuff that I have to take care of? Is this obvious? Put it on my path and I'll take care of it. Thank you! [Laughs]

Occasionally, I'm the aggressor in pickup situations; but usually I'll meet someone's eye and it'll quickly become apparent if we both desire each other. At that point it becomes inconsequential who makes the first move. I haven't pursued anyone for awhile, but I've done it in the past. If there was someone I wanted, I went after him. Wanted to know him more and went after him—as a relationship, not just as a fuck.

If I want some guy just as a fuck, I'll definitely let him know. Sometimes, I'll go after it with this intense desire to be ravaged—or to ravage him. To drink in his beauty, absolutely. Oh, yes. Sometimes, I can't get enough of it, I just want to suck all the nectar. I find the anonymous encounter very exciting on a certain level. I've definitely explored that whole arena of the erotic.

I can understand on a certain level why people desire bareback sex. Having just found out that I have hepatitis—which is, by the way, twenty times more infectious than HIV—it's a mystery to me why anyone would want to put themselves in the position of not only contracting HIV but also HBV, HAV, HCV, and however many other variations through the alphabet you can get. I don't understand why anyone would put themselves at that kind of risk. The message needs to be sent to kids that are growing up today: "If you fuck, you fuck with condoms, that's what you do."

I mean I have my limitations as far as condom use goes. One lover wouldn't suck my dick without a condom. That has zero appeal to me. Several times I've allowed an HIV-positive man to enter me without a condom. Every time, I made him pull out before he ejaculated, but still, it's a risk. I'm aware of the consequences of that. HIV has different mutations. Obviously even pre-cum can be infectious, but I've only done it a few times since my diagnosis in 1985.

I think the idea of barebacking has to do with the desire to be absolutely free with someone. It's a mentality that's running rampant. People want no restrictions, no constraints. To them, condoms are a constraint that doesn't have the appeal of a love toy, it's not part of lovemaking. People want freedom at all costs. It's part of being American. It's tied in with our religions, with our government, and our desire to evolve beyond all of that as human beings. We want freedom, we want to explore the spirit. Therefore we take risks. And part of that is the sexual.

Of course, I could be proven wrong about barebacking. Maybe ultimately it will help us. Maybe it will facilitate our bodies to deal with a totally new mutation of the virus. I'm totally going science fiction here. I'm just trying to find the positive in this when the whole thing is really negative.

I believe you have to see the balance of things. To put a judgment on something immediately is nearsighted. You really have to pull back and ask yourself: "What's the big picture here?" Like the French say, *metre en question,* meaning put it to question. If you're passionate about something, you have to put it to question. To see if it comes from a good light or a bad light. I'm trying to age gracefully by being mindful of that balance. I try to see the whole picture, the picture made up of extremes. I try to see where the extremes are and pretty much take the middle road! Like fish that have big eyes on both sides, that's how I go through life. I try to be tolerant of everyone. When I feel intolerant or powerless, I try to live by Mother Theresa's words: "At the very least, thank God we can smile."

In the spectrum of male and female, I see myself at opposite extremes. Very male and very female. The very male characteristics, aggression, ambition, going forth into life, sports, all of these things, are very easy for me. I'm a total computer geek. I'm always dealing with computer-related codes and laws. All of these are considered male qualities to a certain extent. The female in me is concerned with languages and interpretation. I love the French language. They say French is cultivated from the garden. Just knowing how to use the verbs and knowing the sequence of words is poetry in motion. A female quality. Sometimes I desire to sexually be a woman. I take that to an extreme. Both extremes are very clear to me. They intrigue me greatly. It's the evolution of the human spirit; how our sexuality helps us evolve.

I believe sex can be, should be, has the power to be, a spiritual connection. Look at the radical fairies and their beautiful idea of sharing the spirit through sex in a pagan ritual. I think having that must be one of the most beautiful things to behold, because it's without judgment, it's without shame, fear, all of the things that control us every day. I think that would be the essence of beautiful sex. They have rituals, ceremonies, and it's all about healing. I believe it's possible to get back to that essence. All we have to do is look up at the sky and we can see the answers. But we don't look up at the sky. We're always looking at the ground. I think there are answers in the ground as well. We are from the earth; but we have to look into the skies, to the beyond, into the universe. Two moons ago, it was the flower moon, and on that day [he indicates the garden], every single one of the rose bushes out here and every single rose bush in Provincetown opened up. I speak in Indian now. "Two moons ago." [Laughs]

5

Lito: It's a Natural Thing

Bottom, Age 42

A native of El Salvador, Lito has spent all of his adult life in North America. When he was eighteen and just out of high school, he, his mother, and two brothers were forced to leave El Salvador as a consequence of their political participation in the cause against the dictatorship. Lito's other brother was a political prisoner at the time. Although the government did not officially send them to exile, Lito and his family knew that leaving their country was their only option.

They moved to Canada and settled with some relatives in Quebec. Soon after that, Lito went to Montreal to enter the university. Since then, he has obtained bachelor's degrees in comparative literature in French and Spanish, in education, in human sciences, and a master's degree in the psychology of education. He came to Boston three years ago to look for a job, but ended up enrolling at Harvard to get yet another degree, this time in the philosophy of education. He considers himself very lucky to be so well educated since, he says, "The general Latino experience in North America is pretty bad." He's now forty-two years old and is looking forward to finishing his education and to settling down with a professional job.

I meet him at Wordsworth Bookstore in Cambridge and he and I seem to hit it off right away. He's a small, roundish man, about five feet six inches, with black hair and black eyes and greets me with an elfish smile. We go on a search to find a place to talk together. He's more familiar with the Harvard campus than I am and he leads me to the Adult Education building. We sneak all the way up to the third floor until we discover an empty classroom where we shut the door and settle in to talk.

I ask him how he would describe himself. "I am maybe average guy. I don't know," he says with a smile and a heavy accent. He periodically has trouble articulating certain thoughts and his accent is often difficult for me to understand; but as soon as we get into the nitty-gritty of the subject, those barriers in communication seem to naturally dissolve into a particular style of communication. He's a gentle, thoughtful, remarkably honest, and approachable man.

*   *   *

In many ways, my cultural background gave me a different perception of who I am and of other people. I travel a lot and I have a lot of friends and relatives who support me. I discovered in America to be happy with my orientation, you know? Being gay. In Latin America, this is another story. The macho image is sometimes very difficult. For me, it's a nice experience to be in this country.

I am gay and a bottom. Passive. I don't have any problems with saying that. I'm very caring, very honest, and I'm a hard worker. I'm persistent in projects. I'm realistic, but also idealistic sometimes. I'm a very good friend. I enjoy being with other people and helping other people. I like to give them my time, not only my money. I'm also a member of Amnesty International. I was expelled from my country because I was politically engaged and I was gay. I was idealistic at the time and leaving my country was not a real choice. My father was in the military and he always respected my opinion. He didn't try to crush the way I thought or felt. He always encouraged me to express myself. So I've learned to be very clear when I speak to people.

I realized I was different at the very beginning of my existence. I remember when I was very young, maybe four years old, being attracted to men. To the naked male body. It was a surprise for me. Because even though I realized how I was, it was also very clear in my mind that it was wrong. It's because the cultural pattern where I grew up was very straight. You are a guy or you are a woman. Girls have to do something, boys have to do another. Boys don't express their emotions. Maybe it's changed a little bit, but in my time it was very clear. In my home we were three guys, myself and my two brothers. My father was in the military and my mother was at home. So the realization of this attraction for me, was, oh my God, nice. Beautiful. But at the same time I realized that it was different. And I was afraid. I said, "Wow. What happened? Why am I this way?" So for many years, perhaps until I was nineteen, my reality was to combat that difference. I tried to be the best boy; I was the best student in school and had the best behavior. I tried not to think about that, not deal with that reality.

Then I had an experience with a guy, which was wonderful. He was a car mechanic and I used to pass by his shop when I was walking somewhere. I'd pass and I'd pass, several times a day, just to see him. I was very attracted to the way he looked. He was maybe twenty-four and I was seventeen. One Saturday, he was alone in the afternoon and he smiled at me and he made a signal for me to come in. I was very confused. I thought, "Oh my God, what is this about?" But my desire was stronger than my hesitation. I went in and we started to talk. He said I was nice and he touched me. He asked me why I was so afraid. I said to him, "What do you want?" Pretty soon it was nighttime and I was so afraid. He took off his pants and it was the first time I saw a dick. I performed oral sex on him. He was so masculine and he had a hairy chest, which is still an important detail for me. He wanted to fuck me, but I was so afraid that it didn't work. It was too difficult. I was with him two more times after that and we only had oral sex. For me, it was a kind of liberation. Even though at that time I had to be very careful.

When I moved to Quebec, I lived with some relatives and there wasn't an opportunity to do anything. But when I went to Montreal to study at university, I had the opportunity to have sexual activity with my roommate. We discovered each other's sexuality after we moved in together. He realized that he wanted to have an experience. I think he was gay also and more experienced. One time, when we were in bed together, he said, "Turn your back, I want to caress your behind." It was very nice, but soon I felt something hard. I was afraid the first time he fucked me because he didn't tell me he wanted to do that. Even if it was a psychologically enjoyable and deeper experience, it was difficult for me. It happened only because my psychology and my body were connected.

I can have oral sex casually at the movie theater or whatever if I have the opportunity, but anal activity for me is different. It's a higher level of communication. I'm still pretty tight, so in many cases I have to be very relaxed and have a lot of confidence in the guy. It's not easy if I don't have the feeling, if I'm not at a level at which I can give or receive a lot of pleasure. To be fucked to me, is, in a way, being at the mercy of somebody. You know? For me it takes a particular guy. It has to be a special thing for the anal sex. Perhaps it is trust. The desire to share with the other man a different level of my personality. To be in very good communication with him not only in sex, but also to know him very well. Spend time with him. It's a kind of submission. Many guys may not agree with this, but there's always power involved. To be under the control of someone else is another experience. If I meet someone tonight and we get together we can have caressing, kissing, oral sex, but to move into the anal thing will take much more for me. I won't allow it in general. Only after two or three meetings. I like getting fucked, but I have oral sex much more often.

Being a top does not interest me. I'm not attracted to doing that. I don't feel comfortable with it. It's like I don't like cooking. I try it all the time, but for me it takes a lot of patience. This is my choice. It's a matter of taste.

In my native culture, being fucked is considered a kind of degeneration. The macho Latino guy just wants to fuck and it doesn't matter whether it's a guy or a girl. The more important thing is to be on top. If a guy wants to fuck someone, he's just being a man, even if he wants to fuck another guy. This was the case the first time I had sex, with that mechanic, because he could only do it in that particular context. Some of these macho guys maybe have a wife and children, but they go out and have sex with men too. In many cases a guy has to be married and make children in order to cover his feelings and desires, but the guy being fucked is a transvestite or something. In my case, it was a kind of political statement because although I want to receive pleasure from a guy, I don't want to be like a girl and wear women's clothes. Sometimes the macho guys want to use the feminine pronoun for the other guy. "Papi" is used for men, but if a Latino wants to fuck you, he wants to call you "mami," which is for a woman. For me, that's unacceptable. The language is very important to me. Why does this guy, who appears to be very happy to be with me, have a difficulty saying papi and switches to mami? I'm just a guy who likes to get fucked. I'm not a woman.

Another thing I discovered in having sex with Latinos is that they're very afraid to express their emotions. It takes two or more drinks for them to be tender with another guy, to get close.

The only relationship I had was in Montreal, with my roommate, which lasted one year. He got a job in Vancouver and moved away. He was macho, but also very tender. He cooked for me, gave me flowers, and took care of me. He was very careful. He wasn't feminine. He was a normal guy. I would like to be in a relationship one day, but it's difficult right now because I want to complete my studies and get a professional position. Sometimes I see some of my friends; they meet someone, they have sex, and just move in with the guy. And I think, "Wow." I will wait.

I'm Catholic and I believe in God. Even if the Catholic position on homosexuality is designed to make you feel very guilty, I don't have any conflict about it. I have a very good relationship with Catholic friends. I think God loves us, every one of us, and he loves me even if I have the orientation that I have. I don't believe I'm an aberration or that I'm not loved in the eyes of God.

I have been with younger men, but I find older, more experienced men to be more tender. In my experience, if the guy is younger, he's very anxious and quick. He doesn't pay attention. Although being with a younger guy is another kind of experience which I can enjoy.

There is a lot of discussion about whether being gay is genetic or has to do with social factors. In my own experience, even when my father was absent for a long time because of his job, my younger uncle was always in the house. I went out with him, we had fun, we went to the movies and traveled together. I always had a masculine presence in my life. There is a kind of sensitivity in me and I'm sure I was born gay. I think it's more genetic than social.

As a teenager I didn't want to accept my reality. I wanted to hate my parental figures. I hated everything connected with the army, things that had to do with my father figure, but one day I realized how much I was attached to it. I was in Montreal with a friend and I saw a cop in uniform and he was so beautiful. We were sitting in an outside café and he was right in front. And I told my friend in Spanish, "Oh my God, look at that. He's beautiful. He's so cute," and so on. The cop maybe heard me, but I didn't think he was Latino although I couldn't be sure. So we continued to eat. As we were leaving the restaurant, the cop came up to me and in perfect Spanish said, "Thank you for your appreciation." I was embarrassed. He was a lovely guy. He was not afraid. He said thanks for appreciating me. I like the guy in the uniform.

The masculine body is beautiful. When I was in college in Montreal, I used to go to the gym. I don't normally seek out or pay attention to the body of someone who spends hours and hours each week at the gym. But this, oh my God, it was a kind of contemplation. A divine moment to see those wonderful, different bodies. I think the male body is built to fuck as well as to get fucked. The man has the possibility to give and to receive, which is beautiful. To me it feels like a natural thing.

It doesn't matter to me if a guy has a big penis or small one. Big penises can cause pain and it can be difficult, especially if you're stiff. The expression is the more important thing.

I'm very attracted to black guys and Latinos. I have a very good Latino black friend. The mythology is that they have a big dick, but the reality is not like that. I had sex with only one Asian guy, many years ago in Montreal. He was delicious. He was nice. Very tender. He was one of the more careful or more affectionate men I've been with. So perhaps I'm interested in them also.

The best sex I ever had was with a friend last summer in Montreal. He's from Cuba and he's an openly gay man. I spent the weekend with him and it was magical. We're good friends and we share many different things together. The first night we slept together, we didn't have sex. We talked and drank. We had sex the second evening and we had anal sex and it was nice. Oh my God, for me it was the best experience. It was a wonderful one time thing.

Rationally, I can say that I don't like to have bareback sex and I don't want to do it. But in reality I have to accept that I have the temptation. Making a mistake is the human condition. I feel sex without a condom is a deeper communication. The first time I got fucked, in Montreal, it was without a condom, but I haven't done it like that since then.

Sometimes I meet people on the Internet. I don't like to go to the bars. I just meet people. I was at the bank recently to deal with some kind of problem, and the man I was dealing with was lovely and we started to talk. Finally I told him, "You're very nice. Can we have a drink together?" And he said yes. He's a black man. We're going to meet soon.

My strong feeling is that there are more bottoms than tops. Maybe because the bottom experience is deeper and more real. My gut feeling is that there is one top for every five bottoms.

The best thing about being a bottom is to feel the cock in the body. Physically and also psychologically. It's the communication. For me, it's a magic moment. Having complete confidence with someone to allow near complete fusion with him. It's very deep. One guy told me once that at the moment he was fucking me he felt me in a very different way. He felt he was happy to give me pleasure and to be in that close a communication. He was surprised at my eyes. I can't explain it because I didn't have a mirror, no? He told me afterward that my eyes were in a different place of expression. He was surprised at how much pleasure he was able to give me. It's a wonderful way to love, to be with somebody.

6

Danny: Giving and Receiving

Top, Age 21

Danny had just finished his sophomore year at Emerson College when I met him on a sweltering summer day in Boston. He'd described himself over the phone as having "short black hair and glasses and chocolate skin." He has a small-framed, athletic build and a boyish, bright smile. I met him near the Boston Common, in a crowded shopping area, and offered to buy him lunch. He wanted a burger and fries so we got something to go at Burger King and walked to the park to find a shady spot under a tree.

Originally from Louisville, Kentucky, Danny was raised by his mother, who holds down two jobs to pay for his college education. His father, who Danny hasn't seen since high school graduation, doesn't offer any financial support. There isn't enough money to return home for the summer, but Danny's not discouraged by the financial stuff. He sits cross legged on the grass and smiles with optimism. He quickly devours his fries, but saves his burger since "It will make a nice dinner this evening."

*　　*　　*

I'm a top. I don't like to present myself that way, but it's just what I do. Like the old cliché: better to give than to receive. I have a lot of fun. It's never crossed my mind to be a bottom. I don't know why. People who are bottoms tell me it's a sensational feeling, but I don't know. I don't know if I'd ever try bottoming because I get plenty of pleasure being a top.

I'm only twenty-one so I came out fairly recently. I didn't come out to my family at first. When I came here for school, my freshman year, no one knew—except my roommate and he knew because he walked into a situation. [Laughs] But I tried to keep it under wraps for a while. When I went back home my first summer from Emerson I decided I'd better let my mom know—and once I did that a huge load lifted off my shoulder. I told everyone else after that. My mom said she already knew, which was kind of embarrassing.

I was a child of the eighties, you know? I mean I'd always been dancing to Boy George songs and everything. I was a mischievous child. I used to like to go out and play ball and stuff, but I also liked to stick my head in situations. My aunt had some older gay friends who I loved to hang out with, like Dana who died of AIDS. He was a good guy. It fascinated me and I was always comfortable with it.

I knew gay stuff was going on with me when I was younger, but I couldn't identify it that way. I didn't have anything to relate it to. My aunt had these gay friends and people would joke about it all the time. The kids in the neighborhood would say I was a sissy and that was very hurtful. They'd say I was a mama's boy and things, and I kinda knew it was true cause it was all natural, you know? But back then I was like, "No, I'm not!" I was very offended by it all. So I just buried it for awhile.

I hooked up with somebody for the first time in high school when I was seventeen. This is funny. In the locker room. I played football all the time, and this guy had just quit the team. He was very despondent about it and all and he'd be complaining, "We're not going to the NFL," and shit. And I'm like, it's fine or whatever. And he's like, "Man I'm sick of it. I just want to go out and do my own thing. Nobody here really understands me." I could tell he was dodging around the issue and so I was like, "What is it, man?" And he like came out to me. And I'd been always slightly attracted to him. He was a goofy guy, but he was really cute. I don't know what it was. So I reached over and kissed him. And after a few days we had sex. It was kind of awkward. It was at a keg party and he was drunk off his ass. It was very awkward, actually.

He performed oral sex on me. He was a little more experienced than I was. And I was like "Wow!" I'd had sex with a girl before then, but I knew I liked sex with men. I found out that I like the company of men.

This was four years ago. After that, during the same summer, I met this older guy. We sorta went back and forth with the oral stuff.

I didn't try anal sex until my senior year in high school. I was meeting with this group of poets. They met every Saturday, and this guy asked to take me home. He invited me to his house for drinks. I don't know what he did professionally, but I read his writing and I thought he was a good writer. We went to his place to cool out and drink beer and he asked me to fuck him. So I did.

There's a mind-set about being a top. It's not even like being in control of the situation. It's kinda like maintaining the ship. It sounds kinda odd. If I was a bottom, it's sorta like I don't think I'd be as confident of myself. I just do it because it goes naturally and it's just fun and it feels good. And when I'm with someone who appreciates it, it makes me feel good. I don't want to brag or anything, but I usually get a good response.

Whether tops and bottoms fit in with the masculine or feminine roles depends on the partner. I've been with people who are very like, machismo and things, and they liked to bottom. I've also been with bottoms who are very effeminate. It all depends on the partner.

I'm not a dominant by any means. I usually go in and get naked and whatever happens happens. We can go out to a club or a bar or we can just hang out. I'm not too particular as far as that goes. So when it comes to masculine or effeminate, I'm the same way. You're gonna enjoy yourself as long as you come to a mutual agreement. I see my partners on an equal basis. Like I'm very casual about age. Most men I've been with have been older than me and they always mention how weird it is that I'm so casual about it. I just like to hang out or go somewhere and have a conversation. I don't busy myself assuming any kind of roles.

People have asked me to bottom. I've considered it because they're like, "It's such a good feeling." But I've always said no. I have yet to cross that line. Perhaps I'll cross it if I have a lover or something. I've been licked on my asshole before. It kind of tickled. It was fun. I liked it.

The longest relationship I had was with this guy I met when I was a sophomore in college. We went out for a while. Our school is always like inside peoples' business. So we'd be alone and go places by ourselves. We never made ourselves known as a gay couple. We were both busy, so we'd go somewhere on the weekends. There's something about these Emerson kids when they come out. They live through their sex. It's like I'm a gay man and gay people act this way. I've always disagreed with that. I'm more Danny than I am gay. The relationship lasted a semester. He graduated and left for LA. We try to call each other every now and then, but I have a feeling he's doing his own thing out there in California.

I think people doing barebacking are a lot bolder than me. For me, if there's no condom, it's oral sex. In my relationship, I always used a condom. I always carry one around with me. Barebacking is the final frontier, man.

You can't always fuck. I enjoy giving and receiving oral sex. It's a partnership of sorts. It takes two to tango.

7

Max:
"The Bottom Has to Work with You"

Top, Age 37

I'm browsing through the muscle calendars by the cash register at Glad Day Bookstore in Boston, while waiting for my next interview. Glad Day has the most diverse inventory of gay-themed books I've ever seen anywhere: history, fiction, biography, philosophy, books out of print, and a good collection of porno, including magazines and videos. It's not unusual to find the occasional celebrity browsing the magazines (I once spotted a television celebrity flipping through *Drummer*) or to run into a nervous high school kid who's in a gay bookstore for the first time.

Max has sent me a recent photo of himself, taken on the ski slopes of the Alps. I'm expecting a lanky, skinny man with a bushy beard. I notice a handsome guy watching me, but he looks nothing like the photo so I turn away. He approaches me from behind and taps me on the shoulder. Sure enough, Max is all clean-shaven now, an attractive man with dark hair and hazel eyes.

We're both hungry so we decide to grab a quick bite to eat at the outdoor café downstairs. He orders a hummus sandwich (he's picky about food, he says, he won't eat just anything) and I have a cup of chowder. Afterward, we cross the street to The Boston Public Library and find a remote corner in the courtyard where we can have some privacy, soak in the sun, and talk.

Born to a Swiss father and an American mother, Max has spent most of his life in Europe. He's thirty-seven, a physician, and has arrived in the United States only a couple of months ago to continue his studies at Boston University. "Americans are so goddamn repressed and constipated about their sexuality," he scoffs. "I responded to your ad because I thought you'd certainly not be getting many responses.

They're friendlier than Europeans, but generally badly educated. In the boondocks, people are so ignorant that if stupidity could hurt, these people would be rolling in the streets in agony."

Despite his harsh judgments, I eventually realize that Max has a wider than usual view of the world. He's also warmhearted, if ungenerous with his observations as an outsider, and genuine. His mild Germanic accent and his elegant demeanor soon win me over.

He's in a long-distance relationship with a man who lives and works for a large bank in Switzerland. They met on the Internet roughly three months before Max came to the United States and they hope that the boyfriend can transfer to a branch in Boston so they can be together again.

*   *   *

In my earliest fantasies, even when I was having the slightest thoughts that I might be gay, I always saw myself as the one on top. The one who would be giving it rather than receiving it. It's just sort of the way I see myself or feel myself.

I'm a pretty high-strung personality. I'm a physician, but I'm moving toward consulting and management. I used to think that being a top had something to do with my assertive, energetic personality, but nowadays I don't think it's related at all. I think it's just the way I am, and maybe it's based on my own experience.

When I was twelve or so I used to fantasize about having sex with a boy from my class. Already in that fantasy I was the guy on top. I wasn't even fantasizing about anal intercourse then, but I was on top of him.

I was a competitive wrestler back then. It's interesting. There are quite a lot of gay or bisexual wrestlers. It's very closeted, but judging from some things that happened after practice, I had a feeling that a lot of those boys were tops. I can't tell you why. Probably guys who like to wrestle are predominantly tops.

Maybe it has something to do with personality, but I think it has more to do with your environment and how conducive it is to exploring different aspects of your sexuality. If you don't get to experience both sides of anal intercourse, you don't know what you're talking about, really. It's a learning process. Through my evolution as a gay man, I learned an awful lot about myself from having sex with other men. I didn't know that so many things could be pleasurable in sex. I never read about them and nobody told me about them. Like being jerked by another guy. I didn't know how good that could be. It all depends on how conducive your environment is to exploring different facets of your sexuality.

My initial fantasies about gay sex continued for years. I knew something was different about me, but didn't quite understand what it was. I didn't know the word "gay" yet. I had feelings for boys my own age. They were the object of my masturbation fantasies. Mostly fantasies of rubbing against each other. Something actually happened when I was thirteen or fourteen. After that it became a—not a fetish or an obsession—but something that I constantly wanted to do with someone. But this was not something you did in the sexually conservative environment that I grew up in. I sensed that my parents wouldn't want to hear about this.

Somewhere around age sixteen the other boys started dating girls and I realized I wasn't interested. I was interested in girls to talk to, to go out shopping with. [Laughs] I love going shopping with girls and watching them try on clothes and have them watch me try on clothes—but I realized at that point that I had not the least sexual interest in them. When I understood the meaning of the words "gay" or "homosexual," I didn't want to be that way. It took me years to come through with that.

I had my first real sexual experience when I was seventeen. The other boy was fourteen. We basically lived out my fantasy about frottage. It happened a few times and then I had a series of girlfriends. I had sex with them, but it was never fulfilling. I always felt, "No, this is not right for me, it's not fun, it doesn't turn me on." The ejaculation took much longer than it would have with a man.

I was dating a girl when I was twenty-five and became madly infatuated with this guy who was in med school with me. He was very handsome and I was sexually attracted to him. Unfortunately, he was straight; but my feelings for him were so strong that I confessed to my girlfriend how I felt for him. She said, "You're gay. You've got to be with guys." She was so matter of fact about it, she didn't even seem to care that much. That was a turning point. Although it took another year for me to be with a guy, I never looked back from that point on.

For the next five years I did the coming out thing. I tried to understand what it meant to be gay. I came out to my best friends. I was deviously hoping the rumor would make the round to my parents without me having to stand up for myself. When I came out to my brother, he told me he already knew. My sister had figured it out on her own. I told my mother. My parents are divorced and the only person I still had to come out to was my father. He lives in Germany with another woman. When I finally told him, he was totally cool about it. All he said was, "Well, Max, I don't want to see a whole procession of cute asses around here, but if you have a steady boyfriend, bring him home." And I said, "You wouldn't mind it if it was a procession of cute *tits* and ass." And he said, "Yes, but that's because I'm straight. I like girls." [Laughs] He took it in stride.

I didn't know much about gay sex back then. I had only a few one-night stands. Would you believe that I never actually saw a porno movie until I was twenty-nine? Because I never dared to go into one of those shops to borrow a video and I wouldn't know where to buy one.

The first time I went into a gay bar was when I was thirty, during a medical congress in Berlin. I met this other gay doctor at the congress and we made a date to meet. I arrived there early and paced up and down in front of the bar. I did this for about forty-five minutes before finally deciding to go in. He was there, but he was pissed because I was late and he thought I was a no show. That's how long it took me.

Soon enough I got together with a man from Sweden and he and I were together for four years. After we broke up, I went to Switzerland to work. That's when I decided to become more adventurous. I did my first park and my first gay sauna. I discovered what can happen at an autobahn rest stop. I realized for the first time what cruising on shopping streets was about. I was in a department store once and this guy started to follow me and eventually we ended up in the toilet and that was my first sex in a public rest room. All of this was enjoyable at first. The first couple of times you're looking for someone to have sex with in a park is exciting, new, and dangerous—but after a while I got bored with it. I felt I'd been there and done that. I wanted to be in a relationship again.

During that time the sex I had was mostly hand jobs and blow jobs. After I knew someone for a while, I'd have anal intercourse. Over the years I had a lot of experience fucking men. I know that some men are tops, but they experiment with getting fucked and decide that they like it and become bottoms. I've been fucked a few times, but I didn't like it. I always knew it wasn't for me.

There are definitely physical attributes that attract me. I like a man with a nice butt, nice legs, well-trained calves, and square shoulders. Masculine. I've always liked that. I'm attracted to men with a generally friendly look. What shocks me here in America is that they're totally, grotesquely overbuilt. I don't find that attractive. Someone who has a well-toned body from doing sports, that's fine; but if it's overdone, they begin to look comical, like Popeye or something like that. That's a turn-off for me. Although I've been with a few dark-haired guys, I have a preference for blonds, being dark haired myself. I prefer white men or black men. Asians have not been my thing. Probably, they're not tall enough for me and the height is important. They should be close to my height. Too short or too tall doesn't feel right. Anyway, those are the kinds of guys that make me turn and look at them on the street.

The men I've been with have mostly been close to my age. Some have been slightly older, maybe in their midforties. Two years ago, I slept with a guy who was eighteen. He was the youngest; but I find young guys, these college kids, kind of boring. They have nothing to talk about and they usually don't have enough sexual experience to be interesting in bed. They're just too nervous about everything. They're not relaxed.

Some gay men say that there are more bottoms than tops in the world. I think this is a misconception. It's something that derives from a gay self-stereotype. Like in the gay bashing world they say, "Those fags, all they want is to be fucked in the ass." It's a mistake when gay people think of themselves that way. That's not all that's happening between us. I've met a lot of casual tricks who were tops and anal intercourse did not happen, but we did other pleasurable things. I don't think there's a lack of tops.

I enjoy pornography occasionally as long as it doesn't involve children. And I have high respect for sex workers. There are a lot of men, gay or straight, who have no other way of getting any level of sexual activity. Prostitution makes sense. It should be legal and prostitutes should be paying taxes and social security just like everyone else.

I grew up at a time when the risk of AIDS was well known. I've never fucked anyone without a condom. I also don't cum inside while I'm fucking someone. I've never had unprotected anal intercourse. Whenever I encounter someone on the Internet who wants to have bareback sex, I warn the person off. Some people are saying bareback sex is now okay because we can treat AIDS. They don't know the devastating physical and psychological effects of being infected.

Over time, I've gotten very good at fucking. Most guys I've had anal sex with, with the exception of one or two, have all said that it was very pleasurable. If you fuck guys regularly you learn after a while how to technically do it. I watch the guy very carefully to see how he's reacting, to make sure it doesn't hurt, and that he's enjoying it. That's very important to me. That my partner's having fun. It's really great when I'm fucking a guy and he gets a hard-on while I'm fucking him and he cums while I'm fucking him. That's a real turn-on for me.

My experience is that about fifty percent of the guys I fuck are very excited and have hard-ons. If I wank them as I'm fucking them they want me to stop because they don't want to cum too soon. Especially the guys who are uncircumcised—there are many of them in Germany and Switzerland—they cum very fast if you wank them while fucking them. You shouldn't touch them, basically. About fifty percent of the guys lose their hard-ons while getting fucked. It depends.

I enjoy some anal stimulation. I don't mind being rimmed. I can sort of handle being fingered. I don't like it that much. I don't know why I don't enjoy it. It's never been pleasurable for me. Being tickled around the area is okay. But I've never found being actually penetrated with anything very pleasurable. A lot of men are sensitive around their nipples, but I'm not. I do it for other guys, but I'm not personally sensitive. My boyfriend knows me well enough and he's capable of stimulating me almost everywhere—but that happens when you get to know someone and you've slept with them many times. You discover each others' bodies. He's found erogenous zones on me that I didn't know were there before.

I don't associate being a top or a bottom with being masculine or feminine, nor with which one has more money or which one is older. When it comes to active and passive, I think the top has to be a bit more aggressive and the bottom has to be a little bit more passive, but my experience is that the bottom has to work with you. He has to do certain things to give his partner more pleasure, especially in the age of condoms. The sensual feeling is slightly reduced with a condom so the bottom has to do certain things with his sphincter to give the top a more intense feeling. Then the bottom is actually an active partner. So I wouldn't use the stereotypes active and passive because both partners have to work at it, so to speak, to make it successful and more pleasurable. I like having someone mount me while getting fucked. I like that. I've tried just about every position.

I'd say that I'm a more active rather than passive pursuer in the chat rooms on the Internet, but in bars I'm much more reserved. In pickup situations, sometimes I'm the pursuer and sometimes not. I find bars a very difficult pickup place because they're often smoky and loud, so you can't talk to anyone. And you don't want to take a crazy nutcase home who's going to stab you or something.

Effeminate men don't bother me. In fact, sometimes I find men who are slightly effeminate quite attractive—especially when they have an open face or an open expression or interested eyes. I'm not looking for the macho construction worker. In fact, I should be wearing a shirt that says: "I hate construction workers." [Laughs] I especially hate guys who are gay computer buffs, but pretend that they're construction workers. Just because they go to the gym twice a day and eat steroids and shit and wear construction boots. That's tacky. Having worked in occupational health, I know what construction workers are like. They've become construction workers because they had no other choice. They usually don't know beans about the world. They're certainly not people you can talk to about anything. I ended up having sex with a construction worker two or three times and I must say it wasn't very enjoyable. It was like the McDonald's of sex. It was fast food. It all tastes the same and when you walk out, you smell. One time after I had sex with a construction worker, I couldn't stand the smell of myself. I had to get under the shower as soon as possible. I'd been so horny that I hadn't noticed that the guy had a terrible body odor.

I don't wear anything—a handkerchief or arm band or so on—to signalize that I'm a top. In fact I think it's more exciting to meet someone and find out what they like during the ensuing conversation or even during the erotic entanglement. Fucking for me is not essential. It's okay if the guy is not a bottom because there are other ways to enjoy sex.

I think I've lived out every fantasy I've had. With my boyfriend I'm a little bit inhibited to ask to try out a fantasy or a fetish, but with a one-night stand I'm completely uninhibited nowadays. If I feel like leather sex, or if I feel like wearing my wrestling singlet during sex, I just ask them and most men will go along with it. I've found that when I get going with that stuff, the other guy tends to let go and get into it as well.

I became fascinated by leather in my early thirties. I bought my first set of leather pants and I thought they were very, very sexy—but it took me a long time to do anything about it. I don't go to leather bars because they're smoky and I don't drink and the guys who go there are usually not attractive enough for me. I don't like dark rooms or dungeons and I'm not into S&M, but leather looks nice and feels nice—although I got my testicle caught in the fly of my leather pants once and it was very painful.

I think there must be some sort of genetic program that makes us gay. The theories about the weak father and overprotective mother are just junk and have been proven wrong by psychology and the behavioral sciences. I was at a zoo in Holland once and there were these apes—I can't remember what they were called now—and they were relieving tension by fucking all the time. It didn't matter what kind of fucking, heterosexual, homosexual, you name it. I think the genetic program for sexual activity is more or less expressive in different individuals. As gay men, we have a gene that finds more expression in our actual outward behavior.

In evolutionary theory, homosexuality makes sense. Because in an environment with scarce resources—we're not built for bad weather conditions or starvation—it makes sense that we shouldn't procreate so much. There has to be some form of relieving sexual tension and that's where homosexuality comes into play. When you understand the notion that there is some reason for homosexuality to exist, it must make some biological sense.

I talk openly about this with my straight male friends; although most of them say that they cannot picture themselves having sex with another man, they can understand the notion that a man would know exactly how to give another man pleasure. Because a man knows. I think homosexuality is a perfectly natural aspect of humanity.

Although I'm not sure if I would do it, I believe very strongly that we should have the right to marry and adopt children. A lot of lesbian and gay parents could give kids a good home. Certainly a better home than some of these kids have in abusive straight households with drunk fathers and drug-addicted mothers. Gay marriage should happen with all the consequences, all the positive and negative aspects, the legal commitments and benefits.

As gay people, we make great contributions to society. We've set the tone in the world of culture and glamour for hundreds of years. We've always been the team leaders when it comes to creativity.

I don't see religion as a way of explaining the world or the universe. I think it's an arrogant creation of man. It's also a male, chauvinist, heterosexist way of interpreting the world. I believe there is no God and that we are totally insignificant in the universe. If we'd just accept that, we'd devote the rest of our time on this planet to having fun and living with each other in peace.

I have certain social principles that I stick to. What I feel deep in my heart is a desire to help people who can't help themselves. I felt that way when I was a kid and that hasn't changed about me. I admit that I can be harsh sometimes. I'm trying to be more relaxed about that.

My current relationship is the first one that I've ever thought would last a long time. We're both old enough now. We've both had considerable sexual experience. The notion of playing around is not so important anymore. He is versatile, so that creates some tension because I like to be the top all the time—but I've come to realize that it's important to be with someone who's affectionate, loving, and caring. It's not only about sex anymore. Sex is important, but it's moved to second position.

–8–

Mark: Control and Stereotypes

Top, Age 43

I was at a social gathering in Boston and someone asked me what I was working on. The mention of this book began a heated discussion. Someone jokingly announced that I should interview Mark because he was a "notorious top." This was the first time I'd met Mark and his movie star looks and self-assured, masculine demeanor had not escaped me. I asked him if he'd be willing and, to my delight, he said he was. We met a couple of weeks later at his apartment in Brookline.

Mark grew up in California and moved to Boston to attend college. He came out in his early twenties and has been in two long-term relationships since then. He's forty-three, but looks about thirty. His apartment is decorated with simple, practical furniture, a reflection of his own refreshingly straightforward manner.

* * *

I was very circumspect about this subject in my earlier days, when I was in my first relationship. Friends would always try to assume one of you was the top and the other the bottom, and they would ask, often in a direct way. I'd give circumspect replies or refuse to answer. I refused to talk about it. I didn't think it was anybody's business. But in the last fifteen years or so it's become much more open. I don't know if I've changed or if the community's changed. People are way more open about talking about it. When David described me as a top that day it was pretty jarring. It still feels funny when someone describes me in that way. Part of me still thinks it doesn't need to be public consumption.

Back in the seventies when I was in my early twenties and coming out, a lot of people said that if you didn't get fucked you were homophobic. The idea was that every gay man should be fucked and there should be no shame about these things. People were very political about it. It was about taking away the shame. That militancy seems to have disappeared now and there is more of an acceptance that certain people like certain things. They don't just assume that you're homophobic or that you have issues of shame or whatever. I mean if everyone liked the same things, there would be a problem.

I pretty much classify myself as a top. I don't know how common I am in that regard. When I first came out in my early twenties, right before AIDS became prevalent, I was very conservative. It took me a while to go through the coming out process. I remember one of the first people I met stuck a finger up my ass and I was like, "No, no, no." I was clearly not comfortable with getting fucked. Of course, then AIDS came along and, like many other gay men, I decided that if I hadn't gotten fucked by then, it was probably not a good idea to be fucked now.

Eventually, I met my first lover and after we'd been together for a while I decided to experiment because I was curious. He tried to fuck me and I really didn't like it. I couldn't relax and it was uncomfortable and painful. He kept saying, "Just relax, it'll feel better," but I just couldn't. It was interesting because we never talked about it, before or after that. For the next eight years I never once suggested that he should fuck me and he never once tried to do it. So we never tried it again. I never told him I didn't want to get fucked anymore. I remember at some point thinking that if he ever wanted to, I'd be willing to try it again.

That was also true in my next relationship. I started out as the top and he was clearly the bottom. I never told him I didn't want to be fucked. Once in a while we'd be out at dinner with friends or something and he'd jokingly indicate that he wouldn't mind being the top once in a while. But then, in the three or four years we were together, he never once physically initiated that he wanted to be the top and I never once asked him to do it. I figured that although I didn't really want to, I probably would if he wanted to.

I thought, over the years, that I should try it and that it might be fine if I relax into it. That I'd do it if someone suggested it. But then again, I realized that in my fantasies I'm never the bottom. I mean I never, ever, ever fantasize about getting fucked. The active part is what always turns me on. I would try to fantasize getting fucked, but it never turned me on. I've been intellectually curious about it, but it never triggered the thing in me that needs to be triggered.

I knew I felt different from a very early age. I have very good memories of going to the gym with my father when I was five or six, and sort of being in the shower with him and all these adult men and smelling all their body odor and liking that. I never said to myself when I was five that I was a faggot. By the time I was eight or nine, I had a crush on the guy who sat in front of me in class. I couldn't take my eyes off of him, but I didn't tell myself I was gay. I definitely knew that these were feelings I shouldn't tell anyone about. I knew that I had to hide it.

I do believe that being gay is something that's set at an early age, but I don't know if we're actually born that way. By the time you're four or five it's probably determined and it's not something you can turn on or off.

My first girlfriend in high school was a Mormon. She was the perfect girlfriend because she was conservative. Holding hands and a chaste good night kiss were all that would be tolerated. We were great for two or three years.

When I was sixteen my family joined a health club. I used to go work out and go into the steam room. I remember this guy who was probably in his twenties sat next to me and we were talking and I thought, "God, it would be nice if he reached out and touched me." I don't remember if I thought I was gay or not. People didn't talk about it. They used faggot as a derogatory term in school, but I didn't even know what it meant. It wasn't until college that I began to understand what it meant, let alone the behavior associated with it.

When I was eighteen or nineteen I dated some women, but there was no sexual interest on my part. I knew there was something wrong or different. I tried once or twice to have sex with them, but there was virtually no sex. A couple of times I couldn't even get an erection. They were not positive experiences, let me put it that way.

By college I pretty much knew I was gay, but I hadn't done anything about it. For three or four years I didn't want to be gay. I thought if I met the right woman, I'd change. So I would go out on dates, but of course the switch never happened. Finally I said, "Well, it's not working with women, we'll see if it's any different with a man." I definitely didn't fly out of the closet like a lot of other gay men did. For me it was gradual process.

I wasn't a drinker so the idea of going into a gay bar, especially by myself, was unthinkable. I responded to an ad in the *Boston Phoenix,* and I met this guy for lunch and we went to the museum. A few days later we went to his place and he gave me a blow job. And it was like, "Oh my gosh, this is it!" It's twenty years later now and he and I are still friends. He was like a brother more than a boyfriend.

Soon after that I had anal sex for the first time. By this time I could go to the gay bars. I was hanging out at a bar with a friend, looking around the room and commenting on people. I saw this guy and I told my friend that he was adorable. The guy saw me looking and pointing at him and gave me this big smile. At that point, I figured I had to go up to him. We came back to my place and started fooling around and he started rubbing his ass against me. So I thought that must mean he wants to get fucked. Clearly by this point I understood the concept although I hadn't done it before. I had some lube and I fucked him. This was at the cusp of AIDS and we had unprotected anal sex. Fucking had clearly become a high risk category by then. I saw him once or twice after that. I remember at one point thinking, "I hope he makes it." I lost track of him and I have no clue if he's still okay.

The first time I did it, it was okay. It took a little bit of practice before I learned how to do it properly. I was twenty-four years old and, you know, hard as a rock. With him, it was more animalistic than it became later, in terms of the rhythm and doing it in a way to allow the other person to relax into it. You learn as you do it more. There was no light bulb or anything that went off in my head telling me that I was a top.

The next guy I dated was actually a top as well and he wanted to fuck me. I really didn't want him to so we always just jerked off. It was fun.

I met my first serious boyfriend when I was twenty-seven and he and I stayed together for eight years. He liked to get fucked every once in a while, but not regularly. I would suggest it way more than he wanted to do it. Our sex tended to me more jerking off. If we had anal sex once a month, it was probably a lot. I definitely liked it by this time and it was my favorite thing. About five years into the relationship we had a conversation about what we really liked. He said, "When I'm relaxed and I'm enjoying it, I really do like to get fucked." But he tended to be a little nervous and oftentimes he couldn't relax. We didn't have a lot of anal sex, but I didn't know what I was missing either. It wasn't really an open relationship, although once in a while something might happen. If I was gone, or if he was traveling someplace and if something happened, that was fine. When we were together, we were together. Once in a while we'd do a threesome. He wanted to be more sexually promiscuous than I wanted to be and that was one of the issues we broke up over. I was thirty-five when it ended.

I was single for five years after that and I'd say that was the more interesting period in terms of being a top. When you're in your twenties or early thirties you're omnisexual and you don't think about what you like that much. It isn't until you relax and create sexual intimacies that you start to say, "This is what really turns me on and the other stuff doesn't matter that much." By the time I was in my late thirties, what got me excited and what didn't was pretty clear to me. I tried to date men who were about my age, but a bit younger, hopefully within five years. Clearly, when I would meet someone the antennae would go up about whether we'd be sexually compatible or not. Once in a while, I'd meet somebody and it was just clear that we were incompatible because we were both tops. I'd never think about sleeping with that person. Even if I'd started flirting with him, the interest in flirting would fade pretty soon. I'd never seriously act upon it. I treated people in this way and I could see some instances where other people treated me in this way too.

It wasn't only around the issue of anal sex. It's more complicated than that. It also has to do with control. I mean if you're dancing, someone has to be leading and both people have to be comfortable with that. I've had sex with very aggressive bottoms who were completely compatible with me in terms of the physical act, but in terms of the pacing and timing and everything else I just wasn't comfortable with them. I wouldn't do it again because they were too aggressive. They made me feel almost like a dildo, like they were just using me. On certain occasions that's fine, it can even be fun sometimes, but it has to be done in a way that feels comfortable for both people. Occasionally, I felt like it wasn't about him and me; it was more about him using me.

In a bar situation, it has to do with unconscious signals. It has to do with the way people hold themselves, the way they touch you, the way they make eye contact. It works on a chemical level too. Sometimes, I meet someone and there's something chemical that gets me excited. It takes me by surprise. As I'm getting older, the range type of man that gets me excited has narrowed. In my early twenties anything that breathed could get me going. Every once in a while it takes me by surprise because I meet someone who I'm not really attracted to visually or physically, but there will be something chemical going on. There is something at work on an unconscious level. On the other hand, I'll see someone who is visually and physically perfect for me and I'll zero in on him and we'll end up going to bed together and it doesn't go. Clearly the package is there, but we're still incompatible.

The physical act of top and bottom is only one component of that. There are all sorts of emotional things that need to fit as well that complement that. It may be okay for a fifteen-minute thing, but if you want to do it again with him there's got to be something else that clicks.

I met my next boyfriend when I was thirty-nine. It lasted for about three and a half years. I met him when I was spending a winter down in Florida and that's where we started dating. After our first date, he moved in with me for the next month. After I came back to Boston, I'd go down there and see him on the weekend about once a month. Finally, he decided to move up here. He just loved to get fucked. At the beginning, we were having anal sex four or five times a week. I mean, if we weren't fucking, he wouldn't even think it was sex and it wouldn't count. If we were just jerking off, he'd just as soon not do it at all because we weren't having intercourse. At one point fairly early on, after we'd been doing this for six or eight months, I remember saying to him, "We're fucking so much, I don't want you to feel like I'm taking advantage of this," and he was like, "No, it's great!" He couldn't get enough. I wouldn't be surprised if I never met someone I'm as sexually compatible with as I was with him. We just clicked.

Our relationship was pretty much stereotypical. I'm very practical, he's very artistic. I'm very analytical, he's very emotional. We were just opposites. So everyone assumed correctly that I was the top and he was the bottom. I'm sure there was a part of him that didn't want to be pigeonholed as that, but we were comfortable with the way things were. Sex was not an issue in that relationship.

It ended because of alcohol. He couldn't control his drinking and he wouldn't get help for it. I told him he could either control it on his own or get help for it or we're over. But he wouldn't. One of the problems was that when he drank he became more sexual and more relaxed and he loved that. He loved sex when he was drunk and he was a fun drunk. It also meant that he'd stay out very late, he'd sleep the whole next day, he'd be late for work, he'd forget things, and be unreliable. It got to a point where I couldn't trust him anymore.

It wasn't an open relationship. I don't really have strong feelings about open or closed relationships. What I do have strong feelings about is that I don't want to be in competition with somebody else. If you're going to sleep with someone else, you have to do it in a way that won't affect me. So you do it when I'm not around or when I don't know about it and it makes no difference. Then I don't care. We both didn't tell each other that we couldn't sleep with other people. I didn't do it, but I know that he did on occasion. I was sexually happy in my relationship with him so I didn't feel the need to sleep with anyone else. Toward the end, when it was clear that we were breaking up, I did have sex with a few people; but while we lived together I was monogamous.

With my first boyfriend I always thought I was not a very sexual person. He always complained that we weren't having enough sex, even when we were doing it four or five times a week. After eight years, we were still having sex three times a week and he still complained. With my second boyfriend, sex eventually became less frequent. Toward the end, if we were doing it twice a week, he was happy. If I wanted it three times one week he'd be like, "Oh, no, not tonight." But we were closer. Every once in a while it would be the other way around, with him suggesting sex and me saying no. Sometimes, I'd say no because he'd come home after the bars closed at two o'clock in the morning and I'd already be in bed and he'd want to have sex and I'd be like, "Forget it!"

I think there is a grain of truth to the stereotypes of tops and bottoms. There are exceptions. There are lots of aggressive bottoms and lots of tops who like to be controlled. I think the stereotype somewhat applies to my personality. My second boyfriend and I definitely fit the stereotypes, but in my first relationship we clearly didn't. For a lot of gay men, especially single gay men, it's the prism through which they look.

Every relationship needs a glue that binds you together. Sex was clearly the glue or the arena in which intimacy was built and conflicts were resolved in my first two relationships. There was not a lot of verbal processing, we just knew. Sex was a major, major part of it and sex set the pattern. It allowed decisions about what we're going to have for dinner to be made. You just do it. You don't have to discuss it.

Recently, I've started to date someone and I have no clue whether we'll be sexual. It doesn't strike me that we're going to have a big sex life, but that remains to be seen. Sex is not setting the pattern at all. The glue to this one seems to be incredible compatibility. We're dealing with issues of control in an arena I've never dealt in before in a relationship. We're having to deal with them verbally, not sexually. They're having to be talked out instead of just knowing. It's a whole new and different way of trying to figure out how we're going to be a couple. He describes himself as versatile. I think our sexual relationship is going to be more about intimacy rather than anal sex.

I've never thought about whether God created men to have anal sex, but I guess the answer is yes. It clearly is natural because you see it also in animals and it's also occurred in every civilization. You can make a moral judgment and say God didn't mean for that to happen, but I don't think God has anything to do with anal sex. To me, it's not a moral issue. What's to fight? There's nothing wrong with who I am. I'm not hurting anybody. This is who I am.

Things have changed over the generations. Men who are ten or twenty years older than my generation had a lot more shame that they had to deal with. There was a lot of rationalization going on. Like if they liked to get fucked they weren't real men so they must identify more with women. For people who are younger, getting fucked absolutely doesn't take on that kind of meaning. It just means they like to get fucked. Younger people are more likely to think that bottoms have as much power as tops and that it's reciprocal. They don't feel the shame and they don't necessarily identify it as feminine anymore. Things are definitely changing.

When I was in a relationship, we didn't worry about safe sex. There was an element of trust there which some people thought was stupid. It's rare that I don't use a condom with tricks I've picked up, but it does happen on occasion. My view is that I'm not putting myself at that much risk. If there's no discussion about it, I pretty much assume the other guy is positive. I find it difficult to believe that someone who is negative would let a perfect stranger fuck them without a condom without any discussion. Apparently it does happen.

I was in San Francisco recently and a lot of people there wanted to bareback. I took this guy home and I was on top of him and before I even knew what was going on, he had me lubed up and inside of him. I pulled out and put a condom on. The sensation without the condom was way better, but it also makes me a bit uncomfortable to do it.

Another time, I went to this guy's motel room and we were having sex and it was clear that he wanted me to fuck him. I asked him if he had a condom and he said no. So I didn't do it. We finally went to sleep and at four-thirty in the morning suddenly I woke up and he was giving me a blow job. I was enjoying what was going on, but I was definitely still in dream land and not fully aware of what was happening. Suddenly, he sat on me. Clearly, I woke up at that point and knew what was going on, but I was willing to be passive. So I let him finish. He jerked off on me and I pulled out and jerked off too. It was fun. That's why I let it slip.

I've probably watched a total of ten porno movies my entire life, and of those, maybe four or five to completion. Every once in a while, I'll rent a movie if someone tells me I should see it and it's a great movie, whatever, and I'll try it out. If I like it, I'll jerk off to it and then just shut it off. I'm not a big porno guy.

Once in a while I'll jerk off fantasizing about someone I've seen or someone's picture I've seen in a magazine, but I never look at the magazine when I beat off. I usually fantasize about fucking. Nothing kinky. No fetishes. Very vanilla.

I've had some incredible sex in my life. In terms of sheer pleasure, sex was by far the best with my second relationship. When I consciously decided this guy was right for me, we were in bed. When he moved to Boston to live with me, we hadn't seen each other in six weeks. We basically tumbled into bed and I was just crazed. I hadn't had sex for six weeks and this was a man that I was wildly attracted to. I thought, "I don't even care what he thinks, I just want to be a pig." I just got to do what I got to do. I was just about as piggy as I could get in bed with anyone. I never asked him, I never checked in with him to make sure he was enjoying it. Usually I'm pretty considerate as a lover. I make sure I get feedback. You can tell. You read people. In this instance, I didn't care. I just wanted to do what I wanted to do. We finished up having sex and we were lying there and he literally rolled over to me and he said, "That was the best sex I've ever had." And I was feeling guilty because I'd been so selfish! So that told me. After that, I never felt guilty again and I was as selfish as I ever wanted to be, and we had incredible sex. He couldn't get enough.

I couldn't believe he wouldn't quit drinking for me. I saw him in California recently and we had sex. There's no way that we would get together and not have sex. We would always have sex. But there's no way I'd get back together with him. The bottom line was, even though it was the best sex in my life, it wasn't enough to sustain our relationship.

9

Jay: An Assertive Personality

Top, Age 51

Jay says he tries to create and honest and open discourse in his work in HIV safety. "That can only be achieved by bringing specificity to the discussion," he says. "We used to tell people they should be concerned with body fluids in general; but then it became clear that it wasn't all body fluids that caused concern, but certain specific ones. We had to talk to people about that in a plain and frank language that they could understand. We couldn't just tell them, 'Don't have sex.' We had to tell them specifically what kind of sex. Sometimes when we used the term 'anal sex,' people didn't know that we meant buttfucking. Even today, when anal intercourse is discussed, people often don't distinguish between the insertive and receptive partners. Therefore the risk factors are not clear. The more specific you get, the clearer you are and the better people understand."

It wasn't only his work in HIV safety that drew Jay to call me. He was also interested in exploring his own evolution as an "aware gay man." A beefy, masculine man with a dark goatee and shaved head, Jay looks younger than his early fifties. He divides his time between Boston, where he makes a living, and Provincetown, where he owns a small condo on the water. He has an introspective, gentle, but notably assertive demeanor. On several occasions he's compelled to correct some of the terminology I use, or to point out that I'm making an inappropriate assumption. When I try to lead him to talk about a specific issue, he laughs. "All right," he says patiently, "I'll let you be the top and take the lead. But only for a little while!"

*   *   *

I generally categorize myself as a top. I have an assertive, take charge personality. I exhibit some of the typical male, testosterone behavior, not all of which I'm proud of. We men tend to interrupt and talk more than we listen. I certainly try to cultivate both the male and the female aspects of my personality. I think it's important to be a listener and to be able to take in and absorb from other people and the world, but I know what my personality is and what I enjoy most in bed. Usually, before having sex with someone, I like to find out their likes and dislikes to get a measure of compatibility. While I think of myself generally on top, I really think it's important not to choreograph what's going to happen in bed. The best sex is not just with that nice looking body, but with that person inside that body too. Everybody's different. What really makes sex good for me is to experience that person. So if somebody I'm really attracted to doesn't fit in to that dichotomy of top and bottom, but is drawn to me, I would like, at the very least, to explore the possibilities without limiting myself by saying, "Well, you're not a bottom, so forget it."

I think the notion that the top and bottom roles relate to aggressiveness or age or economic position does exist and I personally experience them. I'm an empowered person. I don't want to sound smug about that. I'm a white male and I don't want to apologize for that because I had no choice in the matter. The joke is that everyone in the world either wants to be a white male or to kill one. I can understand those feelings. Second, I have money and I'm well educated and I can get around in the world very well. Basically, to a great extent, I can have what I want. I don't want to sound arrogant. For me, it's important to recognize the dignity and humanity of all people, including and especially the disempowered. That's why I do a lot of work in Boston and elsewhere with the homeless. I don't regard myself as superior. I'm privileged and more fortunate than most of humanity, alive or dead.

All of this, to a certain extent, relates to my sexual orientation. It's not completely a question of what I prefer. If you go to a smorgasbord and there are fifty different kinds of food, obviously you can't eat from all of them, so you eat from the ones you prefer. There is some amount of preference too. If I were in a relationship with somebody on a desert island and if that person was exclusively the top, and I had to be exclusively the bottom, I probably wouldn't enjoy the sex as much as the sex I have right now. It's not just a matter of preference, it's also nature. It's just what works for me, what arouses me, what excites me. I don't really understand that. I've spent a lot of mental energy trying to understand it.

I took a big detour early on, by thinking more about what should be and what's right, rather than what I really liked. When I was younger, I thought I should be versatile. I thought I should be as comfortable getting fucked as I am fucking—and I used to really enjoy getting fucked. I still do once in a while, with the right person in the right situation; but being on the bottom has come to take on a lot more meaning for me. Sometimes it's hard for me to stay hard when I'm being fucked; so for me it means sacrificing that part of the sexual pleasure, as a gesture to demonstrate how special I consider that other person to be. That I want to do something for that person, I want to give him pleasure.

The last time I was fucked was two years ago with my lover at the time. We had done a lot of things that we liked sexually and we'd reached a plateau. He thought of himself as a bottom and I had to cajole and coax him to take the role of top, which he did somewhat begrudgingly. It was hard for me to understand his reluctance because I was asking him to do something that I enjoy so much. I thought he might enjoy it too. I wanted to experience him, I wanted to take him in. I wanted to have him inside me, because I loved him. I really was asking him to fuck me because I wanted the experience of having him inside me. Of taking in who he was. For me, I guess the act of fucking is an act of acceptance. The person who's getting fucked is in some way making a physical, sexual gesture of accepting and taking the other person in. If it's with someone you don't know very well, it becomes about accepting the person you imagine your partner to be. But when it's someone you're close to—like I was to my lover—at the moment of getting fucked, you're taking in the person you know and love; an accumulation of all you've been through together.

I became a teenager in 1960 and I came out very early. I was always attracted to men and started to have sex with them at the age of thirteen. I played around with some peers, but the sex I had was with older men. When I was five or six years old, I went to a baseball game with my dad. During the break we went to the restroom at the stadium. I don't remember this, but my dad told my mom that after I finished peeing and he'd taken me to the sink to wash my hands, I went back to the urinal. Dad said it looked like I wanted to massage the urinal. I know that I was always curious, from an early age, about other guys' cocks. I wanted to see dick. What better vantage point could there have been than to stand by the urinal and see twenty urinals all in a line, with no separators, so you could see, at one glance, five or six dicks of every shape, size, and color. I don't actually remember that, but I'm sure it was wonderful. I do remember consciously having an interest in seeing cocks when I was eight or nine.

When I was twelve, we'd pass through an area we called The Tenderloin on our way to visit my grandparents. Mama told me never to go to that part of the city because all the worst people in the world, thieves, pimps, drug addicts, and homosexuals hung out there. And I said to myself, "Homosexuals?" So as soon as I was old enough to buy bus fare into the city, I made a beeline to that place. Thank God AIDS wasn't around then because I'd have died before I reached twenty. That's one reason why I do prevention work with teenagers because I was a very sexual kid myself.

I began to have sex in cruising spots, like public bathrooms, when I was thirteen. I took advantage of every opportunity to have sex with men during my years as an adolescent. It would happen on my way home from school or when I had an appointment with the orthodontist or on the way to dancing school. Once in a while I'd meet an older guy and make a date and play hooky from dancing school to have sex with him.

Today, a person who has sex with a thirteen-year-old boy could be sent to jail for a long time. While I do consider sexual molestation and abuse real serious issues, I want to be very clear that I don't feel that those men abused me at all. They may have taken advantage of my willingness and my desire to explore sex with them, but I was the one who was there specifically looking for sex. I was looking for it. I personally don't believe that men involved in that kind of a situation should be punished. If an adult has sex with a minor against that minor's consent, that's another story.

My parents found out I was gay when I was seventeen. I was already seeing a psychiatrist because I'd run away from home. Once they found out, they cried for two weeks and then invested themselves in getting me anything, doing anything to change my orientation. I was brainwashed for many years by a psychiatrist. He told me for four years that I was sick. He tried to convince me that my sexuality was caused by something in my childhood and that we were going to get to the cause and eliminate it. We now know that there was no basis for him to make that assumption. It's just totally unforgiving and arrogant. He billed my parents tens of thousands of dollars and spent endless months convincing me that my life, my future, would be a disaster if I didn't allow him to cure me of my homosexuality. We were all misguided and it was terrible. My parents were misguided in hopes of happiness at a time when homosexuality was scorned. It was inexcusable for a professional to lead us on under the guise of science.

I had this sense, particularly in my twenties, that things should be even, that I should be versatile and comfortable both as a bottom and a top. All of that became more complicated after I got anal warts when I was nineteen or twenty. This was in the sixties and a very homophobic doctor told me that only prostitutes got those warts on their vaginas. Then I let this guy take a knife to my anus. I don't know whether he did a good job or a bad job, but getting fucked became physically much less pleasurable for me after that. In my thirties, I had some more minor surgery which took away some of the pleasure I had previously experienced. I've been fucked since then and it hasn't been painful. If someone knows how to fuck well they can do it with a minimum degree of pain and a maximum degree of pleasure.

When I was in my early thirties, I began to reexamine my sexuality with a therapist. A straight, male therapist, I might add. He and I examined my sexual compulsions and appetite and the fact that, as far as anal sex was concerned, I enjoyed fucking more than getting fucked. He was very proactive and he would often give me assignments. One time, he asked me to try to repress all my sexual behavior, just as an experiment for a week or two. Then, at another time, he asked me to exaggerate and really delve into sexual behavior absolutely, as much as possible. So I could see how I felt and where my head was at during those different periods. I realized at a certain point that there were a lot of guys out there who were just as happy to be exclusively on the bottom. I understood that not every gay man was into anal sex and that those who were, were not all just as horny to fuck as to get fucked. Some of them really liked being on the bottom. And I thought, "Well, gee, with so many guys out there like that, there's certainly one that might be compatible with me—someone with whom I wouldn't want to make rules about who can do what to whom and how. There's somebody who would be happy with me, being on the bottom." Since then I've come to realize that being a bottom is more than just a physical state that a person can enjoy. It's also a social, psychological, spiritual way of being. It's a type of personality. Human beings are very, very complex and it's really hard to predict.

It was only when I saw that therapist that I started to see myself as a top. I realized that the right thing to do was to be true to myself and to my partner too. Because of the anal surgery I'd had, being a bottom had become more associated with pain than pleasure; but it wasn't just the pleasure and the pain that veered me toward being a top. There was much more to it than that. For me it has a whole lot more to do with power and being in charge. I enjoy being in charge. I may not necessarily like the fact that I prefer being in charge and I try to make up for that in some ways. I try to be a good team player in projects and a good listener to people I care about; but even being a good listener, in a sense, is a strategy to being a top—because being a good listener puts me in a position to help people. Having heard what their predicament is, and having heard their situation, I'm able to reflect and give them some help. I'm not always a good listener. I'm easily distracted. I feel that at this point in my life, being able to let go of control is a valuable commodity for me. It's a way of showing myself at my maturity.

For me, the most fun about having sex is not sticking my cock in somebody's hole, it's knowing that person. You can't get to know that person unless you allow that person to be himself. There are very aggressive bottoms, very verbal bottoms, down and dirty bottoms or celestial, "Oh I love you" bottoms. One of the most interesting bottoms I ever connected with wanted to see himself as a woman. He physically became hot as a woman often does when she's sexually aroused. His language and his gestures all became that of a woman while he was getting fucked. He even had some kind of an orgasm which resembled an orgasm a woman might have while getting fucked. Everyone is different. I like novelty and I like difference. How can I experience that if I don't allow somebody to be himself?

I indicate my preference to be a top by hanging some keys from my left side. If I want to be more brazen, I might wear a navy blue hanky in my left pocket which sends the message: "I want to fuck a butt." And while I enjoy fucking butt, I'm much more interested, at this point in my life, not just in fucking a butt, but a person. I'm more interested in who I'm going to fuck. Sometimes a brazen signal like that turns people off. Even if they're drawn to me because of my appearance or the persona I project, the blue hanky might make them think, "Oh, he's just looking for somebody to fuck."

I met two men at The Vault last night. These men assumed that since I live in Provincetown, I must be at the bars every night. That every night of the winter and summer I go to The Vault, which is crammed with available men, and that I pluck someone out of the crowd and take them home and fuck them. Well, that's just not the case. I've only been to that bar three times in the last seven months. I also don't like the smoke and I'm not that fond of drunk people. When I go out cruising for sex, I usually wait for the bars to close and then take a walk or a ride on my bike. No matter what I said, those two guys continued to make that assumption about me. I was drawn to one of them because he was sexually attractive and his work and his background were interesting; but I think—and this is strictly what I'm projecting—he saw me as jaded or saw himself as a sexual object and lost interest.

In some ways I'm so glad to be in my early fifties because I've reached the stage where I just don't apologize for who I am or what I like. I'm also very thankful that everybody in the world is not like me. I would hate to be in that kind of a world. I'm attracted to masculine men; generally men who are slender. I also like what would be called "secondary masculine features," like a mustache or a beard. I don't like to get much more specific than that because I don't want to limit myself. I also must see something in a man that's different than me. Whether it's a difference in ethnic, cultural, experiential, or class background, I need to see that person as someone different from myself. Even though, in essence, I'm still the top, I search for something in them that I want to take in. I can enjoy being with a man who is somewhat effeminate, but I have to see him as a man. I've never been to bed with a man in drag.

The size of a cock doesn't make a bit of difference to me. I like a big dick, but I like a little dick that can fit nicely in my mouth. I like foreskin, but it's just like facial hair or ethnicity. I mean, there's too much else in play for me to say it's got to be a big dick or a little one.

When I initially meet someone and we establish that there is a mutual attraction, I like to find out what the other guy's hopes and expectations of the sexual encounter are. I don't want to get involved with someone who might be incompatible with me. I really don't like guys who are extremely vague about what they like sexually. I like somebody who is able to communicate about that. I've recently been having an affair with a deaf man and although I don't know any sign language, we still don't have a problem communicating about that.

The longest relationship I've had lasted five and a half years. He lived far away and we spent, on average, five or six days a month together. I ended the relationship because I felt it was keeping me from having something more accessible. At the time, I'd been looking for a companion who would be intellectually and culturally more compatible with me. I think I undervalued some of the qualities that he had. We're still close emotionally, but we haven't seen each other at all in the intervening years.

I also had two or three live-in relationships and each lasted two or three years. I'd like to meet someone and settle down, but because I'm a top, I'm assertive and perhaps pushy. I snore and I'm not the easiest person to live with. I'm very much empowered and the guys that I often find myself drawn to are culturally or socioeconomically so different from me that the disparity causes a problem. This is of some distress for me.

The word *should* is ethic shorthand and I try not to use it, especially when the discussion is about barebacking. I have barebacked and I will again. For many people, in many situations, barebacking is reckless behavior. I've lost many, many friends to AIDS. But when all is said and done, it's an individual decision. We always need to have autonomy and control over our own behavior. If someone wants me to fuck them without a condom, to me, that's a real warning sign. They don't know me, they don't know what I have or don't have, and they're making an assumption about me. It's surprising how often that happens. That's one more reason why I like to learn the other guy's values before I have sex with him. I'd run out of fingers if I counted the number of guys who said to me, "If you need to use a condom when you fuck me, then I don't want to do it." The level of denial that these guys have amazes me. Being the insertive partner makes me less likely than them to be exposed to HIV, but I lived through the seventies: I had gonorrhea countless times, nonspecific urethritis, and even syphilis. Fortunately, those things were all curable with penicillin. I remember asking myself in 1975 how many times that year I'd been on antibiotics and how many times I'd caught some sexually transmitted disease. When someone tells me they want to be fucked without a condom, I wonder how many other bareback cocks have been in that butt hole and what they've left up there for me to pick up and take home. The thought and the action of bareback fucking is very pleasurable, but it's something I'm concerned about. Often, when I wind up getting into it, I feel some remorse and a sense that I've let myself go too far. The only time that there was an actual agreement to have bareback fucking was with my lover at the time. Part of the agreement was that it would not happen outside of the relationship, that my unclad cock would not be in anyone's butt hole but his, and that was practiced. And he didn't get fucked by anyone but me. So the criteria for barebacking in that case was that it was someone I trusted.

Since then, however, I've fucked other men without a condom. I met this guy when I was traveling abroad. I knew very well that he wanted me to fuck him and I remember thinking, as I was getting out of the car, that I should grab a condom and put it in my pocket; but for some reason that I can't remember or understand, I decided not to. He didn't seem to give it the slightest thought. I fucked him without a condom and I had a tremendous crisis about that. There was a cultural and linguistic barrier. Even though I spoke his language, there was a certain communication difficulty. It was a small city and he was strange to me.

More recently, I picked up someone here in town and we were fooling around and when it became clear that he wanted me to fuck him, I reached over to the bedside table and pulled out a condom and put it down on the bed. But sometime after that, before I had a chance to put the condom on, my cock penetrated him partly. We talked about it afterward and he wasn't too happy about it. He said he saw me grab the condom and thought I'd put it on, but clearly he didn't see me put it on because I didn't put it on.

I'm not fanatic about it, but I get tested regularly and I'm HIV negative. When I fuck someone bareback, I don't cum inside the other guy—as much as I would love to. It's been fifteen years since I did that. I didn't even do it with my lover. For me, wearing a condom, or failing that, pulling out and letting someone see me cum, is a demonstration of respect for that person. It's a demonstration that I acknowledge that person's humanity, vulnerability, his right to a happy, healthy future. With or without me.

10

Jackson: "I Enjoy Both"

Versatile, Age 25

When Jackson calls the sex lines to meet potential tricks or to jerk off, he describes himself as a twenty-five-year-old gay black man who's energetic, intelligent, loves music, singing, writing, watching TV, and hanging out with friends.

He was raised in a poor home in Kansas City and has overcome great obstacles to get an education. "This was the first school on my list," he told me as we shuffled around in the snow on the Harvard campus, searching for an empty classroom to talk. He settled on Colby College in Maine where he got his BA in English and creative writing three years ago. Today, he makes good money doing legal work for an investment company in Boston. One of his three brothers was shot and killed in a street fight when Jackson was in high school. Another brother is a year older and the third is his twin. Both are straight. Jackson says he and his twin are like night and day.

We finally settle in an empty room on the top floor of the Adult Ed building and settle down to talk. Jackson is relaxed and ready to reveal everything. He has a bright, beautiful smile, and his honesty and sense of humor are infectious.

* * *

I knew I was gay as a young boy. I've always looked at other boys, as far back as I can remember. I've never been sexually attracted to girls or women at all. Although I began my sex life as a bottom, I consider myself versatile at this point. I'd say I'm versatile, but mostly top.

My first sexual experience was when I was eleven. It was an unfortunate incident. There was this guy in the school system who was a friend of the family. He was thirty-eight when I met him and he was involved with the little league agencies. Within a year of meeting this man, he began to take me to his place, you know, as a reward for doing really well in school. He had this thing with my brothers and me. Whoever had the best grades for a particular quarter, he'd take us out to eat, like to McDonald's or somewhere. Then he'd take us swimming. We grew up in a poor family so to have somebody outside of the family take us out to eat or to go swimming was a great joy. It was like, "Wow, we get to get out of the house!" By this time, my brothers all had their friends out on the streets, but I was a homeboy, going to school and coming home to study. So it was great for me to get out. He was a very nice guy and very smart and being with him made me happy because I considered myself an intellectual at the time. [Laughs] He was saying all the right things as far as my future and my education, about what I could accomplish. He was married and his wife taught at middle school.

Before I met this man, me and one of my friends would talk about how we would never let anyone give us a blow job, because we thought it was sort of gross. I knew it was about a woman putting her mouth on a man's dick, but I didn't know what else it entailed. I didn't know what sex was all about.

One day, after we went swimming, I took a shower at his house. As I was coming out of the shower, he brought me a towel and sat on the toilet. I was all embarrassed and I thought, "Oh God, why is this man sitting here?" What did I know? Then he reached over and proceeded to massage my penis. And I was like, "Whoa!" It was kind of irritating because it was a sensation that I had never felt before. I'd discovered by that time that I could get an erection, but I'd never done anything about it whatsoever. I hadn't even masturbated yet. So I was like backing up, and going, "Okay." It wasn't because I was ashamed or anything—I didn't even know it was wrong—but it was weird and the sensation was just like, "Wow, this is kind of different!" I just thought it was odd that he was rubbing on it like that.

Anyway, I didn't ejaculate and he didn't get undressed or anything and he stopped massaging my dick after a few minutes. But then this thing continued for three years after that. It never went beyond that particular thing. It only happened when I went swimming and it wouldn't occur every time.

Over the next three years he told me about the sex he'd had with other men. That sort of opened my eyes. I'd go to the library and try to find stuff on gay sex. I took *The Joy of Gay Sex* to the back of the library and stood there and looked at the pictures. That was my intro to gay sex.

Overall, I wouldn't say it was a bad experience. It was nice to be around him. At that time I didn't know it was wrong at all. My brothers started to make jokes like, "Oh, you're spending too much time with him," and that made me feel self-conscious. I kept hoping no one else knew about it.

Toward the end of the three years with him, I finally ejaculated. I'd never seen him naked except when he took his shirt off or was putting on his trunks. He was building up very gradually. The last time we were together he showed me his penis and I touched it. He told me we would explore everything the next time we met.

Then, out of the blue, one day I'm watching *Oprah Winfrey* and the show is about sexual abuse. And they're describing how sexual molestation occurs and what kinds of signs abused children have and so on. I saw this program and I thought, "Oh my God, that's me. This is happening to me." I went to bed and thought about it all night.

I was in counseling at the time because I was having some family issues. So the next day I went in to see my therapist and I told her what was going on. In the state of Kansas, if a child tells you that they're being molested, the therapist has to report it. She told me what her obligation was and I was scared as hell. I told her I wanted to tell my family first. I told my twin brother and he and I went and told my grandmother. She's from the old school, you know, you don't talk about stuff like that. She would've easily put it under the covers, told me to never see him again, and that would've been it. But at that stage I was feeling completely upset and betrayed. And the legal action had already moved into place.

Within a few days I got called into the security office and there stood a detective. That really scared me. I had to describe to him some of the incidents and a bunch of other things. It moved fairly quickly after that. Within days, the guy disappeared from town. They found him and he pleaded guilty to avoid a trial and got sentenced to three years in prison. He came up for parole every year so I went to the parole hearings by myself and they kept him in. It was my choice to show up. This made the paper because he was a school official, so tons of people from the school district would be at the parole hearings and there would be little me. He served his time in prison and I have no idea where he is now. It's so weird, I found out later that he abused other kids too, but none of them pursued the case. My brothers also mentioned that this man had attempted to do things with them.

For the next few years, until I was seventeen, I'd get magazines and look at the men and masturbate. My eyes had been opened to the joys of gay sex. One day, a friend gave me the number of some sex line. So I called the number and met this guy. He sounded really cool and we exchanged numbers and decided to meet. We were going to meet around the corner from my house. The day he was coming over, oh my God, I was so scared. My family had no idea at the time and it was top secret. To me he was this established, experienced gay man and this was quite an adventure. I couldn't believe I was doing this behind my family's back.

We met and I was like, "Oh, you're cute." He was twenty-seven. We walked to the park and sat there to chat and get to know each other. After about an hour, I got up to go to the bathroom. So I'm in the bathroom in the park and he comes in. I'm standing there urinating and he's standing next to me, urinating too. Next thing I know, he's kissing my neck. And I was like, "Oh, my God! He's kissing my neck at the urinal!" And he pushes my pants further down and I'm like, "This is interesting." We were in a public bathroom and I was like, "What if somebody comes around?" He kissed my neck, kissed my back, and then suddenly he sticks his tongue in my ass. And I'm like "Whoa!" Out in the open, not even in the stall. It was exhilarating. I put my mouth on his penis, but I didn't really suck him. He proceeded to lick my ass and jack me off and I ejaculated. It was the second time I'd ejaculated with a guy.

I felt guilty for the rest of the day. It felt like the whole world knew what I had done. I grew up a Baptist and I thought God was looking down on me. Every time the preacher would say anything related to sex, I'd think, "Oh, God, he's looking at me, he's talking directly at me." It had a profound effect on me because I was a teenager and there were other things going on in my life.

A week later, I went over to his place and I couldn't believe I was in another man's house. We did everything that day. We performed mutual oral and then he penetrated me. He basically "made love" to me. He did everything I expected sex to be. My only problem was that he kept wanting to do it. He didn't want to stop, and, you know, the first time you get fucked, it hurts. It took like thirty minutes to get it in. Once it was finally in, it was okay.

Being a bottom seemed natural. I was attracted to older men and being a bottom with an older man seemed the right thing. He was more experienced and he would lead and I would follow. I finally told him I was only seventeen and he was fine with that, but I only hung out with him for about two weeks.

For the next two years, whenever I got together with someone it usually ended up in anal sex and I was pretty much a bottom. In the beginning I'd lay there and let the guy stick his penis in me. To them, it was the greatest thing because here was this eighteen year old with a tight ass who'd never been fucked. I was inexperienced at the beginning, but I eventually came to like it. The more I did it, the more I liked it.

To me, everybody I met at the time became my boyfriend. I met this other guy and he wanted to fuck me all the time. By now, I was a little more experienced so I told him, "What if I fucked you?" He agreed and I finally got that experience and it felt very good. Except as soon as I got it in, I was like, "Oh, my God, I'm cumming!" It happened too fast and I didn't like that, and I was still the bottom in that relationship.

I classify myself as versatile now, but I'd like to be a top more. I like penetrating a guy more than being penetrated. I think I was a bottom during the first years because there were other issues related to that. Back then, I'd meet someone, we'd go out, and I'd think he was my boyfriend. Being a bottom was always about meeting someone older, the guy getting some ass, and then leaving. That happened too many times. These guys would seem so genuine, they'd tell me I was cute and all that, but then we'd have sex and they'd get some ass and they'd be gone. That happened from when I was seventeen 'til twenty-two or so. It still happens occasionally. It affected me emotionally. It felt like they were leading me on to think that something good was going to happen. I'd be waiting around for them to call and I pretty much let my personal life be led by them. My emotions went up and down based on a phone call or seeing someone or what they told me. I didn't have any emotional support from my family, so I put it on the men I met. I wasn't old enough to get in the clubs, so I always thought the older guy was off somewhere at the clubs, doing someone else. It was horrible. I felt used.

There was one particular individual that I really liked. The day I met him, he said he'd been on his way to kill himself, but that I'd saved him. I'd met him cruising the park and he was a good guy. I thought he was nice. I thought I had this particular bond with him, that, you know, meeting me had an effect on him. I sort of fell for him. I don't know if I can say I was in love, but I was really, really in lust, or infatuated with this guy. I tried to have this long distance thing with him, but later I found out that he was the biggest whore in town.

Nowadays, it's very rare that I bottom for someone I've just met. My idea of relationships has changed. My life doesn't depend on another man anymore. Now if the guy doesn't call me back, it's like, "Oh, well." What do I care? I don't get emotionally attached. I haven't had a long-term relationship to this day.

I have a friend and he and I have been sort of sex buddies for the last three years. We go back and forth fucking each other, and that works for me. Occasionally, I'll meet someone and I'll feel the urge to get fucked. I do enjoy it now. I enjoy both, and when I get fucked now, I don't have that emotional attachment that I used to. If I'm contemplating getting in a relationship with someone, I always tell the person that it won't work if he's a total top. If he's a total top and is unwilling to budge, it's not going to work, because he won't bottom for me. If someone told me that they're willing to try it every once in a while, you know, that's fine. Just try it once with me. Don't completely shut me down and say, "No, I'll never do that."

I've found that most guys who say they're total tops just want to be serviced all the time. So you're sucking them off, licking their nipples, pleasing them, and the top is pretty much laying there. He'll kiss you a little bit or do a little sucking, but for the most part you're taking care of him and doing all the work. Even when they're fucking you, they're not necessarily doing all the work. A lot of the time they don't really care whether the bottom cums or not. So fuck you. They cum and they're ready to go.

There's this guy who wants to have a relationship with me now, and he's smart, makes good money, and all that stuff. We could have a great relationship, but he wants to be a total top. We've had sex a few times. He's one of those tops that I mentioned: he'll kiss you a little bit, but he refuses to suck a dick, refuses to do anything. He just wants to lay there and have you service him, lick him over, and he wants to fuck you. Then you have to jack yourself off while he lays there. I told him I wouldn't do that. I'd go crazy.

I think some power issues are involved. Nowadays, I feel empowered when I'm not the bottom, when I tell someone no. Like we get together and they're putting their finger down there and I'm like, "No, we're not doing that." It's a great feeling. When I was younger, I'd say yes to everything. I wasn't terribly promiscuous, but if someone wanted to fuck me, I'd go along with that. Now, I can say no and it feels very good.

I changed my ways when I got to college. I became leery about anyone fucking me. I was being more careful about STDs and the people I met. There was a gay club in Augusta, Maine, and I'd go there every now and then. I was always a hit when I went in there. It was mostly white guys and I was the new black man that walked in. I seemed to be in demand there. It was great. One of my friends said it was like I was holding court. [Laughs] I got into oral sex and I had some threesomes. Nowadays, I don't do anal as much anymore. Unless I meet someone real cute and I just have to have that.

I've had thoughts of being gay as far back as I can remember. I never seriously pictured myself with a woman, married and stuff. I meet married men who mess around with me and they tell me, "Oh my God, I always felt that this was what I wanted to do and I had to get married because of so and so." I think we all have the potential to be gay or straight; and honestly, if I hadn't been molested, I probably would've gone the other route of marriage. I'd have gotten married and repressed the feelings that I had.

I'm not as religious as I used to be, but I believe in God. I believe that everything we do in life is the will of God and that there's a reason for everything, whether it's right or wrong. Everything we do, to me, has been predetermined. As a child we learned that God knows how many hairs you have on your head. God knows everything that can happen in your life before you do. I don't think God would've given us the ability to fuck men unless there was a reason. He wouldn't have given us the ability if he didn't want us to experience it. So I do believe that we were created to have anal sex, as long as we're cautious and safe about it. That's where people go wrong.

I've been safe for the most part, except for a few occasions. The first time I got fucked was safe. Once I fucked a guy without a condom and he fucked me without a condom, too. Me and my fuck buddy, we don't use protection. We keep each other up to date on our HIV status. I'm negative. I feel guilty when I have unsafe sex with him, but I have no one to blame but myself.

I'm trying to be truthful about this: I think the size of a man's cock does matter. I don't want someone overly large. My fuck buddy has a big one and he and I can tolerate each other. A lot of guys with big dicks don't know how to fuck, and it hurts. Medium size is fine with me and it would depend on how small. I encountered a guy once who had a one or two incher and he attempted to penetrate me and I didn't feel a thing. I was just put off by that.

My best sexual experience was about a year and a half ago and I was actually a bottom. I met this guy on the phone. He said let's get together tonight, but I was hesitating. He called me again that evening. I'd just taken a shower, and he sounded really, really nice, so I was like, "Okay." I hopped on the train, which I normally won't do for anyone, and went to his place in Jamaica Plain. He opened the door and, oh my God, he was cute! He was in his thirties. He was my height and my weight, professional guy. I was like, "Oh, God, you're cute," and he was, "You're cute too." We ordered dinner and ate and lay on his bed and watched television. Then he leans over and says, "Can I kiss you?" and I'm smiling and I'm like, "Sure!" So he kissed me. It was great because he's versatile too, but that time I bottomed for him. There was mutual oral sex and he got into kissing my nipples, my neck. His goal was to make me happy. He got up the next morning and made me breakfast. It was beautiful. We still see each other occasionally and he enjoys getting fucked just as much.

For me, there's no emotional attachment to being a top or a bottom, but being a top seems to be empowering somehow. Like, "Oh, goodness, I'm a top!" It's not a masculine/feminine type thing, but there's something about the power of being a top. I just enjoy pleasing my partner. When I'm a bottom it means that I really, really want to receive it, and I get into that and it feels good once it's there. The guy who's doing it should do what he's supposed to do and I should do what I'm supposed to do. Which is him penetrating and me responding. Years ago, when I first started doing it, I'd just lay there and it was always my goal to get them off quicker than they wanted to. But now I'm an active bottom. Now that I can choose the situation, about being a bottom or top, being a bottom is great. Being an active bottom means you're not just laying there, letting the other guy fuck you. You're moving and getting into it. You're fucking back, you're enjoying it. I'm amazed at bottoms who just lay there. I'm like, "Okay, work with me."

When I'm bottoming, I like to be on my stomach and have the guy fuck me from behind. Every now and then if I'm on my knees, doggy style, I'll jack myself off. I'm not too concerned with jacking off because, like I usually tell the guy, I'm getting fucked for a reason. I'm more in tune with the pleasure that my ass is getting from his dick. It's kind of hard for me to jack off when I'm getting fucked if it's a good experience. When I'm a top, I like the guy in the same position, on his stomach while I fuck him.

I wouldn't have a problem being with someone who always wanted to bottom unless he was an overly feminine man. I also don't think I'd want an overly feminine man fuck me. Not that he would want to. I believe the tendency is that feminine guys are more bottoms than tops. As far as money and age, I've always been attracted to older men, but most of the guys I'm with, I'm usually making more money than they do.

My most recent sexual encounter was with my buddy, at my house. I fucked him. We laid on the bed to watch TV and I could tell he wanted to do something. So I thought, "Okay, this man is here and he wants to have some sex." I opened up my pants and I pointed to my dick and said, "Okay, you can take care of that." And he was like, "Alright!" He was excited. He'd mentioned that he'd shaved his ass so I said, "You want me to fuck you, don't you?" He was like, "Yeah." He lubed himself up and got on the floor. I had him on his stomach first and it was great. He likes his legs over his shoulders so he can jack off so we did that next and that was beautiful too. He's a bit taller than me and it was the perfect fit with his legs over my shoulders. We spoke yesterday and we complemented each other on how great it was.

Next time, it's my turn to get fucked. I look forward to fucking him most. He likes to be a bottom more. He's twenty-three. But me and him, we'll never have a relationship. We talk about it periodically, but we're fine the way we are.

11

Randy:
"Boston Is a Very Bottom Town"

Versatile Top, Age 26

Born to Greek nationals who immigrated to the United States when he was very young, Randy embodies typical Mediterranean character- istics: lean swimmer's build, angular features, dark brown hair, and goatee. We meet on a rainy day on the Boston University campus and walk to the Psychology Building where, he tells me, most of his time as an undergraduate was spent. He studied criminal psychology with a desire to join the Behavioral Science Department, but didn't follow up on those plans. He says his ideal job, so far, has been bartending on the beach in Florida where he had a great time and made lots of money. Now he teaches health and human behavior at a high school in the Boston area, but is still ambivalent about what he ultimately wants to do. "I'm asking my high-schoolers what they want to be when they grow up so I can get some ideas for myself," he says.

*　*　*

I was a top when I first started out having sex, but now I consider myself versatile. I realized I was gay at a very young age. I started to look at other men sexually when I was in the sixth grade. My first sex- ual experience with a guy was in a cruisy situation when I was nine- teen. It happened in a public bathroom in the Liberal Arts Building at Boston University. At that point, I had no idea what went on in those bathrooms. I was pissing at the urinal and he came and stood at the urinal next to me. I think he was in his late twenties. He looked over then kind of pulled back to show me what he had. Then I pulled back and showed him what I had. He motioned me over to a stall and he sat down and sucked me off. It felt great. I came in his mouth, I said thanks, and left. I went to class and I was in shock.

After that, I started to go to the bathrooms every once in a while, but I wasn't happy with myself. It was kinda nasty. BU police mentioned that they were going to crack down on it. So I said, "Okay, if BUPD is on it then I'm not gonna bother doing this anymore." It lasted for about a semester, but I stopped after that.

The following year I went abroad to study. I went to Australia and I was out and about there. I went to the clubs on Oxford Street in Sydney, which is the big strip down there. I was having a great time. I was the stupid American abroad. I'd have anonymous sex, mostly. I'd go out dancing, get drunk, and get hooked up. I wasn't looking for a relationship. I still hadn't had any anal sex at the time. I was giving and getting head.

After Australia, I spent a summer in Paris and I went to a sex club there. This guy was talking to me in French and I had no idea what he was trying to tell me. It turned out he wanted to fuck me and I was like, "No, no, no." It wasn't happening.

When I returned to BU for my last semester, I met someone in one of my classes. We quote unquote dated for a while. We tried anal sex, but I wasn't into it. I was like, "I don't know if I want to do this." He was older than me and he wanted it. We'd be in his apartment and we had to be quiet because his roommates would be in the next room. He wasn't out to his roommates and all kinds of nonsense. We were supposed to be studying. I was trying to top him, but for some reason, I was having trouble staying hard. I guess I was nervous and apprehensive. Then he tried to top me and that didn't work at all. I was like, "You're not doing that to me ever!" So that was that. In retrospect, I think we weren't really into each other sexually. Like we were more friends, I guess. We shouldn't have brought sex into the relationship. Then I graduated and that ended, thankfully.

After graduation I went to Hawaii for a couple of months. There was a nude beach in Maui. It was pretty cruisy so I did the good ole anonymous sex thing there. It was in a tropical location and I didn't complain about that, but there was still no anal sex.

The first time I had anal sex was here in Boston, at the Safari Club.* I went there one night and I had some condoms with me. I got together with this guy and I wanted to top him, but he said, "No, let's

*Bathhouse that was closed by the city in 1999.

flip for it." He won and ended up topping me. It was my first anal sex ever and I didn't like it at all. I didn't like the feeling of having no control and the physical pressure. He used a condom, but he didn't use enough lube. It hurt. I thought, "This isn't pleasurable at all."

Shortly after that, right before Christmas of that year, I met a guy that I dated for over a year. He was a bottom and wanted me to fuck him all the time. Ninety percent of the time we had sex I was the top. I'd say he topped me maybe twice in the year or so that we were together. Three times at most. He was thirty-seven and I was twenty-three at the time. After that, I moved to New York and broke off that relationship.

In New York, I was in school and didn't do much at first. Then I said, "I'm in New York City and I'm going to have a good time." I really didn't care about school that much anymore. I had some friends and we'd go out every weekend, sometimes every night. We'd go to Greenwich Village, Chelsea, or the East Village. Sometimes I'd pick someone up and sometimes I'd get picked up. I had a few bottom experiences during that period and it was better. It's better if the top knows what he's doing. I had a few top experiences as well. I dated someone for about a month, but nothing serious came out of it.

After New York City I went to Florida. There I met a guy and the first time I tried to fuck him I couldn't get it up at all. I don't know if it was psychological or what not. But then he said, "I'll fuck you," and he did and it felt great. I dated him for six weeks and I was a bottom. Then we broke up because he's insane and I got together with someone else and I was a top. That felt really good. In all my relationships, I was either a top or a bottom. I don't know of any truly versatile relationships, although I think some people switch every once in a while.

I would say that I'm a versatile top. Being a top is my preference because I enjoy it physically. The different positions and styles of doing it feel good. I also like being in control. When I was younger, I thought being a bottom would make me more feminine and that's why I didn't do it back then. But that masculine-feminine dichotomy does not apply to me anymore. I'm not more of a man because I'm a top. Now I'm just like, whatever. You can be aggressive as a bottom and also passive as a top. There's no denying that bottoming feels great too, if the guy knows what he's doing. It feels great both ways.

I'm not hung up or confused about sex anymore. I think being gay is definitely a biological thing. I can't imagine it being environmental. I never thought it was. Anal sex is a good way to experience pleasure. And the body was meant to experience pleasure and since that's sex for gay men, I'd have to say the anus was created for that purpose as well. I don't know, however, if it's a genetic structure.

The only time I had bareback sex was with the guy I dated for about a year. Outside of that, it's always been with a condom. I don't think I'll ever have bareback sex and I don't think I will ever want to.

I think Boston is a very bottom town. I don't know why, but most of the guys I've hooked up with here have been bottoms. In New York you never know. You can go home with someone and you'd be in dungeon equipment. It's a weird town, but I love it.

My biggest fantasy is to have sex on an airplane. I got a hand job on a plane once. It was an empty flight and we had eye contact. He came over and sat next to me. It wasn't a very exciting episode. I'd like to have sex in every time zone in the world. I'm close to half there.

My most recent encounter was two nights ago. It was a blind date. We'd been talking for two weeks and we met for coffee on Davis Square. He was about thirty and he invited me over to his place. We talked some more over there and it got to be about eleven o'clock. I had to get up in the morning so I said, "Are we going to do something or not?" He said, "What do you have in mind?" and I said, "Nothing very serious because I have to get up in the morning." We started to make out. He put his hand down my pants and got me hard. He gave me a blow job, but I didn't cum. I got up and left. It was better than spending Wednesday night at home watching TV.

My best sexual encounter in my whole life was on the beach in Maui. I was lying there reading *The Brothers Karamazov.* I wasn't looking for anything, but this guy came up and we started talking. He saw my book and said, "Wow, I never thought I'd see someone reading that here." He was from Colorado. He looked me up and down and I looked him up and down. Maybe it wasn't the all-time best encounter physically, but the setting was great. We went to a little clearing and the water was right there, the trees, the sun, the clouds, the whole setting was great. You don't get that every day.

Another one was in New York. This guy and I worked together and hung out together a lot. I was really into him, but he had a boyfriend. They were breaking up. I kept flirting with him and he flirted back. One night he said, "Just come over and let's rent a video and drink some cheap wine and do whatever." So I went over, we had dinner and two bottles of Chianti and got real messed up. This was a guy that I really liked. I actually thought I had emotions for him. I wanted a relationship with this guy. We were on the couch together and he started to rub my head and I was rubbing his legs. We got naked in about fifteen seconds. It got very hot very fast. First we did some oral and then I could tell that he wanted to be fucked. There was no condom and I was reluctant, but he really wanted it and I couldn't resist. I fucked him raw and it was amazing. I'd wanted to have sex with him for so long. The reward actually exceeded the expectation. You know how you chase someone and when you get it, it's not so great? Well, this one was truly great. I was so into him and he was so into me that I didn't care that we didn't use a condom. Then the next morning I was like, "Fuck, I fucked him raw." I knew that we both didn't have HIV, but still . . . I went to class and told my friends what happened. They all knew I'd wanted this guy for a long time, and they were like, "Wow!" I definitely had the glow.

12

Peter:
"A Hard Dick Has No Conscience"

Versatile Top, Age 37

Peter and I made a date to meet the day after his return to Boston from a week's vacation in Florida. He called that morning to confirm. It was the middle of January and snow was in the forecast. I tried to dissuade him from making the two-and-a-half-hour drive to Provincetown, but he insisted on coming, saying he was bored and a drive would do him good. He kept addressing me as "buddy" on the phone, which was somewhat charming, but the "I'm just a blue-collar naughty boy" attitude rang false. He drove up to my house in a red SUV, wearing a baseball cap, jeans, and a flannel shirt.

Peter is thirty-seven years old. He tested positive for HIV some years back and got sick for the first time about a year ago after he broke away from a sixteen-year relationship. He was hospitalized with *Pneumocystis carinii* pneumonia and also suffered from viral meningitis. He was laid off from his corporate job and since then has held down jobs as a temp, a receptionist and, more recently, as a sales associate for Eddie Bauer.

* * *

I came out when I was nineteen years old. I was engaged to be married. I hadn't even masturbated before. I met this guy through a friend at work. We spent a lot of time together for about a week and then we got together one night. I made the first move to touch him, which surprised him, but he made the first move to be sexual. That was my first time. It lasted for about a week. We'd have sex in the morning and meet for lunch and have sex and meet again at night and have sex. I was primarily the top. He actually tried to fuck me once, but it was a total disaster. He didn't explain the mechanics of it. I didn't understand that I had to relax and bear down and all that stuff. It was a lot of pain and I said, "We're not doing that anymore."

Shortly after that ended, I met another guy at Buddy's* one night. I met him at eight o'clock and the next thing I knew they were putting the chairs on the tables. It was two-thirty a.m. We spent the night together and the next morning he made me memorize his phone number because I wouldn't write it down. This was the second time I'd had sex. He had a huge, huge dick. He was a total bottom, and because he was a bottom, I ended up being the top. Except once or twice a year, I'd get this itch and I'd go out and look for a top. So once or twice a year I'd be a bottom. We spent sixteen years together and we broke up about a year ago.

I used to watch his face when I fucked him and realized he knew something that I didn't. I see the same expression on the faces of porn stars when they're getting fucked. So since we broke up, I've been experimenting with toys and fooling around and I think I'm gonna be a born-again bottom. [Laughs] So I'm looking to learn to be a bottom, you know? Considering how extremely unpleasant my first experience as a bottom was, I'm surprised that I ever let anybody do it to me again. Much less *want* someone to do it to me.

I wasn't exactly forced to be a top. I had an unpleasant experience as a bottom and then I jumped into an almost monogamous relationship, or a steady relationship, with someone who was completely a bottom. I wasn't forced into it, but circumstances sort of dictated that I would be a top.

My relationship was monogamous for the most part. Once in a while, in the beginning, we'd do a threesome, and once in a while he wouldn't come home and once in a while I wouldn't come home. Later on, I had a few regular people outside the relationship and I had sex with them numerous times.

In the beginning, me and my boyfriend had sex at least five times a day. Every single day. It was mostly fucking. A lot of alcohol and a lot of fucking. I drank quite a bit then. He still does.

I became HIV positive after we were together for four years. I know when it happened and who infected me. It was in Brookline on September 9, 1986. It was through someone I met at college. I got re-

---

*A gay bar in Boston.

ally, really drunk and he wanted me to dump my boyfriend and come live with him. He had four bottles of champagne and I drank all of them by myself and made the decision to have unprotected sex with him. It was the wrong decision. I don't even remember him fucking me, but I guess it happened. Four bottles of champagne go down really well.

Being a top wasn't bad. In fact, it was great. I used to have sex with women back in the eighties too. When I was a top, as far as I was concerned, it didn't matter to me who was beneath me, as long as I was getting my dick off. A hard dick has no conscience. To me it really didn't even matter if it was a man or a woman.

I feel I can be a lot more passionate with a man than with a woman. With a woman you're supposed to be controlled and it has to last a certain amount of time. You don't have to worry about hurting a man. You can be a lot rougher. With a man, I can do it as many times as I want to and if I get off in thirty seconds, it doesn't make a difference to him, as long as he gets off too. Men are more accessible and less complicated. You don't have to dig into a whole relationship to fuck a man.

Being a top makes me feel more masculine. More in control. I had a friend who was a complete bottom in college. I asked him why he wanted to get fucked although it hurt so much and he said, "First of all, it doesn't hurt. Second of all, I'm in control. If you're the top and you think you're in control, you're mistaken." I had no idea what he was talking about, but I think I'm beginning to understand it now. I always thought I was in control when I was a top. If I didn't like it, I'd just zip up and go home, but my friend and I had the same idea. As a bottom, he can just say "no" like a woman can and it would be over with. I'm the same way. It's no skin off my nose. If you don't like it, I'm going out and finding someone else. It's just the way it was in the early eighties.

I think there are more bottoms than there are tops. So when you're a top in a bar, you're in demand. Once I had four guys in one night. I was seeing all four of them on the side and they all showed up at a bar close to my house. I lived only a block away, so I went back and forth from my apartment to the bar, and I had all four of them in one night. All it requires is four changes of sheets. I never had a problem picking up guys like that.

After I'd been with my partner for eight or nine years, our sex life started to decline. We started to have sex less often. It became once a month instead of once a week, because I'm HIV positive and he was afraid of getting it. He was having problems with his work which caused him to get depressed. Anytime I touched him, he thought it was for having sex. All I wanted to do was hug or kiss or stroke, but to him, touching at all meant sex. So I started to get starved for affection. We went from once a week to once a month and from once every three months to once a year and then to once every three years. It wasn't good. He was very much overweight and he smoked three packs of cigarettes and drank half a gallon of scotch a day. Finally, it had been three years since he touched me and I just told him that I could live without the sex, but I wanted him to work on the smoking and drinking. And he said "no." So I moved out. In the middle of Y2K, with bad credit and two dogs. One month later I had my first opportunistic infection and almost died. My doctor thinks a lot of it was caused by my breakup. I'm still very much in love with my ex. If he were less self-destructive, I'd get back together with him. I miss him terribly.

I was always fascinated by the look on the faces of the guys getting fucked in porno movies. Some guys, you know, are in it just for pay. They're hustlers. But there are guys in porno movies that are really having a good time getting fucked. There's a book about Joey Stefano written by Chi Chi Larue* about his life as a porno star. He's dead now, but he used to be a big-time bottom. He talks about totally loving getting fucked. It's all about enjoying the sex and the drugs and all that kinda stuff. Anyway, he was one of the people that I specifically know was enjoying getting fucked like eight hours a day. No matter who it was and what position. The look on his face was like, "Uh, I can't believe I'm doing this for a living," you know, that kind of thing. People like that make me wonder what I'm missing. I'm always a little paranoid anyway so I wonder what I'm missing. Somebody has a better look on his face than I do. When I see his eyes roll back in his head, it's like, "Mmm, I think I'd like that dick in me."

I don't know if I have a big dick, but I haven't had any complaints. I've seen much bigger cocks, but I've also seen much smaller. My partner, my sixteen-year relationship, had a dick almost a foot long.

<hr>

*Charles Isherwood (not Chi Chi Larue) (1996). *Wonder Bread and Ecstasy: The Life and Death of Joey Stefano.* Los Angeles, CA: Alyson Books.

You can't really do anything with that. You can do it orally. I've tried to take it anally and it's okay for him, he gets off, but you just can't enjoy that. I'm sure there are people out there who can, but I can't. I mean the guy has like a road cone on him. I'm not in that place. I don't enjoy sex with really huge guys. I know that's the opposite of what most gay men say. I prefer somebody reasonably sized. I'd rather have a smaller or medium dick. If I work my way up, I suppose, I could eventually become a size queen. Try buying toys that aren't geared toward people with tight asses. It's difficult. They're all like cast from porn stars.

Over the years, I learned to enjoy getting fucked on occasion. In eighteen years, I've been fucked by five guys. That's it. I enjoyed four of them. The fifth one was too big.

One of the guys I enjoyed it with was almost as big as my partner, but not quite. It was amazing. It was the first time I had outdoor sex. He took me on his motorcycle out to a big hill out in Jamaica Way in the middle of the night. He laid his leather jacket down and shoved my face in it and just fucked me. It was the whole scene, I guess. It was great. Whenever he and I had sex after that I always went back to that feeling. He's also positive, if he's not dead by now.

Another one of the guys I enjoyed having anal with was a good friend of mine. We knew each other very well and we got to know each other sexually. We made sure each other had their needs filled, whether we were topping or bottoming with each other.

One of the good things about getting fucked is that afterward I feel really, really relaxed, whether I enjoyed it or not. I feel like [he lets out a big sigh], "Okay, we're all set, let's go back to life and do whatever we have to do." I feel I'm in control when I top and being a bottom is the exact opposite. I actually feel like someone else is in control and is taking care of me.

During my relationship, a lot of times I'd get fucked when I was out of town. I'd be on a softball tournament away from my partner, and I'd take care of my needs where I wouldn't be throwing it in his face. There was no chance of getting caught. I'd come home and let myself into the apartment and find little boys. He liked them really young and really dumb, and I like them older and intellectual.

I always knew I was different. I just didn't know *how* I was different. I currently hold the record in the most varsity letters earned in a high school career. With gym class and wrestling practice and all the sports I did, I showered with those high school athletes at least twice a day my entire high school career and it never dawned on me that I wanted to have sex with them. I would look at them and say, "His pecks are really developed today and I gotta work on mine," and "I've got to work on my biceps because his are looking better than mine and I'd like to look like that." But do I want to put that in my mouth? No. That never crossed my mind. Until I was in college. That's where I met some people that were open about it and it made me think about it for the first time in my life. Whether I wanted to be gay. I guess I'm not really gay, I'm bisexual. But people have a whole lot of easier time dealing with gay instead of bisexual. It's like pick a team. For the past thirteen years, I've mostly been with men.

I'm a recovering Catholic. I went to Catholic school and was an altar boy, the whole nine yards, but I fell away. I was born left-handed and the nuns wanted me to be right-handed. Being left-handed was considered the devil's work. I still have scars on my right hand because I couldn't form the letters correctly and the nuns would come by and slam down my hand with a metal-edged ruler. Never mind that all the artwork done in the Sistine Chapel and the Vatican was done by left-handed men. There's only one thing I still do left-handed and that's to masturbate. So I gave up religion, but now I'm going back.

I think God made us gay because he has a sense of humor. It's sort of like breeding dogs. Once in a while you get a different strain. In nature, those strains are like a mule that can't reproduce, and we can't reproduce either. It's not a mistake because God doesn't make mistakes. He just has a sense of humor. It's a joke. It's my life, but it's a joke.

I've come close to barebacking, but I've never gone there. Some guy wanted me to fuck him without a condom and I told him no. We fooled around and he wanted to sit on it without me wanting him to. We had a little altercation. It didn't happen. He was positive too. But the idea of barebacking fascinates me. What's the point? If we're both positive, what's the point? To me, it's a quality of life issue. I mean, if I get fucked bareback is it going to take a month off my life? Well to me, a month of my life is worth a little unprotected sex and total freedom like I had back in the early eighties.

Physically, my ideal man would be bald. He'd be in his late forties to early sixties. A big, hairy chest. Little bit of a gut. Gorgeous bubble butt. Big, heavy legs. Big, hairy feet. His dick would be like medium size.

I have a huge collection of porno magazines and movies. A few novels here and there. I really, really get into gay cartoons. If you're taking pictures of a guy, you gotta get a model, which means he's going to have imperfections here and there. If you're drawing somebody, he could be perfect. He can be anything you want him to be.

My biggest fantasy is to live happily ever after. I'm still keeping my hopes up on that one. My sexual fantasy is to get fucked and enjoy it the way the guys on screen enjoy it. With my eyes rolling back in my head. I'd like to be in a relationship, have somebody that I could have every night. An equal partnership with someone who's available to my sexual tastes. Someone that could be my every man. Which is never going to happen, but at least someone who's not a bottom all the time.

My ideal sexual encounter would be to fuck someone and have him fuck me too. There's a bar up in Canada, there are hustlers there. I want to go there and take the perfect hustler home, fuck him, and let him fuck me. And do it all over again the next morning, and then send him home. I want to be able to dictate what I want to do in bed and not worry about, "What do you think of me," you know? I don't care what he thinks of me because I'm paying him. I'm not going to see him again so what difference does it make? Whereas if you're dating someone or you're going home with them, you're wondering, "Is this the guy I want to spend the rest of my life with?" A hustler is probably not going to be the guy I'm going to spend the rest of my life with.

I think the asshole is meant for fucking as much as a mouth is. Women have anal sex too. I've been with several women who liked it. They have no prostate, but they liked it.

This past weekend in Florida I got into some new scenes that I'd never gotten into before. I met this guy and he invited me to his place. When we got there he asked me if I'd like to be hooded. And I'm like, "Hooded? You mean uncut?" And he says, "No." So he showed me the hood and I'm like, "No, I've never done that!" I was kinda like wondering if it was a good idea. He asked to tie me up and I'm like, "I don't think I want to be tied up in someone's home without someone else knowing." I had no car key. He drove me there. No one knew I was there, but he seemed like a nice guy so I decided to go along with it.

We spent four hours in bed together and it was amazing. It had nothing to do with actual sex, but it did have a lot to do with role-playing. He spent a lot of time shaving me. I was scared. He was doing everything. I was just laying there, bound and hooded, wondering what he was going to do next and if I was going to survive this. He was kissing me through the mask and when he was kissing me he was forming a seal and pinching off my nose and breathing into my lungs so it was like total control. The very breath I was getting was from him. There was no control on my part whatsoever. He could've killed me. It was probably the best sex I've had in my life and there was no fucking involved. There was definitely tops and bottoms involved, but there was no fucking. When we finally got off together it was like amazing. I shot all over the place. For the last year or so I've been sexually dysfunctional and I dribble at best—but I was shooting six and eight feet around the room. Not just the headboard, I mean all over the room. That was the high point of my week. We just kissed a lot and jerked off together. It was exciting, it was thrilling, it was different. I mean if it happened to me every day it might not be quite as thrilling and exciting.

When I first came out I thought top and bottom implied masculine, feminine or weaker, stronger and so on, but since then I've met some very, very effeminate tops, and very masculine bottoms, so I don't think that anymore. I'd go out thinking I was going to get myself fucked and pick up the most masculine guy in the bar. We'd get home and the legs would go up in the air, and I'm like, "All right, we'll have to try again tomorrow night." Try again. So lately I've been asking them what they're into. And if they're not what I'm looking for that night, I just move on. That's probably why I haven't gotten laid in the last couple of years. [Laughs]

13

Bruce: Too Much Alone

Versatile Top, Age 42

I knew from our phone conversation that Bruce had a speech impediment. I also understood that he never let his stutter get in the way of what he was trying to say. Although I didn't know much about stuttering, my instincts told me to always wait for him to finish what he was saying, and to never complete his sentences for him.

He greeted me at the Boston Common with a big smile. We got some muffins and coffee and sat on the grass to talk. He's forty-two years old, has dark hair and bright gray eyes. He's down to earth, free of pretense, and laughs freely when he has too much trouble articulating a certain word. Sometimes, flustered, he laughs and gives up and uses hand gestures or facial expressions to make his point instead.

* * *

The tops and bottoms issue always makes me wonder why people do certain stuff. I've been pretty much a top, mostly, but I can't say that's been my choice. I've been a bottom on occasion, but mostly I end up on top. I'd probably like being a bottom more if it didn't hurt. [Laughs] But it just hurts. Some people really love getting fucked and I can see why they like it. I liked it on a couple of occasions where it didn't hurt as much, but often I'd have some bleeding which wasn't good. When it was all done and I went to get rid of all the luby crap, it would be all bloody. I think if I did it on a steady basis with somebody, it wouldn't be so bad. I was once in this relationship thing where, you know, I was the bottom most of the time. I kinda liked it. We kinda took turns a lot. He pretty much had the upper hand. Every single time he fucked me, it would be all red and bloody. I think it was because I was tight and he wasn't small. [Laughs] I got good enough at it after a while and I didn't mind it so much. It stopped hurting so much, but it was still uncomfortable.

I guess I'd consider myself versatile if I got fucked more easily. The idea of getting fucked is a turn on, but being the fucker is more of a turn on. And that doesn't hurt. [Laughs] The people who get fucked, you know, they don't seem to mind it. They enjoy it and that's good.

One of the things I like about fucking is getting the lube on. Not KY, but the other stuff. That stuff turns me on—and the sex is wonderful. I like getting head and all that, but fucking is better. I like to give pleasure to my partner. I get really bummed out if the other person doesn't cum. I feel bad that they didn't get off.

I was doing stuff back in high school, but not like a real lot. A couple of gay friends in high school wanted to do some things, but I just wouldn't. I wasn't sure. So it took me a while after that.

One day, a bunch of my friends in high school and I were playing soft ball on the street. Six of us, I think. All of a sudden they were gone. So me and this other kid started looking for them and we found them behind this bush, and they were all jerking off. I had no idea what they were doing. I was like, "What the fuck are you doing?" That's how I found out about jerking off. I was in the ninth grade. And then I started doing it and I remember thinking, "Well, this is interesting."

At the beginning, I didn't specifically think about men or women when I was jerking off. I was just fascinated by the fact that such a thing could happen. But pretty soon I got hold of a book, *Everything You Ever Wanted to Know About Sex But Were Afraid to Ask.* Somebody in my family had it in his drawer and I'd spend like all this time with it. That started to make me think about girls. But that would change.

One day, me and a friend stole some straight sex books and went down to his basement. We were just going to read them, but we ended up jerking each other off. I realized I liked it more than he did. I hadn't thought I had a preference for men, but I knew that it was there. It was an underlying thing. I didn't want it to be true. I was like, "No, no, no, it's not!" But it just was. I liked all the young stars, like David Cassidy and them, you know? The young, cute guys. And I was like, "Why do I like them?" I'd get all those teen magazines, and I'd be looking at those pictures of them half undressed and all that. And I thought, this is obviously something bad.

I went out to the bars for the first time when I was in my early twenties, which was when I fucked someone for the first time. I walked into the bar and I was like, "Wow!" First time in a gay bar. Within ten minutes someone walked up to me and he pointed at me and he was like: "You." So I left with him and we ended up in a car, which was awkward. The guy was wicked drunk. He was cute, but the sex wasn't great. This was my first time and all this guy wanted to do was get fucked, which was fine with me so I fucked him. That happened a lot more times after that.

I don't feel like I have any power or anything when I'm fucking someone and I don't feel any kind of superiority. It doesn't enter my thoughts at all. Sometimes, I feel like the other guy feels that way, which bothers me. This one guy who fucked me, I think, felt domineering over me. I didn't like that at all. It felt weird. In my mind, getting fucked is not about being weak or being dominated.

It seems like in porno films the star of the show gets to fuck everyone. Also, especially in videos made in this country, the guy who's fucking cums and the one who's getting fucked has to masturbate while the other guy just watches him. It seems like in European videos, like *Bel Ami,* they both get fucked and they both cum.

I had a couple of relationships that I hoped would work out, but nothing went beyond two months or so. I don't know whose fault it was, but I think in some cases the fault was mine. I was thinking, "If I can get a guy, I can get the world." I think everyone wants that and I had a low self-image anyway. I still have issues. A lot of them lasted one night. That was okay for a while, but it gets old quick.

For the longest time, I'd go to the bar and I would hook up with the first person that came up to me. I didn't make any first moves. I would just wait until someone came to me and that worked sometimes. I wouldn't go up and talk to anyone. That would just take a lot out of me. Then I walked into a bar one night and it was jammed. I go in and it was packed, and it seemed like every single frigging head was turned to the door. And I was like, "What the fuck are you doing?" It finally hit me. I just wanted to get out of there.

That's when I stopped going to the bars as much. I thought there were other things in my life and a long-term relationship wasn't the most important thing. But I'm still looking for the right guy.

Nowadays, I try to meet men through different groups. A friend of mine from high school, who I didn't know was gay, came out to me recently. So we said, what can we do to get out more and to meet more people? So we tried some of the social groups. We found one in the Malden area and we went there a few times. It was a kind of social scene. Most people there were couples and they weren't my type. There were some nice men, but they were more the Ramrod type; their idea of fun is having a leather night. My friend is a big, balding guy and he looked like a lot of them there. He fit in perfectly. Soon enough, he met someone and they're living together now. They moved into a luxury condo. It happened in a year. Bang, bang, bang, bang, like that. And here's me saying, what the fuck, what the fuck, you know?

I did the personal ads, I did all the groups and bars, and I talk to my shrink about this all the time. What's next?

I really think that we're born with the gay gene. I don't see how all these people would have the same kind of thing happen in their lives that makes them gay. There are millions and millions of us on the planet, and in history. I can't believe that each one of us had the same kind of social thing. It's just in us. Not to say that people who are basically straight don't experiment. I don't think they're lying or whatever when they say they're straight, but there are people who are like, no, no, no, never! What makes that happen?

I'm not out to my family. They're staunch Catholics. We live in a two-family house. I live downstairs from them. They have no idea what goes on in my place. As far as the Catholic thing goes, I don't have a sense like I'm going to hell and all that. If I wasn't made to be like this, then things would not have been like this. I really believe there's a God out there and that He wouldn't have made so many people like this. I think there's a reason for us to be like we are. I have a younger sister and she has two kids, and my brother is a devout Christian. I know how they feel about all this stuff. I don't want to be cut off from my family, but as the years go on, they're starting to ask me, "Are you going to get married?" or "Do you have a girlfriend?" But I sorta work out a lot and I don't have a real settled job and that's my main excuse; but that gets old.

My main concern is that I just don't want to be alone anymore. The thing I've been feeling for the past couple of years is that I may be bisexual. Because in high school I went out with girls and I had sex with them sometimes and I did like it. So I don't know. It's funny because I've met so many cool people that I wouldn't have met if I were straight. But if I had been straight everything would have been more normal. More acceptable. That's why the bisexual thing is occurring to me more and more lately. Because I feel like I'll have somebody. I just don't know how to go out and meet women. But it's what I've done all these years with men. Although if I had to pick the right woman or the right guy, I'd pick the right guy. But there's a better chance of forming a good partnership if you pursue women. I know men who have been gay or bi and got married, and they're thrilled. They have kids, a house, and the whole shebang. They've met somebody they truly love. But men are just like, you know, get in line, get in line, next. But the line keeps getting thinner and thinner and thinner. And it's like *next!* And that's the whole thing.

Barebacking is pretty cool if you happen to be a horse. I've done it a couple of times in the heat of the moment. I think if you're a bottom and you bareback, that's how you get AIDS. Using a condom makes the act less pleasurable, but not that much. And about the intimacy thing, you're right on them, with or without a condom, and it can't get more intimate than that. Unless your entire body is like all the way inside of them. You can't get much closer than that and it's still fun even with a condom.

-14-

Eddie:
"We're Being Held Prisoners for Fucking"

Versatile Top, Age 42

Eddie grew up in South Boston, a predominantly Irish Catholic neighborhood. He and his three older sisters were raised by a compassionate and loving mother and a strict father who, at the time Eddie and I met, had just retired from the Marine Corps. Eddie and I had been distantly acquainted for a while. When he arrived at my office on a summer afternoon for this interview, he gave my hand a firm shake and smiled uncertainly, not knowing quite what to expect. As we sat down to talk, I was reminded what it was about him—his direct, blue-collar, regular Joe attitude, his friendly, self-assured demeanor—that I'd always found intriguing and sexy.

Eddie is forty-two years old, at lower than average height, with a stocky, athletic build, brown hair, and hazel eyes. He's a recovering alcoholic and was recently diagnosed with attention deficit disorder. He's highly intelligent (as I'm told most people with ADD are), but remarkably disorganized in his speech. During our talk, I often find myself struggling to figure out what brought us to a certain subject. Caught up in his own wildly erratic free association, he seems perfectly assured that I can easily follow his train of thought—but each time I think I finally understand what he's saying, he's off talking about something else. He seems a bit surprised when I have to stop him with questions like, "How did we get here, Eddie?" or "Can we go back and talk about how this began?" and even gives me occasional what-are-you-stupid kinds of looks. Nonetheless, everything he says is passionate, heartfelt, and often brilliant. Even the catch-up game becomes interesting; every turn offers another surprise, another amazing insight.

Eddie got married right out of high school. He and his wife separated seven years later, when Eddie started to come to terms with his sexuality. His late twenties were a time of great change on all fronts. He got divorced, dissolved his business as a building contractor, came out, got sober, and went back to school to get his degree in photography. Today, he works as a photographer and supplements his income with some carpentry on the side. His aim, he says, is to balance the commercial aspect of his craft with his personal art. His family, especially his father, has not accepted his sexuality. Eddie tells me he recently sent his family a letter telling them they either had to accept him or forget him. He hasn't gotten a response yet and jokingly says that he's become an orphan.

Eddie's been in a relationship with an Asian-American man named Tom for the last year. It's been a rocky course and they've been attending couples therapy to try to make it work. Eddie told me he wanted to do this interview because he thought it would allow him to confront some intimate questions he's never asked himself before.

*   *   *

If I had to define myself, I'd say I've been mostly a top, but I've also been willing to be a bottom a couple of times. I think if there's any help to come out of this conversation, it would be to get rid of the terms top and bottom and just kinda let it flow. 'Cause when people ask you if you're a top or a bottom, usually there are a whole lot of other things going on in their head such as masculine or feminine. All of that is already fucked up in the heterosexual world so why should we bring it into ours? There are a million things to do in bed and everyone puts too much emphasis on just fucking. It should be part of the play, instead of the main dish.

I guess I enjoy more being a top than a bottom because I haven't found a good top. [Laughs] I've only let two men penetrate me so I've been penetrated maybe three times. One of them was good, but we broke up soon thereafter so we didn't really get into it. The other one put too much emphasis on masculinity and all that.

A lot of men who like to get fucked put a lot of emphasis on feeling overpowered. All of a sudden they have to reaffirm their power in the relationship. Even if the guy was begging to get fucked, once you fuck him, he starts to scurry around, trying to reaffirm his masculinity. All of a sudden, he feels less masculine and he's got to prove it somewhere else. Bottoms think that they have no power once they've been topped and actually they really have a lot of the power. You have to teach them that they have the power without giving them the power. You gotta convince them that everything's fine. Actually, I don't think power or masculinity has anything to do with it. If you stay away from the power struggle everything loosens up and everything's fine.

The couple of times I've given myself over and gotten fucked, I thought of it as a bonding experience rather than a power situation. It's really the most intimate thing you can do. People try to convert that intimacy into power. If I'm in a relationship that's going to last a long time, and if intimacy is the thing that's going to separate that man from my other buddies, I'd want something more out of that relationship. Fucking could be a part of that. In a relationship, I wouldn't mind getting fucked seventy-five percent of the time and fucking the rest of the time.

When someone asks me if I'm a top or a bottom on a first date, it's like forget it. Is that all you want to know about me? I'm worth dinner! It's the same power thing as telling me he's bisexual. If some guy tells me he's bi, I go, "Okay, but you're *gay tonight,* right? If we go back to my place, we're gonna have *gay sex,* right?" And that freaks them out. 'Cause this is abuse! He's abusing me! He's telling me that not only do I have to worry about the guys he looks at, but I have to worry about every girl that walks across the street too. Are you a top or a bottom? What's it to ya? I tell people, "I have a dick as big as a baby's arm." And they go, "Really?" And I say, "By the time you find out, you won't care anymore." Don't ask me what I'm into. I'm into *sex.* Lots and lots of sex.

We talk a lot about fucking in my current relationship, but it gets complicated. We try to avoid it so we won't complicate things even further. When we first met, Tom had just come out of a ten-year relationship so we had to get past certain issues. Like the fact that his ex had a beard and I don't have a beard. He had to get used to kissing me after kissing a mouth with a beard for ten years. So I had to take my time and wean him through a lot of things like that. He wants to be fucked, but he's afraid for whatever reasons. I don't like to get into the reasons because it just gets complicated. He's only done it once before and I think it hurt so he has that with him. He doesn't understand that it could feel really good and that it won't change him in some fundamental way. I started to fuck him once early on and there was partial penetration, but the whole thing got so mechanical and labored that I got soft. But as we get closer, I'd like to bring some fucking into the relationship. We've been dating for a year now so hopefully we'll get into some fucking in the next few months. I just had to get all the other stuff out of the way.

When I got fucked five or six years ago, the guy I was with was real gentle and he knew what he was doing. He taught me how to fuck and be fucked. He told me to relax, don't worry. It became a loving, no problem, teaching experience. I said, "Okay, I can appreciate this." I allowed myself that.

I knew I was different at about the age of thirteen. I started to fool around with a friend and that went on for four or five years. It was the late seventies and he was a year older than me. Every couple of days we'd go into his bedroom, he'd kick out his two brothers, lock the door, and we'd watch *Star Trek* and he'd tell me, "We're not gonna fool around." The boys are gone, the doors are locked, and we're laying on the same bed together. By the end of *Star Trek,* we'd be blowing each other and everything else. When it's all over, he's like, "We shouldn't have done that." Then, three or four days later, we'll be up in his room again, he'll send his brothers out, he'll lock the door, and tell me we're not gonna have sex. This went on for five years. Sometimes, we'd go down to the basement to do photography, but not many photos came out of that basement.

There was no fucking. Fucking would've been too way over the top. Kissing was out for Stan. Stan wouldn't kiss. We could blow each other and jerk each other off, but we couldn't kiss. I was the one who wanted to kiss. Almost every time we fooled around, he'd blame it on me. My father used to say, why can't you be more like Stan Owen, and his dad used to ask him why he couldn't be more like me. We were inseparable and I think our parents knew.

When I told him I loved him, he joined the Air Force and I never saw him again. I didn't think I was gay at the time, I just thought I loved Stan Owen. I told him, "Stan, I think I love you." He freaked. "You can't, you can't, you can't!" Two days after that, we were up at the cemetery where a bunch of us guys played touch football. Stan was a quarterback for his high school team so he could throw a good ball. I was on the opposite team. I'd be on defense and he'd gun the ball at me and then he'd tackle me. I wasn't a football player and this was only touch football. He did this six or seven times in a row. Tears were coming down my eyes and tears were coming down his eyes. No one could figure out what was going on. He came over at me and yelled, "Stop catching the ball!" And I said, "I'm gonna catch the ball every time you throw it at me, Stan." People started to realize something was up.

That was the last time I saw him. He joined the Air Force a week later. He married an English girl and had two or three kids. I kept tabs for a while. To this day, if he got within eyeshot of me, he'd probably shake like a leaf. I asked him to usher at my wedding, but he wouldn't do it.

When I graduated from high school, the president of the chamber of commerce wanted to take me to Greece for two months. He was about sixty years old, single, and well known to be homosexual. My father called the state police and a couple of friends of his and had him checked out. My parents sat me down and they said, "You can't go." And I was like, "Why not, why not, why not?" They said, "He's homosexual." And I said, "I know that." They freaked. "You know that he's homosexual and you still wanna go?" I said, "Yeah, he ain't gonna touch me." I ended up not going, but I figured way back in my mind, if I was gay, I wish someone would tell me.

A year after, that I freaked and I bought into marriage. I said, "Okay, I'm not gonna be gay, whatever that is." All I knew was that gay guys were old men who were married and wanted to touch me. And if being gay is being miserable and unhappy like those men then I'm not it, I'm not gonna be it. So I bought into the system.

For four or five years after I got married, I didn't have sex with men. But these feelings weren't going away. I had my own business doing carpentry and building houses. Once I got to a certain level of success, I had some time to think about who I was. I also had some money to go out and get drunk. I'd get drunk and I'd have sex with friends. This was when my drinking got much worse. I was thinking if I wasn't drinking, I wouldn't be gay, and if I wasn't gay, I wouldn't be drinking so much. [Laughs] I had to separate the two.

I had a summer cottage in Limerick, Maine. I'd bring four or five guys who worked for me there to work for the weekend. We'd do some carpentry work or build a deck or something like that and then we'd just go out and drink. It was a binge type of drinking. We worked hard and drank hard, that type of mentality.

There was this one guy, Kyle, who worked for me and he was really cool. He was six feet two inches, red hair, big hairy chest. He could pick up two cinder blocks with one hand, without breaking a sweat. One night, the other guys were out partying at a bar, and me and him were in the cottage together. He was married and unhappy and I was married and unhappy. We were talking about getting divorced. We had lots of beer together and our feet touched and our knees touched and we joked around and went "ha-ha-ha" and pretty soon I was doing *Star Trek* again. I wasn't the first guy he was with. We had sex four or five more times after that. We always had to get drunk to do it. We'd go to the cottage together and play footsie and one thing would lead to another.

He wanted me to fuck him all the time. "Fuck me, fuck me, fuck me." But I said no. At the time I didn't know about fucking. He had been fucked before and he liked getting fucked. He had a huge dick, a huge dick, and he wanted to fuck me, but I said no way. No way was that thing going in me. Even by today's standards that thing wouldn't be going in me. He wouldn't kiss me, but he wanted me to fuck him.

One day Kyle said to me, "You wanna go to camp this weekend?" I said, "Yeah, let's tell the guys we're going up," and he said, "No, just me and you." I said, "Okay, fine. No problem." [Laughs] At this point, we'd already fooled around two or three times. So we go out there and we have sex and we wake up the next day and he's like, "Boy, were we drunk last night." And I said, "Right, I had two beers." That freaked him out because he'd only had two beers too. So we weren't so drunk and we knew it. We'd actually done it because we wanted to, not because we were stupid.

I had a secretary, Janice, and Kyle said, "I'm going to take Janice out to Maine." He was trying to make me jealous. I said, "Go on, go ahead. Here's my keys, have fun." I knew that he didn't want her, he wanted me. I was like, "Fine, be an ass, go for it." And Janice was like, "Oh good, I get Kyle."

So next time I saw him it was Labor Day weekend and I was partying at someone's house. My wife and I were gonna go up to Maine. He was pouring some concrete in the basement of a new house, but the job wasn't done yet. It was pouring rain and he comes over to the party, he's soaking wet and he says, "I wanna come party." I said, "Is the cement dry yet?" He says no, and he starts to yell and scream at me in front of all these people and I give him some beer and he goes back to the job site.

Afterward, I swung by to see if the concrete was dry and I walked down to the basement. He was drunk and he walked up to me, started yelling and then he grabs me by the chest, picks me up, and starts to shake me. He goes, "You're not going to Maine without me!" I just went limp in his hand. He could throw me like a rag doll. All the other guys came over and they could tell that there was something more between us than what was going on. Now, I'm eye to eye with him, and he's like six-four. In the masculine, bravado world, he's supposed to throw me so I'm looking for a place to bounce, but he put me down. By putting me down he was admitting to everyone that there was something more between us.

I guess he told the guys later that I was gay, which is really his own outing, but whatever. He told Janice that I'd touched him. She said, "Well, what did you do? Weren't you pissed? Did you hit him or anything?" This is in front of my ten guys. And he was like, "Uh, no." And everyone's looking at him like, "Why didn't you hit him?"

After I came out and I was free in my mind, I saw him at a wedding. I said, "How are you doing, Kyle?" He says, "I'm okay." I said, "Are you happy?" He says, "No." I said, "That's too bad. See you later." He wouldn't hang out with the gay guy and if his wife saw me with him she'd come over and tell him to get away. So we sat across from each other after that. He was as closeted as I was. He was miserable.

I tried anonymous sex a couple of times back then, but I couldn't handle it. I started hanging around outside a gay bar in Lynn. I was one of those guys standing outside, thinking no one knows why they're standing there. I was a contractor and the police knew who I was. They'd come up to me and say, "Eddie, are you okay?" I'd be standing by the fence outside, not daring to go in, hoping something would happen. I was scared shitless to go in. I thought I'd change if I went in.

When I turned twenty-seven, I said, "Okay, Eddie, you're a gay man in a straight world, so what are you gonna do about it?" I ended my business and got divorced. Once I got divorced, women got in line. They had no idea I was looking at their brother, not them. I went through the whole deal of trying to figure out what was natural and what wasn't natural. I tried to cut more women before I tried the gay thing. After that, I decided to try the gay thing for a year and the rest is history.

Sex with women was okay. I didn't have trouble performing with women. I just thought that was as good as it got. It was like a glass of warm milk in the middle of the desert. You're in the desert and you're thirsty and you get to an oasis and there's a glass of warm milk there. You drink it and that gets you through. You're okay living in the heterosexual world. And you come to another oasis and there's another glass of warm milk. But then you get to another oasis and there's a tall glass of ice water. You drink that and you go, "Aaahhh!" That's the difference between sex with a woman and sex with a man. It was okay with women, but when I met a man there was an emotional connection as well as a physical connection and I was like, "Okay, this is the way it's supposed to be." It went from "God would have me love wrong than not at all," to "Oh my God, this is real!"

Heterosexual wives use sex as a power tool too. My wife shut her legs on me once. Like she learned it from her friends, she just closed her legs and said, "Heh!" And I said, "Excuse me? There are plenty of girls out there (and in my mind I'm saying guys too) who are *giving* it away. If you're gonna use something against me, you're using the wrong tool."

After I came out and got sober, I started dating this guy, Bill. He was the one who taught me how to fuck guys and get fucked. He'd had a rough childhood, he'd been at West Point and he was a big, burly guy. He'd call me on a Sunday morning and he'd say, "What're you doing?" I'd say, "I'm making spaghetti. (That was our code word for sex.) Wanna come?" And he'd say, "I'll come over, but no sex." He'd show up and sit there, you know, like Stan Owen, watch TV, football or something, and then I'd put my hand on his knee. I had an AA meeting at three o'clock and he'd wait until about two thirty before he'd let me get into him. By three-thirty, we'd have had sex, showered, and he'd dropped me off at my meeting. He liked making me late. He liked to prove to himself that I loved him enough to be late to my AA meeting. This happened Sunday after Sunday after Sunday. Most of the time I didn't even have spaghetti sauce in the house and I'd have run out and get some before he showed up. He liked power.

Once we got into sex, he was pretty honest about it. I fucked him all the time and he liked it. He was very promiscuous and he probably fucked everyone else. Mostly blonds. He liked tipping over tall blonds. He loved me, but he needed anonymous sex. Because of his size, everyone who saw us together thought I was the bottom. They'd look at me and I'd look back and I'd think, "You have no clue." He asked me once, he said, "Does it bother you that everyone thinks you're the bottom and I'm the top?" And I said, "I don't care what people believe as long as *you* know what I am." [Laughs] He walked like he was the top and treated me like the bottom. I didn't give a shit 'cause I was gettin' what I wanted. People think that the taller guy is the top unless you're one of the little guys who knows that's not true. You know how quickly they fall.

I dated this other guy—his name was Tom too—and we ended up living together and we started to get into some fucking, and that's where the power thing started. All of a sudden, it came down to if I fucked him, he had to fuck me. He wanted a sort of equality of masculinity. That's when I first saw it as a problem. It was too negotiated. Even today, his friends say if he'd admit that he's a bottom, he'd have a ball—but there were so many safeguards before he could be penetrated. You had to make sure you totally loved him, he had to make sure you wouldn't use it against him. If you fucked him, he had to fuck you. And I'm like, "Are you keeping score? What's the big deal? Once you get into the act who cares?"

I think the power thing has to do with the fact that bottoms feel the sex for hours after it's over, and the tops don't. After you're penetrated, you know you've been penetrated for some time. Topping someone is like knifing them, like a sexual stabbing. It's about having the equipment to penetrate the other person. I think bottoms feel like they've lost a piece of themselves. If they'd look at it at a more spiritual, intimacy level, they'd overcome some of their hang ups. But instead of going there, they bring it down to a mechanical sort of negotiation.

One of my sisters told me, "You know, Eddie, I'm sick of hearing about your sex life." I said, "You know nothing about my sex life, Jane. Just because I'm homosexual you think you know my sex life?" And she says, "Yeah." And I says, "Jane, do you blow Randy?" (Her boyfriend.) "Do you just get down and blow him?" She's like, "That's none of your business." And I said, "You're exactly right. Just because I'm gay, you sexualize everything I say about my life. You don't know anything, you don't even know if I blow Tom."

My father's the most honest man you'll ever meet. He'll put it right out there. He said to me, "Eddie, I don't mind you, but I don't like *them* in my house. You're okay, but I don't want anyone else with you." And I said, "Why?" He's like, "My mind wanders." That's honesty. He thinks about two guys having sex. I said, "I'm one of *them,* Dad. If you can't get over that, then I'm not coming home anymore. You stay out of my bedroom and I'll stay out of yours." Heterosexuals think they don't sexualize their own lives, but when a young girl says she's pregnant, the guys don't think about her at all, they think about her boyfriend. They think, "Oh, someone fucked you and it wasn't me." That's what people automatically think when they know you're gay.

When I was married, I couldn't have kids because I was sterile. So sex has been in the doctor's office for me all my life. The doctor told us how to fuck, what time to fuck, what to eat before we fucked. All of a sudden I come out of that and there's AIDS. And I was like, "Oh my God, my sex life is in the medical society again, oh my God." Back in the eighties people mentioned AIDS under their breath like they were saying, "Some guy is queer to me." So I joined ACT UP and went to their meetings and I met this guy and I said, "What do you do? What's left in sex?"

He says, "Well, do you lick?"

I said, "Yeah."

"Do you suck?"

I said, "Yeah."

"Do you like to lick 'em all over?"

I said, "Sure!"

He asked, "Why is fucking so important to you? Fucking's just part of it."

I used to tell people that I was the Labrador that grew up in a pack of Rottweilers, meaning I'm the soft, gentle guy around all these tough guys. In the last couple of years, I realized some of the things that attract me to certain guys. I like looking up at a guy, a guy who's taller than me. I like a guy who still has a waist that's not the same width as his shoulders. A well-built man. I found that I like darker skin. I like the touchy-feely Latinos who are free to show their emotions and passions. If you'd told me a year ago that I'd be dating an Asian guy, I'd have laughed because I used to make all the stereotypical jokes about them. Like if a guy was driving too slow in front of me, I'd say, "Oh, he's probably Asian." Tom has dark skin, black eyes, and black hair and that attracted me. I knew the first day that I met him that he was talented. Someone said to me, "You know, no two guys you've dated are ever alike." And I said, "They're all alike because they all have one thing in common and that's passion." I need them to have a connection to some passion. Tom's passion is art. He's a computer programmer, but he's taking a photography class and a painting class two nights a week.

I didn't used to care about dick size until I dated a guy and I thought it was going to get caught between my teeth. I felt bad for him. That's why I don't like sex on a first date. When they take that dick out and you gasp, they know. That's why I think you should get to know the person. When it's so small, you can't find it and you're searching around and it's your first date and you don't even know the person and it's like, "Couldn't you have at least told me, or warned me," you know? There's a whole weirdness that goes on.

I don't like sex with a rubber. Barebacking is all I can do. Between being circumcised and being sterile, I'll just refrain if there's going to be a rubber involved. When I was with my wife, I couldn't drink beer and I couldn't eat cheese and I couldn't wear jockey shorts because I had a low sperm count. It had nothing to do with making love. One time I told my wife, "Okay, this is where you're supposed to put your head on the floor and hold your feet up in the air for five minutes." She made me turn the light on so she could see my face because she couldn't believe what I was saying. I said, "This is what the doctor told me. After I cum in you I'm supposed to hold your feet up for five minutes." One time I was inside her and she started to cry on me. She was saying, "We're never going to have a baby." I just threw her on the floor from the bed. She went *bang,* flat on her back on the floor. I said, "I'm here making love. I don't know what you're doing here, but if you just want to make babies go get someone else." I find rubbers to be intrusive in the same way 'cause you have to plan it and when you stop to put it on it ruins the whole thing.

When I'm in bed with a man, I want him to think there are two or three people there with us even though it's only me. I want him to be surprised by what I do. When I touch Tom in a certain spot and he giggles, I go, "Thank you, Rick." If he giggles on another spot, I say, "Thank you, John." These are things I learned from someone else and I bring them into my relationship. Even now, after we've been together for a year, I'll do something to Tom that will freak him out. Just a feel or a grab. The repertoire is never the same twice. That's kinda what I offer. He maybe dated three guys in his life and he says I'm a slut. And I tell him, "If I'm a slut, that's the best thing you've got going for ya."

Guys who are not circumcised have more fun than I can possibly think of having. I touch Tom in certain spots and he jumps off the bed. I think, "Man, I'd love to be able to do that." Maybe it's because I'm prudish or Catholic or maybe I just don't have the same nerve endings. If you get an uncircumcised guy all wound up on his dick, you can touch him anywhere else and he'll go crazy. They're a bundle of nerves.

Joseph Campbell talked about the medicine men who were mostly homosexual. We don't have the need to procreate or to continue our gene. We have the open clarity and the open mind to deal with art. Tom and I live in a subdivision in North Reading and our neighbors who are in their mid-forties and have three kids are jealous of us. They're talking about college money for their kids and Tom and I are buying a tree or something nice for the front lawn. She comes over and she says, "Oh, I'd love to landscape my lawn like you. Once you're finished, can we do the meditation sessions on your lawn?" That's what it's all about. She needs this place and I have the time and ability to do it and give it to them.

As gay men, we have a purpose. We were born gay and God made us gay so we can serve that purpose, except we're not allowed to do it. That's the thing that's confusing us. Our whole electrical system is fucked up because we're not allowed to be who we're supposed to be and to contribute to society what we're supposed to. The art is the culture and it's our history and the art is who we are and who we're supposed to be. So if they fuck up the gay world and the medicine men, they're fucking up all of humanity.

I think the gay culture has one big hurdle, which is the fact that we're being held prisoners for fucking. The whole thing about telling our parents we're gay is that we're telling them, "I fuck guys." The Catholic Church makes sure that we're held prisoners to ourselves because we have anal sex. If we admitted to the cardinal, "Yeah, sure we fuck each other," then they probably wouldn't have that power over us. If we can get organized and say, "Yes, Mommy, I fuck. Yes, Daddy, we fuck. Yes, Cardinal Law, we fuck." If we can get past that, we can take on anyone and we'll be fine, but since they have that power over us, we need to have power over someone else. When I'm the fucker, I have power over you. Until that happens, we're prisoners to each other and to ourselves.

If I were to be born again, I'd definitely come back as a gay man. The best thing that ever happened to me was that I came out. When I told my father I was gay, he was driving my mother's car and I was in the passenger seat. I said, "Dad, I'm a gay man and I'm happy." And he said, "What are you still doing here?" What he meant was why was I still alive. I told him, "Two years ago I would've shot myself in the head right here so the blood would be all over you. I knew I was getting that message all my life, but you're not worth killing myself over." I got out of the car and went off to never-never land.

15

Tom: Control and Volition

Versatile Top, Age 42

A hot, humid August day in Provincetown; the beach at Herring Cove is teeming with gay men of all ages. They're tanning, cooling off in the water, and indulging in sweaty sex in the nearby dunes.

Tom's house is away from all of that, in a newly developed, fairly remote area of town called Pilgrim Heights. I've never been to Pilgrim Heights before. As I drive by the landscaped gardens and neatly designed driveways, I feel like I've left quaint old Provincetown behind and entered the suburbs of an ordinary American city.

Tom meets me at the door and offers to give me a tour. After showing me the living room and the kitchen on the ground floor, he takes me upstairs to show me his bedroom and the two spare rooms that he's rented to summer lodgers. I feel slightly uncomfortable perusing these men's rooms in their absence, but Tom seems to have no problem with that. Clearly, in his view, his privileges as landlord take precedence over the privacy of his tenants.

There's a separate apartment in the basement that opens out to a charming flower garden in the back. Tom tells me he had to fight his neighbors for months before he was able to secure the necessary town permits to make the small apartment handicapped accessible for his ailing mom. By the time he had everything arranged for her it was too late; she died only a few weeks after she moved in. "It was the neighbors who killed her," Tom says indignantly.

At forty-two, Tom is a Caucasian masculine man with dark hair, a stocky build, and average height. He has intense, piercing dark eyes which he locks directly onto mine as we sit down to talk in his study. He never shifts his gaze during our hour-long conversation. I'm a little intimidated by this direct, aggressive attitude, but I also find it refreshing and even seductive. As the conversation progresses, Tom gets so heated up over certain issues that I internally amuse myself as I can't help but look toward the door and contemplate a plan of escape in the event that he gets worked up enough to threaten or attack me. I realize soon enough that beneath all the machismo, Tom is just like many other gay men I know, a gentle soul trying to make sense of his life.

*   *   *

I don't classify myself as top or bottom. Although when I was younger circumstances required me to make a choice and I chose to be a top. That was essential at that point in my life. It was a question of power. I would never bottom and I would never have sex with anyone who was older or bigger than I was. It was always about power.

My first introduction to sex was when I was three or four years old, with the little boy next door. The first negative experience, however, was just a few months after that because he and I, after exploring each other, decided to explore the little girl who was with us. We took her up into the woods and she was three and a half and we didn't know any better. She didn't like what we were doing and started to scream. My friend's grandfather got wind of it and he kicked my friend's ass, literally, kicked him very, very hard. That experience taught me about the opportunity to violate. From that point on, without even knowing it, consensuality became essential to me. Except for the time I got raped when I was nineteen, sex for me was always consensual from then on.

I was born in Springfield, Massachusetts. I come from an underprivileged background. My father abandoned us when I was four and my mother lost her leg and arm in an automobile accident and put us in an orphanage when I was five and a half. After a year and a half in the orphanage, my father came back and we all got out. My last little sister was born and he abandoned us again when I was eight. So me and my three brothers and sisters were in foster homes and orphanages on and off, that kind of stuff.

When I was growing up, I always pursued boys my own age. The oldest person I had sex with was probably three or four years older than I was. I ended up coming out when I was very young because people were poking fingers at me and giving me a hard time about being gay. A gang of boys called me up one day and yelled faggot into the phone. I went upstairs and put on my oldest clothes, came down, went across the street, and pounded on the door. They thought it was funny because I'd never reacted that way before. They came out, they surrounded me and the toughest guy came at me and I punched him once and broke his nose. Blood went everywhere, he started to cry, and I just looked at all of them and I said, "Who's next?" I was thirteen.

Of course, these boys all knew I was gay because we had sex together all the time. Oh my God, we grew up together, we all had gang bangs together, big sex parties. I was always the instigator because I liked it and I knew they liked it as well. It was okay when we were young, prior to eleven or twelve, because first of all, the word homosexual wasn't in the vocabulary, and neither were all the connotations. Sex was just something we did together. You know? We got pretty exploratory. We would blow each other and we attempted anal sex a couple of times, but it was never successful, we were too small for that. Then, of course, the judgments started to come into it and the fingers started to point, and I said, fuck you.

After I broke that guy's nose, I went away for the summer and when I came back he was my best friend and so were the rest of them. They weren't saying anything about being gay or making any antigay jokes in front of me anymore because they knew I would nail them if they did. And they were still having sex with me! Individually. Never discussing it with anyone else. Of course, these were all "straight" boys who didn't "reciprocate," which meant that I always blew them. That's what the game was. But a peculiar sense of top and bottom came into that experience for me. Is giving a blow job a top or a bottom thing? In my estimation, I always considered it to be the top because I got exactly what I wanted, the way that I wanted it, when I wanted it, and so on. I was in total control. Yet, I'm sure in their minds, they perceived me as being the one who wasn't in control, the one who was the bottom, so to speak. Those were the formative years for me.

I got kicked out of high school when I was seventeen and I joined the military. I was a nuclear missile technician. Wanna see a picture? [Shows me a picture of himself in uniform, standing with a nuclear missile, and laughs.] That's my nuclear missile, right there, goddamn seventeen-year-old sonofabitch. I probably had my first experience fucking someone in the military, but I don't remember that.

I ended up getting my GED plus a half year of college before my class had even graduated from high school. I left the military at twenty and immediately went into the university and got my undergraduate degree in philosophy and psychology and my graduate degree in computers and organizational development. I finished graduate school in 1985.

I didn't get fucked until I came to Provincetown, not counting the time I was raped. I don't want to talk about the rape specifically, but I'll tell you the impression it left with me.

When I was growing up my perception of the world around me was that I must control it, otherwise I'd be taken advantage of. One night, I came across this older man and he was getting drunk next to me and he put the moves on me. I said no, but he wouldn't let up. I'm not exactly new to the gay scene at this point, but I don't know what the game is, all right? I'm looking at all of this and I'm looking at my history and a couple of things occur to me.

One is that this world ain't no different from the world I came from. Okay? This ain't no promised land. These ain't my brothers who're gonna care for me, love me, and make certain I never get hurt. Fuck that shit. These people are as bad as anybody else. That was a negative, very bad awakening for me, number one.

Number two is that immediately, immediately I understood that there was a *hunt* at work here. The hunt was at work. Nothing more than that. These were men and this was a hunt. I was going to be the hunter or I was going to be prey. What can I say, that was just what I came from. That's what's going to occur in the sexual realm of things. If the hunt was going on for food and shelter baby, that ain't nothin' compared to the need of the sexual urge. The sexual urge isn't just for the physical component, but rather for what that physical component creates, the emotional thing. If I was entering into a game that was going to be just as crass, just as exploitative as anything else, where was I to find my nourishment? Where was I going to find any level of confirmation of self? Any set of values that I could relate a larger social structure to? I didn't find any of that. I found myself being either the prey or not. That was what I saw. The rape really exaggerated all of that for me. It just made me mistrust any older gay man.

That's why in the earlier years, especially before AIDS, I was a top. The sex I had back then was around a trophy. It had to be a white guy, younger than me, preferably wealthy, and at least as intelligent as me, if not more. Back then, if I saw someone that I liked, and if they met my criteria, and if they turned around and saw me and if they liked me too, something magical would happen. I'd go wow, this guy likes me as much as I like him. My ego would inflate. I felt fabulous, because not only did my body get to experience what it wanted, but my ego did too. I was desired. I could be as desirable as I thought that I was, despite what my society told me because there's this other guy who's perfect and gorgeous and he's doing the same thing to me and I'm like looking in the mirror and I must be okay. To me, sex was essentially about that. In spite of all my accomplishments, I was still trash in society's eyes. I was still illegal, everything I did. Sex as a top was the only way of getting a trickle of acknowledgment and positive reinforcement about who I was.

The other good thing about being a top had to do with trust. The trust that someone was able to give me. The only reason I would not be a bottom was because I could not trust another man enough to penetrate me. In Greek and Roman times they had temples for the worship of different gods of sex. They were called temples of whores. If women couldn't procreate, they would come to these temples and lay there and have sex with as many men as possible in the hope that they would be filled with light and they could have a child. There was a willingness to serve, to be a disciple. I think it's the same, sometimes, with gay men and the acts that we do. Think of the way these acts take place. For the most part they occur anonymously. I know that that's changed substantially in the past twenty-five years, but for me, in the earlier part of my life, I had sex only under anonymous circumstances, whether it was in the woods, in a bathroom, a bathhouse, or a dirty bookstore. At that level of anonymity, there must be a sublevel degree of unequivocal giving. And for that to occur there must be trust. I will give you everything I have, but you must not hurt me.

If they gave me that trust, trusted me enough that they thought I wouldn't hurt them, it gave me a chance to express the goodness I felt I had. If someone trusted me enough to give me everything they had and I didn't abuse that, I was obviously the good person I thought I was. Not the bad person the world had decided I was. I trusted my use of power, I trusted that I wouldn't hurt anyone. It was not my game plan. But I knew that when I was placed in the position of that person, the position of bottom, I'd always been abused or I'd always perceived the danger of being abused and I wanted nothing to do with that.

The presence of that trust allowed the ritual of my being benevolent and in my own mind reinforced the positive self-image. I talk about my HIV status in the same terms. When I participate in something that fills me with a sense of positive value, I believe that my immune system channels that healing energy. The sexual act has always been about that for me. The sense of being good and the sense of being involved in something good.

I've had a few relationships over the years. I think that our society overestimates marriage and companionship. I think gay marriage is bullshit. I think the economic benefits ought to be granted us, but fuck the rest of it. I don't fight for something that looks like somebody else's thing, I want something different. Sure, I'd like to have a companion, but you can't have everything in the world. And boy, do I have a fortunate life.

I've had sex with countless men; I can't tell you how many thousands. Well over eleven thousand and at least eight thousand of those after I tested HIV positive. Which brings me to after AIDS and again the temple whore thing. I believe that when a man ejaculates, he ejaculates not only his sperm, but also his life force. When I suck a guy off, I'm receiving not only his semen, but also his life force.

When I first tested positive, I couldn't have sex because I felt that the thing that made me feel good would also make me a killer. Now, I'm not just bad because I'm homosexual, I'm bad because I have AIDS, I'm a piece of trash and I have no value in the world. What the fuck am I going to do? Fuck my bank account, I don't even care about that. How many men like me? How many really like me?

Then, I looked at it as a level of healing. My healing required that I understand my desirability. So I started having sex again and there were thousands of men who were willing to go along with that.

I believe that in ingesting sperm a homeopathic treatment occurs. You know what homeopathy is. You distill something so far that it really doesn't have anything in it, yet it really does. I figure out of all the men I sucked off at least a thousand of them must've been HIV positive, if not more. So I formed a version of healing in my body by ingesting the sperm. That's as much an aspect of top and bottom as anything else. If you're getting what you want and what you need, and if you're not hurting anyone, are you a top or a bottom?

By this time in my life, I'm comfortable being top or bottom, anally or orally. As time went by, I got a sense of my own power in a more real sense. I've broken the fetish and I give myself permission to go in a variety of exploratory ways—except I don't take a person's cum in my ass unless we're both HIV positive. I have no issue with barebacking as long as it's conscious. People choose. I have practiced that.

I was out at the circle by the breakwater the other day. It's my favorite place and it gets cruisy at night. This guy, he was about nineteen, came over by my van and sat on the fence. I went over and he whipped out his dick and it was hard as shit and I said, yeah, come on. We jumped into the back of my van and I started to suck him off and lick his chest and do his tits and I had him blow me too. I pulled down his pants all the way and ate out his ass, which was really nice. We sucked each other off some more and about twenty minutes into it we both shot our loads.

His ejaculation was formidable, and, oh my God, I ate all his cum, absolutely, without a question, every last creamy drop of it. There's another level to this. The more turned on you get, the more ejaculation you get. The better the orgasm is, the more profound an experience, the more energy, the more life force. So I do everything I can to get these guys as stimulated as all hell. Not only because it's good for them, but it's good for me too and I like it. It feeds back and forth.

I'm not concerned about reinfection because I don't look at HIV as a horror, something to be afraid of. Can you imagine what goes on in a top's mind when he's with this guy who'll give everything to him, including his life? The sense of power he must feel and the sense of life force that must get ejaculated in response to that? Again, the homeopathic component. The psychology of our medical science is that of the cold war. It's us and them. Gotta kill the enemy. I'm sure that's not the way medicine will go in the future. We have to have a paradigm shift. Not everything in the world is an enemy. Right now we have more microbes in our bodies that are required for living than we even have cells in our bodies. It seems to me we could look at the sexual act as a gift rather than a torment or torture. I'm not the only one who conceives of these psychologies. There are negative men who go out and have initiation parties and invite twenty known HIV positive men to infect them. It's pretty rampant. In effect, it's the church of HIV.

In the seventies you were either a top or a bottom, but there's no sense of top or bottom for me anymore. Suppose I'm in a bathhouse and I'm laying there on my stomach and I'm a bottom. This guy comes over and he fucks me. Is there any remote connection between what's in his mind and what's in mine? I don't know his name, his profession, all I have is some image that I can slap my own fancy onto. So I could be the top even though I'm physically the bottom. I want him to fuck me and I get what I want, therefore I'm in control. That's what my mind says. Control is all about volition. That's all I'm trying to say. My sex life has always been predicated on what I conceive as volitional. Sometimes, it's important for me to test my own sense of vulnerability. I jump out of airplanes, I scuba dive, I do things that frighten the hell out of me because I want to push my limits. Sometimes, getting fucked is just like that.

16

Cole Tucker: A Man's Soul

Versatile, Age 45

Interviewing Cole Tucker, a.k.a. Rick Karp, is a cinch; set him off and he goes full speed ahead. He's opinionated, extremely bright and charming, funny, insightful, brassy, assertive, bold, and arrogant. He's proud of who he is and of what he represents. He has an easy, masculine demeanor and gesticulates wildly with his hands and uses facial expressions to stress a point.

We'd made a date to meet at a restaurant on Commercial Street at 11 a.m. on a Saturday morning in mid-August, the absolute peak of the Provincetown tourist season. It's nearly impossible to maneuver my bike through a crowd of tourists—most of them gay, hungover, hungry, and not yet quite awake—and I'm five minutes late. I spot Rick standing in front of the restaurant looking despondent. I fear this is going to be disastrous. I bravely introduce myself; he barely responds and walks inside. We settle at a table in the back and he gruffly tells me he'll be fine once he gets his coffee. Sure enough, once the waiter approaches the table and pours him a cup, Rick is a different man. He reaches under the young man's shorts and gives his butt a squeeze. The boy smiles, enjoying the attention. "See, this is perfect," Rick tells me as he takes his first sip, still caressing the waiter's ass, "I can actually see you now."

Interviews with Rick Karp—or rather, with the cigar-chewing, foot-stomping, macho, top porno star—are all over the magazines and the Internet. I'm honored that he granted me this interview, which is more personal and candid than most. He was forty years old when he made his debut in adult films and achieved unheard-of success in an industry obsessed with youth. He has more than twenty-four films to his credit, including the classics *Big Guns 2, Catalinaville,* and *House of Games.* He won the Probe Award for best top in 1999, when he was forty-four.

*   *   *

My name is Rick Karp. I'm also known, in public, as a character named Cole Tucker who's an internationally famous porn star. I'm six feet, one hundred eighty-five pounds, tattooed, extremely muscular, kind of dramatic, square jawed, and hard looking. Because of those physical attributes and my demeanor, in the porn world they've totally cast me as a top. Most of the people who hire me to make movies put me in a top role, even though in thirty to forty percent of my movies I go down like the *Titanic.* I bottom. But most people who see me bottom in the movies don't cognitively acknowledge that I'm bottoming because of the way I do it.

As far as Rick, where my heart is, I'm pretty well a fifty-fifty kind of guy. I love men. Masculine men. When I'm in bed, I love giving pleasure to men. That means, whoever I'm with, if they're predisposed to being a top or a bottom, then I will go to the other side to give them the most pleasure in bed as possible. When I bottom, or I lick boots, or I suck dick, or I take a dick or an arm or anything up my ass, or even when I'm dominated, I don't feel any of that compromises my masculinity. At times, I feel more masculine as a bottom. Some of the things I do, only top guys can do. It ain't for the faint of heart. I'm a pretty strong, vibrant, powerful man and I take that to my bottom side. Again, what I do in bed comes from a genuine space of enjoying to please. Now that in itself may be a bottom concept. Pleasing the other man. I'm not sure. But it means if you stick your arm in his ass or you slap him around or you choke him with your dick or you fuck him silly 'til he cums, that's technically considered a top role. So what's the difference? Is it the physical act or is it where you're coming from in your head?

A physical act doesn't really make a top or a bottom. It's a function, an organic function of what you do. It's the dynamics of where you come from. I believe I come from a truly neutral place. My male energy and my masculinity never diminishes in either side. So it may look like I'm bottoming, but it's coming from a top place in my head. To be honest with you, when I'm being fisted in a sling, the stuff that comes out of my mouth is very top. [He growls.] *Do it! Move it!*

Right! Often, when I'm fucking a guy, I'm more gentle with him. I'm very cognizant of his pleasure.

I have this terminology: *You either give a fuck or you take a fuck.* Most men who fuck other men are taking a fuck. They're fucking for their own pleasure, for their penis. Most guys are not even cognizant of what's going on in their lover's butt, whether it feels good or not. I'm not like that. I'm always asking the person if it feels good. Often, I don't have to ask them at all; I can tell by their body motion if it feels good. So when it comes to being inside a man, I'm much more gentle than any other thing I do because I'm doing it to give him pleasure. If he gets hot, I get hard.

I'm very open-minded and I'm very secure with my masculinity. I'll be honest with you: there are times when I'll almost fantasize being a woman. Like getting fucked like a woman gets fucked. That gets me very hot, but I don't feel like a woman. I don't want to be a woman. Sometimes, when I eat a guy's ass, I transfer it to eating a pussy. I get into it, I eat it like a pussy, which is a very top thing. So I'm willing in my mind to get into these fantasy scenarios that do cross gender. One of the things I love to do, I visually love to watch a straight man fuck a woman. I love it. I love the way it looks.

I've found that in homosexual sex, or homosexual relationships, what happens between two people outside the bedroom does not necessarily fall in line with what happens in bed. Sometimes, you're very surprised. There may be definite top/bottom roles in bed because it may be a true preference, but if you look at the household and the lifestyle, the chores are very sporadically divided by who does what better. That's just healthy. If I can cook better than the other one, but the other one can clean the bathroom, that's who should be doing those jobs. I suck with the laundry. I think it should come out folded and I don't think there's such a thing as sorting. I don't understand it. I shouldn't be doing laundry. But when it comes down to cleaning the bathroom, if I'm in the mood, I can get that thing shining.

I think social dominance and aggression is different than dominance and aggression in bed. A lot of interesting, high-powered people have come across my doorstep and one of them used to live here in Provincetown. He was the most brilliant, the most autocratic, self-ruled, self-running, arrogant son of a bitch. He made big corporate decisions all day. But when it came time to close the bedroom door he wanted to be tied down and gagged. He didn't want to make a single decision in bed 'cause he's tired of making them all day. That's more prominent than you'd think. A lot of gay high-powered people completely acquiesce in the bedroom.

There's some masculine things. I love to drive the car. I prefer to drive. It's a very control thing. I like to paint. I can paint a good room. But when it comes time to building stuff, like the wood would never line up. I'm not patient with that stuff. I wouldn't measure stuff. Those are all subcategories of top and bottom. The interesting thing is, these subcategories are not something that gay men cultivated as a culture themselves. They're Judeo-Christian, Western culture mimicry. This whole top/bottom thing is, in fact, an effort, if this is about gay men, to mimic heterosexual roles that were patterned in them as children. From the time we're one day old, we're thrust in an environment where extremely strong identification patterns are programmed into us. Parents are very cognizant about what their boys do and what their girls do; what their boys will wear and what their girls will wear; what the boys will play with and what we should talk about with them and what color their room should be and who they should hang out with and how they should grow up to be a young man or a young lady. All of that is subtext and subtext and subtext. It's horrifying when a father walks in and sees his little boy playing with a Barbie. He may grow up to be the most famous fashion designer in the world, but that doesn't matter. At that moment, it's horrific for a little boy to be playing with a Barbie.

My penis got hard for the first time when I was four and a half years old. I was watching cowboys and Indians on TV in the late fifties. In those shows, the Indians were always played by California musclemen that were dyed dark and had a little feather in their head and a loincloth on. I can distinctly remember seeing the side view of the loincloth with the flap in the front and it gets to the buttocks, and my dick got hard. Now, I would find it very hard to believe that this was socially induced because my parents are overt heterosexuals. I believe that there was a predisposition or a genetics in me. But I also believe that it was highly socially, environmentally induced because my parents were dysfunctional. They represented an unhealthy heterosexual relationship to the max. So I wanted no part of that. So not only did I have a genetic predisposition to be gay, but my image of the heterosexual relationship was terrible. With those two elements in play, I was done for. I was never anything but homosexual. Nonetheless, I don't think it's black or white. I think there are people who are really, really, really dark, and people who are really, really, really, really, really, really almost white but light gray. I don't think there's a person on earth, if you could get in their mind and heart, who hasn't honestly fantasized about what it's like to have sexual relationships with their own sex at some point in their life. Or at least a three-way with the third partner being their own sex. I think the environment encourages or discourages this behavior. You could be eighty-five percent homosexually inclined and grow up in Columbine, Texas, and you can get fucked over royally in the head. So I think depending on what kind of environment it is and how the child assimilates that environment, that environment can steer the tendency in either direction.

I was clearly the bottom in my first relationship. I was nineteen, he was thirty-two. He was the daddy. And daddy loved to get fucked. [Laughs] Just loved it. Just loved it. We had dildos and everything. Daddy loved to get fucked. What's that all about? Was I the bottom in every other aspect? Absolutely. I was submissive, I did what I was told, he always made the decisions. My second relationship was a little more equal. I tried to find someone who could take care of me too. No more. I do a much better job of taking care of myself than anyone else.

There's some versatility in the porn business, but not very much. It's very confusing. In the beginning of my movie career, I was clearly cast as top. Two weeks before I was given the best top award, two movies where I bottomed came out, and everybody's asking *is the best top really a bottom?* In magazines, they show a picture of my dick and a picture of my ass and they talk about the movies I bottom in. The interesting thing is that people who are invested in me as a top, who come to me as consumers, customers, fans, refuse to acknowledge my bottom scenes. It's like they can see it, but it doesn't make any sense to them. They think, *he's a top.* It's a fantasy. It's their image of me. Again, it's that Judeo-Christian mimicry, homosexuals imitating heterosexual lifestyle. They can't break out of that mold. One's gotta be a top and one's got to be a bottom for it to work. A lot of guys want the ultimate top and that's the way most of my fans want to perceive me. They want to serve me, they want me to fuck them silly and they want, you know, all of this extrapolation of what my image looks like.

There are men, and I know them, who have not yet discovered the joy of the other sexual organ, the asshole. There are some things I don't like in bed. I just don't like 'em. They're pretty bizarre stuff. Most of the stuff we all know about, I like. I think there are people who were captured on the potty or something or who think, for whatever reason, that their asshole is a horrible place. They don't want anything going there at all and they're totally ashamed of their asshole. So they believe they're just totally tops. They're so protective and so asshole phobic, that they won't even permit anyone to go near it and find the pleasure in their butt. I know 'cause over the years I've discovered how much pleasure is inside my ass. Real fucker that I am, I love my ass played with. [Wide grin] It feels good.

Some friends of mine who are in their forties tell me that they're tops. And I say to them, "You'd better find out about the other side of your sexuality 'cause you're spending your life missing half your orgasms." I can understand it if someone says to me, "I've gotten fucked and I just don't like it." But when someone says they've never gotten fucked their whole life and they're thirty-five, thirty-six, thirty-seven years old, and they're gay men, I wonder, "What's going on here? Aren't you even curious?" Like in fisting, right? Very rarely will I let someone fist me who's never been fisted because they don't have a clue. In fisting, to be one or the other, you have to have done one or the other. But that's a whole other interview.

From a strictly anatomical standpoint, I don't believe the asshole was designed for getting fucked. It sure is strange. But I don't think God intended the mouth for dicks going in it either. What's the difference? If the principle is that God did not intend anybody to take it up the ass, then the same principle must apply to the mouth. He didn't intend anyone to get blow jobs. Would you really want to go there?

Getting ass-fucked is much more pleasurable for men than it is for women. A major part of a man being fucked is the massaging of his prostate. The way women enjoy getting fucked is they like their clit played with and that's how they get hot. Women actually prefer clitoral stimulation to insertion. There's lots of things that God created that we discovered can serve us in different ways. There's some beautiful flower that cures headaches. Did God make that flower to cure headaches? The flower may have been there long before there was a headache or even before there was a man to have a headache. It seems to me if it creates that much pleasure, there must be something about it. Maybe it's a form of birth control. Maybe the caveman discovered, "If you put it in this hole, no babies come out."

I believe a function of homosexuality is that it's a form of population control. I genuinely do, and of course a culture without homosexuals would lose many dimensions of its richness. Who'd do everybody's hair? There's homosexuality in the animal kingdom. We're a part of that kingdom.

I wouldn't call myself a caveman, but that's where I come from. I use all five senses in sex. All of them. One of them that really gets me going is smell. I love the smell of a man's armpits, I love the smell of a sweaty crotch, I love the smell of a sweaty asshole, all of those smells get my dick rock hard. It's very much like the way the animal kingdom works. How does a male bull find a female bull in heat? Certainly not on the Internet.

I was talking to this big, hunky bear of a guy at the gym the other day. We're talking and I'm looking at his armpits—bears don't usually mind that—and they're perfectly clean. I went, "Pity." And he went, "Eugh!" This big, hunky guy said *eugh.* So I said, "What do you mean, *eugh?*" He said, "I'm spotlessly clean all the time." So that put him right to the bottom of my list. And you know, I just know the animal kingdom works in smells and taste and everything. If you watch a male animal approach a female, first thing he does is he smells her and then he licks her. Then, he gets hard and he mounts her. *Hello!* Works for me. So I tell this guy about the smelling and how the animal works, and he says, "It works like that in anything but evolved animals." And I said, "Could you name, besides us, other evolved animals?" He says, "We are the only evolved animal." I just saw the flaw in that right there.

With Calvin Klein we Polarize. We Irish Springize. Not only do our clothes have to be clean, but we have to throw some ridiculous cancer-causing piece of paper in the dryer to make it smell like Irish Spring, Rain Day, soft blue sheets, fresh sheets smell. What are we hiding from? What is unpleasant about an actual smell? Now there's dirty. *Very* dirty. And then there's the natural smell. I find them all very pleasant. We've been socialized against our natural instincts.

What excites me during sex, what brings me close to cumming, is when my partner cums. I like his cum on me. Then, what I do is I flip him around and I have him lay his freshly cum dick over my face, his balls on my nose, so I can see his asshole. The vision of my lover's male hole, male section, is especially orgasmic. There's actually a smell that comes out of a man's balls after he comes. A kind of very musky smell. That's what makes me cum. Sometimes, I like cumming while eating his ass, while my tongue is in his ass.

I'm homosexual by definition because I like my sex. Maybe I've been socialized, to a degree. I like the masculine aspect of my sex. The aspect of the male that we identify as masculine, which is a form of Judeo-Christian, Western culturization. These are men who go to football games and drink beer and fart in public. I don't know if I just bought into that role. That's what makes me hard.

I'm not particularly hairy. I shave myself for business purposes. But there's nothing more beautiful than when I'm in bed and I see hairy thighs and I just go [gasp], "This is what sex is to me!" I've bought into that hyper masculine trip. I love it. I've been to bed with men who are not the epitome of masculinity, for whatever reason. It's okay, but I prefer masculine men. It's almost a prerequisite. I have nothing against men who are less masculine or more on the feminine side as friends, but as bedmates that's not what floats my boat.

Now, I could, uhm—oh, boy, I'm going to get in trouble for this—I could more easily go to bed with a woman who's sexually totally open than with an effeminate man. Effeminate men don't do a lot for me because there's a lot trappings that go along with it. There's a grueling meticulousness to them. There's often a cologne, a style, and interest in more womanlike social qualities. I've met a few women who approach sex like men. They're fun. You know? They're in touch with their pussies and their assholes and they love cum and you stick a finger here and tongue there and they go wild. That's nice. That's animal. I like animal. That's why I'm a caveman.

At age twenty-two, I made a lot of mistakes with people I went home with. But at forty-five, you get home and they're totally a mismatch in bed. You know. Cologne and hair spray. That's a bad sign. I've been fooled a few times. Most recently, I was fooled by a guy who had a tremendous amount of bravado. He's like: [growls], *Yeah!* It was here in P-town. [Baritone, macho voice] *Yeah, fuck yeah, we'll get down and dirty, yeah, yeah.* Great. I get to his house, we open the door, and not only was it fully decorated, but every magazine was perfectly laid out within a perfect inch so you could see the title. Every glass was speck and dust. There was nothing. Nothing. It looked like, you know how they make a house that they're gonna blow up with an atom bomb, this was a test house for that. It was perfection. The moment I walked in the door, I went, "I'm in big trouble." And sure enough I was. Because this was a totally anal retentive neurotic man. But he hit it well in the bar.

Being in the business that I'm in I will not, never will, do a movie or a public performance which does not, try as best as it can, as close as it can be, to light gray in the safeness quotient. I don't know as anything as pure white. I think everything takes a risk unless you get in hefty bags and bump pussies, you know? But I have an obligation as a sexual role model, an icon—that I guess I am today for whatever amount of time—to go out there and proudly represent the safest sex I know how. I also have no problem with two HIV-positive men making private decisions in their bedroom, and making open, honest, cognizant, completely revealing decisions in the privacy of their bedroom. I do have a problem, a little bit, if an openly HIV-positive man barebacks an absolutely known negative man. I think, in that case, the positive man has to take the responsibility. If you're negative, it's healthy to assume everybody's positive.

I'm happy with condoms. I've learned how to use them. I make them work for me. I get really, really hard for films, get really, really hard. What people don't do is they don't lube the inside of the condom. So if you put lube in the inside of the condom, it changes the whole feel. It's a very small thing to do to ensure safety. I don't believe in bareback videos. I just don't. We have to teach the younger generation.

I have a friend who believes that HIV has actually promoted kinkier forms of sexual behavior. Many of what's considered kinky forms of sex are absolutely safer than plain apple-pie sex. Water sports. Fisting with gloves. Bondage. All of these things are much safer than, you know, fucking without a condom. Tying guys up and jerking off on them is very safe.

No matter how safe you are, there's always an element of risk. I had a partner that I saw for a while and he was negative and we played safe. Sunday morning, he was making breakfast and he cuts a bagel and slips and cuts his wrist. Not a bad cut, heals up. Sunday night we're in bed thumping and jumping and thumping and jumping and of course my cum always goes away from him. I cum on the sheets. We're in afterglow, he goes like this [reaches over with his arm], and his cut touches the cum on the sheet. No matter how careful you want to be, shit happens. I had a tremendous amount of guilt and he went nuts for a while. He did prophylactic treatments, blah, blah, blah.

At this time, right now, I prefer positive men, because I've been positive for fifteen years. I've never been sick. I'm super sensitive to my body. I'm so in tune with my body that I can tell that I don't feel right long before I used to be able to.

Here's my most recent sexual experience: I met this guy, Kevin, the last time I was down here. We met at the beginning of my vacation and we didn't part company until he left town. We had a marvelous time. We discovered that we were acclimated even on the finer levels in bed. We had a wonderful time. So I was coming back to town yesterday and he was going to be here too, so we decided to see each other. I hooked up with him briefly, but like the true homosexual I am, I told him I wanted to be on my own my first night out. So he said, "That's fine, it's okay."

I went out and in my best whoriness—and I tried the best that I could—I got turned down three times. *Three times.* So the bars close and it's pizza hour and I see Kevin coming down the street and I say to myself, "What am I doing? I know how good he is and how much I like him." So we decided to go home together. On our way home, one of the gentlemen that turned me down is following us. We turn off and we're almost to the door and all of sudden we hear, *Hey, hey, hey!* And he says, "Can I come in and watch you guys?" Now I think he has a lover, he may even have a woman lover, but he really just wanted to watch. He was very straight acting and appearing. So he's sitting on the chair and we're going at it in bed. His dick was rock hard for half an hour. He's instructing us on what to do and we were putting on a little bit of a show. Finally, he pulls up his pants without cumming and says, "I gotta go." We asked him, *why,* and he says, "I have a lover and I gotta go home." And I say, "So this is your way of sowing your oats, 'cause you don't cum?" He says, "Yeah, I don't cum, I didn't cheat on him, and if I don't touch you guys, I didn't cheat on him." It's like a three-D movie. Okay, so he left. Kevin and I got into an embrace and we made love and it was wild. We were so into each other. We fit beautifully. It was phenomenal. He sucked me a lot and I sucked him a lot. We both love eating ass, deep eating ass. And I fucked him silly. Then I shoved four fingers up his ass and made him cum. It was wild, I was blowing him. I could feel the whole orgasm from my fingers all the way on his dick. I could see the whole thing just build. He was out of control. And then he came all over me and then I took my hand out and I put my face right in that hole area and I came rockets. We fucked every position, every which way, and talked dirty in each other's ear, talked the nasty man talk. And it was great. He's got the most beautiful body, his ass is unbelievably beautiful. He's very quiet, nice, and very sociable, and he's wild in bed. He's so easy to get going. He responds so well to everything you do.

I've decided I'm not letting Kevin go because when it's good, it's really good. I do not believe in tossing the big fish into the sea because *maybe* I might catch a bigger fish. We all do that. That's why nobody gets laid after pizza hour. I was in the bar and I approached several people and they were not saying no, but they were not saying yes. Finally, I said to one of them, "Is anyone better than me coming along, do you think?"

I do a lot of talking to people. I don't specifically ask what they're into, but I'm very perceptive about people. So I talk to them. I can tell you a whole shitload about a person after twenty minutes. Just from what he said. From that, I can feel this sexual energy and I know if it's a match or not. I did this a few times and there was this energy, chemistry, this and that, and I can see the guy's looking over my shoulder. It's like, "Oh, okay." Some of these people knew who I was, but they're almost in automatic pilot. People don't think consciously of it. I don't think they consciously say, "I'm looking for something better." I think it's a modus operandi that's almost built in, like a circuitry. Two of the people that turned me down, and one followed us home, were looking for me afterward. Well, guess what? Your window of opportunity is gone. You know?

I don't mind it if people know who I am. I don't mind that, but once I let someone in, they better get over it. They better permit me to be me. I drop people who are preoccupied with the Cole Tucker thing. I don't have time for that. You're not really interested in who I am or what I think, you're interested in being seen with Cole Tucker. I have enough Cole Tuckerism. Rick and Cole are a little more interchangeable than they were. I expect Kevin to call me Rick. I freak out if he calls me Cole. I have some friends, they want to introduce me to someone at tea dance or something and they stop and say, "What do you want to be called?" Sometimes, I just want to be called Cole because that's as far as I want to go. It's a kind of a wall that I can put up.

It's not a nasty thing because I'm a very easy guy. Cole is a way of protecting Rick.

For me, the size of a man's dick doesn't really matter. The problem with guys with big dicks is they think they're all about their dick. They're totally boring in bed. You're going to bed with a guy and his dick. Separately. I just can't stand that. Both ends of the spectrum create psychological problems in the person, which is more of the problem. Guys who have itty-bitty dicks or guys who have fourteen-inch beer cans, they have psychological problems, I believe. This is my judgment. But the size of the dick, as long as it gets hard and functions and is able to derive pleasure, doesn't matter to me. Our culture puts way too much emphasis on the size of sexual organs. I see these women who go on these talk shows and their breasts are the size of the cocktail table, and it's *ooh, ooh.* To me it's like, that's horrible. It's a freak of nature. Like it means something. I don't chase after guys with size thirteen shoes, you know, it's not important. I'm going to bed with a man.

I'm proud of my dick. I'm told that it's large. I don't see it as large, I've had it all my life, it's my dick. I don't think of it as a big, huge dick. In porn terms, it's not a big dick. It's just a regular dick. In the industry, I have a good to average dick. If someone says in porn, "He has a big dick," this is a *big* dick.

There are three important things in the gay world. The third most important thing is a wad of money. The second is a beautiful face and a beautiful body. And the most important thing is a big dick. If you can do eight on a scale of one to ten on all three categories, you're gonna do real well in the gay world. The most important thing a man can have to get me in bed is an unbelievable intellect: a loving heart and a brilliant intellect. Those are the most attractive things to me and those are the elements for long-term relationships. 'Cause at the end of it you're in bed with a man's mind.

I like to leave the lights on when I go to bed because I like to look at the hairs and juices dripping, and the faces, but most people turn the lights off. So now you spent all night passing one beauty off to the next because one person has a waist that's two inches smaller or biceps that are a little bigger or a nose that's a little straighter, and at the end you take 'em home and you turn the lights off. Hello! You're in bed with a man. You're not in bed with a mannequin. A lot of people go to bed with people as trophies. I know a guy who has to catch the most beautiful thing in every bar. Do you know what his most awful moment is? When he's in the car driving home, knowing he has to go to bed with this person. It was all about leaving the bar with the most handsome man and the sex is just like a routine to get him out of the house. I think that's pathetic.

I go to bed with a man. Heart, soul, spirit. There are people who you'd see with me and you'd think, "Now, why does he want to be with that one? He's forty pounds overweight, he's fifty-five years old, he has gray hair." Well, it's because in the art of conversation, that guy turned me on. That's what I go for.

17

James: The Female Position

Versatile Bottom, Age 47

It was pretty clear that James was calling in hopes of a sexual encounter. He asked if we could meet that evening, but I said I was busy and suggested we meet the following day.

I was already familiar with the apartment complex he lived in. I'd seen one of the units when I was shopping for a rental for a friend the previous summer. It was a depressing, musty building. James' room was poorly lit, the furniture was rickety, and the air stale and thick.

James looks considerably older than his age (he told me he was forty-seven). He's thin and frail. A whiff of stale alcohol emanates from him when he shakes my hand. He seems nervous and preoccupied. When we sit down and begin to speak, his hands tremble and his eyes keep shifting away from me.

* * *

I guess I'm more of a top, but I fantasize about being a bottom. I want to be fucked, but maybe I'm not loose enough because I haven't done it enough. My first sexual experience was when I was twenty-three, in Washington, DC. It was with someone I knew. He had a huge dick and he wanted to fuck me. He did it and it hurt. I have the aggressiveness of a top. I like the idea of fucking. Having my dick up their ass. But my fantasy is to be a bottom and to be good as a bottom. I fantasize about being in the female position, with my legs up in the air and having a man on top of me. I believe when we have sex, as gay men, one of us takes the female role and the other the male role. I think it's a kind of chemistry. I think every gay man is that way and people can reverse. I like the idea of being in the female position and having a man take control of me and fuck me, but I have the reverse fantasy too. There are times when I want to be the man, the aggressor.

I have S&M fantasies, but I haven't explored them much. I've had my ass slapped a few times and my balls squeezed. I really like that. I like a man with a big dick and circumcised. A dick with a big head. I'm attracted to good looking guys, but the dick does matter.

I haven't had a long-term relationship. There was an older guy that I liked. He wanted me to suck his dick, but I just didn't like his dick. He was too old and not very clean. I like sucking dick, but maybe my mouth is too small. When the guy is too wide, it's hard to get my mouth all the way down; but if he's not too wide I like to suck his dick and I like for him to cum in my mouth. I have this fantasy of being fucked and someone sucking me at the same time. That hasn't happened.

[At this point James says he's getting turned on and asks if he could stroke himself. I tell him that I'm not here for sex and suggest that we stop if he's uncomfortable. He assures me he's fine and would like to continue to talk. The tone of the interview shifts here as he's more relaxed and is able to talk more comfortably.]

I think the feminine role is portrayed as inferior in porno videos. When I take the female position I feel like I'm less than the other person. That turns me on. Just the idea of someone taking you and fucking you is exciting. It's the female energy. I think we're born with that and we're born as gay men.

You may have the male fantasy. The male fantasy may be the best sex you can get. The female fantasy is somebody just like [indicating the door], someone just walked in like you just walked in and you take me over and you carry me off and we're gonna live happily ever after. You can have your way with me, fuck me, put your head on my shoulder and hug me and I don't have to worry about all the things that are out there ever again. That's the female fantasy. I know gay men who have that fantasy. The female runs through all gay men.

I know it's not a realistic fantasy. It only happens in movies, and once in a while in life. There's a great song, "Marty the Martian." It's about this woman who's in the park and a space ship comes down and this really good looking guy comes out. He says to her, "I've come from Mars to find a wife." And she says, "The only problem is, you've got eleven arms. How come you've got eleven arms and I've got only two?" He says, "We need them all to hug." And she buys that. They go off together on top of this hill and they walk off arm in arm in arm in arm in arm. That's the female fantasy. Barbra Streisand did it. I think what I want is someone to protect me. That's what a woman looks for.

I grew up with women in my life: my mother and my grandmother. I got negative vibes from the men in my life, which is part of the problem of being gay. It's not that I don't like men, it's that I just don't understand them. I don't understand the way they feel their feelings. They can totally go off the edge. Women are more comfortable with the idea of feeling. There's a flow. I think it's the female energy. Men are not comfortable with it. I mean there's feminine and masculine. It can be in either sex.

[At this point I ask James his thoughts on barebacking, but he says he doesn't know what barebacking is. I tell him it's having unprotected sex and ask him if that's something he does or would do in the future.]

Sex definitely feels better without a condom. I would use a condom if I was fucking someone, but I can understand that sometimes people can get inebriated or whatever and they kind of lose it. I was tested in 1991 and I was negative.

I was on the beach the other night. I was watching these guys who were doing it and it really turned me on. They were fucking down by the boat. I was by myself and I thought I was looking pretty good that night. I was by the ship and there was nobody there. Then these two guys came, and, I guess it's because I'm in Provincetown and not in the city; if I were in the city, I'd have picked up on it I guess. They were an older guy and a younger. The younger guy came up to me and he said, "I wanna urinate on you. Do you have a problem with urinating or something like that?" I said "No." And he said, "Why not?" I said "No" and I walked away and he said, "I'm gonna cut his fucking throat." He said it to the other guy. I walked away, I started to walk away slow, not to get him to pounce on me, to get a little leverage. Then, I felt he was coming behind me and I started to run down the fucking beach. I thought if I can just get to the Boatslip.* If I can see the lights I'll be alright. There was a moment when I thought they were gonna catch up with me. If I were in the city or anywhere I don't know what those guys would've done. I was running on the fucking

---

*The Boatslip Beach Club is a popular guest house and bar on the water in Provincetown.

sand, which was hard, and I finally got to the Boatslip and they asked me what was going on. I said, "There were two men and they wanted to urinate on me and then they wanted to kill me."

That was the only time in my life I thought if I could kill somebody, I could kill that guy. He scared me to death. I mean this is not a safe town. There are people out there, those two guys are out there now. You have to be very careful. I wanted to call the police. I got a guy to walk me home.

There's a testosterone thing that happens in men and if you say no to them, and if they're aroused, some men, depending on their culture, how they're brought up, can go off the edge like that. If I had a daughter or a son who was gay, I'd just say, "You be very careful when you're around men. Even if they seem very nice. You still can't be real sure."

−18−

Richard: To Know Who You Are

Versatile, Age 49

Richard divorced his wife of twenty-three years and embarked upon a life as a gay man which, he says, "is full of possibilities and fraught with uncertainties at the same time." He still adores his ex-wife and the two children they raised together. At nearly fifty years old, tall, bright, and highly articulate, his eyes shine with optimism when he talks about the possibilities and challenges that lay ahead. It's been two years since his divorce and he's still trying to figure out what it means to be gay.

We meet on a gorgeous summer day and I insist that he go to the beach instead. He and his strikingly handsome friend Roger have rented a condo for a week's vacation in Provincetown and I hate to make him sit indoors and talk into a tape recorder. He says he's been looking forward to this interview, which we'd set up a week ago on the phone. He tells Roger to go off fishing and offers me a drink. As soon as Roger's out the door, Richard, giddy with infatuation, confides in me that the agreement they have not to have sex together during this vacation is proving to be difficult. "It's so hard to resist him," he says, "because he's so incredibly manly and good-looking."

*   *   *

So much of this is so new to me. I'm still trying to figure out where I'm going with all this. I'm still in the process of figuring out the tops and bottoms thing. I don't have a clear definition yet. It seems to be so important to know what you are. I mean everyone wants to know. They ask you before they move on to a further place with you. I don't often know how to answer that question. It sometimes depends on the day or the hour. So I felt this interview would be a good way to de-mystify it. I thought this could be therapeutic for me.

As a man who's spent most of his life as heterosexual, I guess I've had the best of both worlds—which also makes this subject intriguing to me because straight men mostly consider themselves tops. They act in a top sort of way much of the time. It's so different for gay men because, you know, there's so much more variety.

I had my first sexual experience when I was in the eighth grade with an intimidating bully. It was very exciting. I was at the low end of my popularity as a kid at the time. This kid was very popular but pushy and we were the same age, but he was bigger than me. He sort of intimidated me into sucking his dick. It happened in the garage at my house. I sucked him and he came in my mouth. We did it several more times in the course of about six months. I never got used to him cumming in my mouth. He was uncut and not very clean either, and I didn't like that. But the prelude to it was the real exciting part. I was thirteen and the danger and the timing and almost getting caught was very exciting. He was pursuing me. It was his decision, always. I just sort of followed the rules because in return, I got to hang around with him and I got popular! [Laughs] I'd hang around with him and he'd, you know, take care of me. Then he graduated and I never saw him again.

My next experience was when I was fifteen with one of my par-ents' really good friends. Married guy. At a shore home that his fam-ily owned, where my family used to go to a lot in the summer. It was on Chesapeake Bay. It was a total seduction. It surprised the hell out of me. In the changing room at the shore. I was there first by myself. He walked in and started to talk to me. He was like forty and, sort of out of the blue, he said, "Do you mind if I jerk off?" I was like, "No." He was between me and the door. So I was sort of there. I could've left, but I didn't. We weren't talking about anything sexual or any-thing. Just out of the blue. So he jerked himself off and he jerked me off, and then he left. I, like, didn't know what to think. Then a week or two later we were there again and it happened again. And it pro-gressed. I actually saw him on and off for about four years. His wife used to go to bingo on Tuesday nights. I used to pretend I was going to the library and I'd go over there. It always happened after his kids were asleep and before his wife came home. Very bizarre.

He and I went all the way; we fucked each other. He fucked me first and it hurt. He wasn't a gentle person. It was forceful and I thought that was the way it was supposed to be. I mean, I didn't know. I just thought that was the way it was supposed to feel. It never got easier with him either. He was always just very abrupt and I don't think he was using any kind of lubrication, but what did I know? He always took the lead and I just always sort of thought, "Okay, he knows what he's doing." I fucked him too which I liked a lot—and he loved it. See, that's why I'm not really clear about the top or bottom thing because I really liked both for different reasons. I bet he's still married. I haven't kept in touch. I stopped seeing him when I went to college. I was dating and I wanted to be straight.

I always had a fascination with the masculine icon type. The Clint Walker on TV, the very manly type man. Both of these guys were very masculine and that was very appealing to me. But I hadn't really fantasized about taking it as far as getting fucked, until it sort of happened.

My preference about topping or bottoming seems to depend on who I'm with. Now again, I'm relatively new to a lot of this. In terms of volume. Not in terms of age. Because I did start early, but then I stopped. For a long time.

I had no other experiences through high school other than those two. A couple of my schoolmates and I got close to fooling around a few times, but I never wanted to do it with guys my own age. It was just not right. I liked that older guy thing.

I didn't have sex with a woman until I was eighteen. In college I was involved in a lot of the antiwar stuff in the sixties. That included communal living, group sex, a lot of things that may have labels today that didn't have labels then. So for me it wasn't a question of am I gay or straight, it was a question of what's the most pleasure I can get or give, with the right person. So I was doing men and women. Not in great quantities, but experimenting with both and occasionally with groups. It really was fun.

The reason I wanted to be straight was not because of guilt or shame. I was just following the rules. The rules were that you became a family man. It's interesting because I followed those rules and there were so many others that I broke. I'm not religious. My family's very religious. I did exactly what I wanted to do in college, took the major I wanted, didn't follow anybody else's suggestion about anything. In fact, the mere suggestion often made me go in the opposite direction. But I followed the marriage rule because in my heart of hearts I always wanted a family and kids.

Being straight came naturally. The first woman that I had sex with was a virgin. I ended up marrying her at twenty-one. I was already out of the house. I was living communally with another guy who ended up being gay, who was married at the time as well. He's now dead. She and I got our own apartment. Being married was fine with me. I enjoyed her sexually, but it only lasted for two years.

Sex with men, up to that point, had always been quick and in a hurry. Sex with women, on the other hand, was eventful. It took time. It was creative, time-consuming, and it involved more of me. It was much more engaging. Actual intercourse was only a part of the whole series of seductive and sensual events. All of which I really liked. I thought it was really cool to get up and make dinner and, you know, watch a movie together. It had a continuum that sex with men did not have. I mean at the time, you have to remember, most men were not out. So sex with men was dangerous, it was unlawful, and it was hurried. That was my introduction to it. With women it was legal, you could hold hands down the street and you could kiss under a street light. All of those things made a difference to me. So I went from a very barren, but exciting experience to a very well rounded one that, to me, had all the stops along the way.

I had sex with a man only once during that marriage and it was very hot. I'll never forget it as long as I live. I was in graduate school and I didn't have classes until the afternoon. I walked her to work one morning and I was heading back home and I stopped at an antique store window to look. This guy walked up to me and stood behind me. I saw him in the reflection of the window and he was a little older. He was muscular and hunky and all those things I like. He just said, "Let's go fuck." And I was like, "Okay." Unbelievable. I had to do it. The sex was incredible. He had the biggest dick I'd ever seen until then. He fucked me and it was great. For some reason he knew what he was doing. That was the last time I had anal sex until three years ago. It was a really hot experience, but then I compartmentalized it. I put it away and it was over. There was no risk at that point. There was really very little communicable disease. It was all easy. It was sort of at the beginning of the era where it got easier.

My first marriage ended because in my second year of graduate school I met another woman that I completely fell in love with. I don't think I was in love with the first one. She was a passage. I'm still in love with my second wife. She and I spent twenty-three years together and I love her to this day. We had two kids and were together from 1975 to 1998. She's probably the reason I didn't come out much earlier. We had an incredibly hot, passionate relationship at the beginning. Our sex life was good for about fifteen years. Then it trailed off as kids got in the way, you know, distractions occurred, and it got to be much more ambiguous—like when to have sex and who was going to initiate it. It became less comfortable to talk about. I would usually be the one to bring it up. And then I quit doing that. I got tired of it. I decided I could do without it until she made a move, which was probably not kind. But it was too much work. In my opinion, pursuing and seducing should be shared. When it isn't, it's not very much fun, you know? Why should one person have to shoulder it?

I didn't see any men on any regular basis during that marriage until about three years ago. My job changed at that time and I had more opportunities because I was traveling a lot. Before that, I did it maybe four times a year. It was a kind of an irregularly regular thing. I had, you know, the occasional bike ride to the part of town for anonymous sex, that sort of thing. That was about it.

Three years ago, I met someone in Florida at a conference: a psychiatrist. We met at this hotel and he was single and very closeted. He was very cute and sexy and very willing to do something adventurous. So I had a long distance affair with him for about a year. I ended up getting a consulting job in Florida two blocks from his house completely by accident. It allowed me to see him twice a month, but it turned out that he was an alcoholic and it got worse. I know it's because he's in, and stays in. He's married now and has kids. So that sort of woke me up to begin with.

Then I was recruited for a job in Boston and ended up taking it. We were going to move there, but my daughter, who was a senior in high school, didn't want to be disrupted, and that was fine. We were going to commute for a year, which we had done before. Soon after I got to Boston, I came up with a blood clot in the back of my leg and I was hospitalized for a week. During that week of laying there with nothing to do, I realized I couldn't move my entire family to Boston because I knew that I was ready to come out. To move them there and then to disrupt their lives again would be a very bad thing. So I took three months and saw a therapist and figured it out. I came out to myself completely, and then figured out the process I wanted to use to come out to everyone else. Which took another year. My marriage ended last June when I told my wife.

Fucking, to me, is the ultimate expression of close, physical intimacy. It's more intimate when I'm getting fucked than when I'm fucking. I'm not sure why that is, but that's how I feel about it. The feeling's more intense when I'm receiving rather than giving. There's more of a closeness that goes with it for me. I'm sort of out of body when I'm getting fucked, which I'm not when I'm a top. It's something I'm letting someone have that I don't let everyone have. It's sort of a personal trust thing too. I have to feel like there's something more there. I need to trust the person who's fucking me 'cause it can either be really pleasurable or really not. And if it's really not pleasurable, it's a waste of time.

One of the things that's appealing about being a bottom is that you really are totally in control. You can let him do it or not. You can tell him to stop or not. You can push it in harder or not. There's all kinds of things for me that are much more "in control" feelings. That does appeal to me. Being able to do that and to enjoy it is the ultimate expression of my masculinity. When I'm really in the mood to fuck someone, I don't feel emotional about it. I have very little emotional feelings about being a top. To me, it's just an act of getting someone to submit.

One of the things I really loved about fucking women is that it's very clean and sweet. There's really no preparation that needs to be done and the fit is just right every time. It's sensual and natural. One of the issues about fucking men and being fucked by men is that there is prep time. Also, I never had a problem getting hard with my wife. I find that a lot of men have a problem maintaining erections. It happens more often than I thought it would. You never know this crap shoot until you go through with it. I mean, with a woman, once I began, I knew exactly what to do. With men it's more of a challenge. There are so many variations: you can fuck like a man and a woman, or you can fuck like two men, and there's all kinds of things you can do that are just different. I'm also a little bit of a clean freak. I'm not really into anything scatological. Cleanliness is very important to me so I usually have an enema and ask the other guy to have one too because I like to rim. I like men's smell, but I don't like all of them. I guess I have a little bit of a prudishness left in me. Women smell good. They smell like women. They smell like sex. Some of the men smell wonderful. It's hard to be around Roger because he smells so good. And he's so manly.

I think the terms "top" and "bottom" are very confining. That's my only beef with them. I understand you have to have something to reference, but within anyone's definition of a top there are fifteen things. Like when I'm watching porno, before they get going I say to myself, "Okay, I'm going to try to figure out who's the top and who's the bottom in this." Physical appearance often doesn't give me an indication. I've been fooled by that before. What usually tells you is who starts what first. Such as who drops to the knees first. That's usually the bottom. And in real life experience it's pretty much the same. Although I have to tell you, I've had some very interesting experiences where someone started out being completely submissive and then got completely aggressive. I find the mystery of that very exciting.

My ideal sexual experience would be in the middle of the afternoon. Unexpected. Thoughtful. Seductive. With somebody who's completely focused on it, who puts everything else aside, and is able to be completely sensual. Like showering together and being very uninhibited. I tend to be attracted to men who are not physically perfect. I like men with real bodies. So somebody with a little bit of a gut or, you know, with flaws like all of us have, makes me feel much more calm. When somebody's perfect, I get very intimidated by them. They're generally more into how they look than what they're doing. They're much more interested in what they get than what they give. So the ideal experience for me would be something that starts out very passionate and spontaneous and then develops into a lot more than that.

I generally prefer to top first and then bottom later. I want to do both. I want to top first because it's easier for me. Less emotionally involving. But when I bottom the emotional risk is much greater. So I like to do that once I know somebody better.

I'd like to be in a relationship where I can have it both ways, but not in a prescribed way. I love it when somebody figures out what really turns me on without me telling them. The best experiences I've had—and they've been rather rare—are the ones where the other person figures things out without me having to say very much. Because that's what I do. I really spend some time understanding their physical interest in me and I don't assume anything. It generally makes it very satisfying for the other person. It's not satisfying for me if I don't get that back.

I'm afraid being versatile is just another one of those big gray areas that I often have to explain to people. It's not a term that's accepted at face value as the terms top or bottom are, even though those two terms are much more complicated than people understand them to be. There's a huge middle ground that means everything and nothing. So I don't use the term "versatile" very much. Not because it makes me uncomfortable, but because it doesn't explain anything. Nowadays, if someone approaches me and wants to know if I'm a top or a bottom I just say, "You have to find out. If you're not adventurous, then don't proceed." That either turns them on or turns them off. Turns them off more than anything. It's too serious. But I'm not willing to commit to someone's need to know that before they know anything else about me. I think if you know me then you'll figure out and understand what works for me. It's not because I want to hold back or test people. It's really about the three-dimensional parts of people. If they don't have three dimensions, or four, I'm just not interested. Now, that's not to say I haven't done a twenty-minute nooner. But that's all it was. And I knew it going in. The beginning, middle and end were clear. But if it's going to be an experience that's going to mean something to me, those things are unpredictable and unclear.

Let me tell you about a conversation I overheard in a bar last night. A lesbian and her good friend, a gay boy, were talking in this bar, among a whole bunch of other people. She was saying to him, "You act like you're a big top, but you're just a flip flopping bottom boy." And he's like, "No, I'm not. I'm really both." She says, "How can you be both? You either like one or you like the other." He's like, "That's really not so. Depending on the circumstances, I like this from this person and this from that other person. It depends." He was trying to really explain this to her and she was like, "I don't care. Define yourself." And that's what I think I run into. I think that's what the problem is. You have to define yourself. Some people don't understand the variations of being gay. Some people are all the way gay. Some people are not. Some people are players, some people are dabblers, some people are committed to it, and some people, God love 'em, go back to being straight. Saying you're gay has lots of other avenues.

It was hard for me, when I was coming out, to explain to people what being gay meant to me after being straight for all those years. I had to pick and choose what I told people because they didn't want to hear some of it. But it's the same kind of thing to me. It's a loaded question, and it defines where you go with a person. To me, that's premature. To define where you go with somebody just based on, you know, what you feel like doing today, based on what their major enjoyment is, is premature. Minor enjoyments can be just as pleasurable, sometimes more.

For me, when I find myself in a situation where I'm a bottom, I must really care for that person. To me, it's a matter of taking that feeling to another place. So there's a control piece there. I've bottomed for younger guys, older guys, and guys who were my age. It really has more to do with the future than the moment. The moment is great. But it really has more to do with whether I'm interested in this person for something beyond this. And on a more personal, selfish note, I want to be taken care of and pleased. I think tops have to do that. So I make them do it. It doesn't always have to be that way, but it is more often than not. There are lots of times when I top when it's a total sensual gift from me to the other person. All I'm doing is pleasing them. I'm second to the person I'm with because that's really what I want to be. And that's what I've really understood that they want and need.

Sex with men is on an altogether different level of emotional connection than it is with women. Perhaps my deficit is that I've never bottomed for a woman. I've never been with a dominant woman who takes charge, calls the shots, and says what she wants. The women I've been with have all been bottoms. I've had several experiences topping with men who really like to be bottoms where I felt like I was giving them exactly what they needed. Just like I'd be giving a woman what she needs.

I have no shame or guilt associated with bottoming. I gave up the guilt stuff a long time ago—because being a closeted gay man who's married and had kids, the guilt will consume you completely if you let it, whether you've had one sexual experience or one thousand. I didn't have the energy for that. The whole thing was, for me, an exploring and actualizing an aspect of myself that I'd been grappling with. It was a long process, probably longer than it should've been. But I didn't walk around feeling guilty. I feel guilt about other things, but not that. As I said, I believe being a bottom is much more of an open expression of my masculinity: my ability to give as much as to receive. I think it takes a strong man to be a bottom. It's easier to be a top.

I know that in our culture the bottom guy is often viewed as inferior, even by other gay men. It's remarkable how hard we are on each other. But I think that's changing a lot.

I'm not sure if we were biologically meant to have anal sex or not. God knows it's been going on long enough. I think we've figured out a way to do it that makes it more sensual and much more acceptable. I don't think the male body was meant to be fucked because it's not as easy as it is with women. With a guy you have to think about it. You have to try things. There are angles and positions that work great for some people and terrible with others. Whereas with women there's like three ways to do it that work for everybody. I know that in gay porno it all looks very natural, but it's probably the tenth take. My experience in real life is, you know, you have to discuss it a little bit. I was dating a man for about three months, a little while back, who considered himself a big top until I fucked him. And then he couldn't get enough because I did it in a way that worked for him. I had talked to him about it and I had to sort of help him figure out what would work for him. The way he had seen it done before didn't work because of the angle of the penis and his particular hole and all that. So it took some discussion. But once we did that it was, "Please, please, please, one more time." I mean, he couldn't get enough. 'Cause it felt great. When he fucked me, I was on my back. When I fucked him, it was on his belly with his legs turned out to the side. It was the only way it worked for him. Any other way hurt a lot, but this didn't hurt at all. So is it natural? Not exactly. Is it doable? Oh, yeah. Is it something we can accomplish by some sort of working it out? Yeah. We do it because we can.

Being on the receiving end, there's a lot of pleasure in having that man that close to you, and there's a lot of pleasure in being able to accomplish it. Because it's tough to take it sometimes, probably because you haven't done it all your life or something. There's a sense of accomplishment in being able to take it. I like being able to surprise somebody by how much I can take. Sometimes, they just can't believe it. I can do it as smooth or as rough as they want it. Men are often very nervous about hurting me because they think I'm older. It's really true, trust me. So for me it's like, "I can do this." Physically, the friction and the pressure are great. I love the feeling and, of course, the whole prostate thing is really intense. I like a finger as well as a dick, so for me it doesn't matter all that much.

I think the idea of barebacking is exciting because it's dangerous. It's emotionally and physically hot. I think I've gotten fucked bareback twice in twenty years. I knew both men were absolutely negative and neither one came in me. But still, I look back on it and think it wasn't wise. I've fucked men without a condom maybe four or five times. Again, you know, with the precaution of not cumming in them. I'm negative and I get tested pretty often. I think all of this, for me, is part of the process. My process of getting every experience that I can that will help me figure out where I am. To never have done it bareback and to pass an opinion on it isn't as clear for me as having done it and being able to say it was this or that, or this is how I feel about it. I think about it a lot because I missed the whole disease-free seventies and eighties. But I believe each person should have the freedom to make a decision for whatever reason. People make bad decisions all the time. I smoke. People should make their own decisions about barebacking. That's politically important to me.

19

John: "People Want Me
to Fuck Them Like Crazy"

Versatile Top, Age 65

John was the first person I met when I arrived in Provincetown in the spring of 1985. It was a foggy, eerie night when I got off the bus, took a cab to the house where I was to stay, and knocked on the door of the small apartment downstairs. A handsome man, very tall, about fifty years old, opened the door and greeted me generously. I was going to stay in the vacant apartment above his and John had the key. He took me upstairs and showed me around. Pretty soon, we were up on the roof, listening to the fog horns afar and becoming fast friends.

John moved to Provincetown in the 1950s and made a living as a portrait artist for some years. He was married at one point and has two daughters. He's an accomplished water colorist and has a small, popular gallery in the main drag of town. He paints beautiful renditions of Provincetown's skyline, which he dismisses as commercial. He claims that he can do one in fifteen minutes with his eyes shut. His true aspirations lie elsewhere. He's fascinated with the world and loves to analyze, philosophize, and observe. He and I spent many hours sitting in his lush and wild garden, drinking tea or vodka, smoking and talking.

Now in his midsixties, John still sports a rugged and handsome six foot four inch figure and speaks with a deep, sexy, baritone voice. He personifies the seductive combination of the mature, masculine hunk, and the awestruck, curious boy. Although he can be arrogant and bossy at times, he has the uncanny ability to charm anyone.

It's a warm day in July when we meet for the interview and John decides we should sit indoors so the neighbors won't hear us talking. His small one-bedroom apartment is relatively unkempt. I remove some books and sit on the worn couch. On the wall across from me, there is a bas-relief sculpture of five white, plaster masks of John's visage, seeming to emerge from the wall eerily and progressively, one next to the other. I place the tape recorder on the glass coffee table, next to a dirty knife (peanut butter, I think) and an enormous ashtray overflowing with cigarette stubs.

A few months ago, after he returned from a trip to London, John had a heart attack and was also diagnosed with emphysema. That motivated him to stop smoking pot, he tells me, but he continues to smoke cigarettes.

As soon as I ask my first question, he produces several sheets of paper on which he's jotted down some of his thoughts about tops and bottoms. He stands in middle of the room and proceeds to deliver them to me. There's no denying that what he's reading is fascinating, but I'm still hoping that the interview will soon take on a more personal tone. Once his presentation is over, John relaxes and speaks honestly and compellingly about his life and his struggle to come to terms with his homosexuality.

*   *   *

[Reads] Okay. Here's what I wrote: Tops and Bottoms. There's no such thing as a real top or a real bottom. There's no such thing. Even if a person is preponderantly a top or a bottom, someone who wants to be identified as one or the other, this is merely a persona that they project. A top is often deliberately projected in a complex combination of physical manifestations associated with tops. Tops have attitudes and behavior of mannerisms. This is not an act necessarily of homosexuality, but of men. I saw this in Texas. Every guy there, no matter his religion, orientation, or age, manifested certain masculine mannerisms in his behavior. It's something they picked up from their fathers and brothers and it's a part of their persona. It's an innate mechanism necessary to the survival of the fittest. Like a cat raising his fur. This male act of being a top, which people walk around, presenting, is a way of warding off being killed. Since the beginning of time, the beginning of human survival. Certain acts are in of themselves totally "top." Aggressiveness, combativeness, men at work, teaching, guiding, leading, et cetera, are all qualities and acts relegated to the top persona, while the opposites, to the bottom.

Sexual attraction: A top could be attracted to a top, a top could be attracted to a bottom, and a bottom to a top. But never a bottom to another bottom. I don't know why that is. I'm not answering these questions, I'm just observing.

Roles: Same person can be a top or a bottom, depending on the situation. In a one-night stand, once the roles are established, they are usually sustained from beginning to end. In an extended relationship, the roles can change from minute to minute. People are relaxed and they can interchange the role of top or bottom.

Threat: In male homosexuals being the bottom means being the fuckee. That can be threatening because it's perceived to be female. Actually, I had this problem years ago. I just could not be fucked without feeling like I was submitting myself to being female.

Top and bottom personas are not necessarily realities, but perceptions. Acting out the top or the bottom expresses a current state of mind, not necessarily a sustained state of mind. For example, when I get on my motorcycle, I get a hard-on because I know I'm just total top. But that's something I feel at the moment, not all the time. It doesn't mean that when I get off the bike and go in to buy some groceries, I'm still that person. It's a mind-set that we can create at will or that can be imposed upon us.

People identify power with either one of two achievements: Either power in control over others (for instance, JFK), or power in one's own independence and self-control (as in JFK junior). I'm personally attracted to, and aspire to be, a person of the latter category. In other words, I find people who are independent and self-controlled to be very attractive. I'm probably perceived as being the former, the person in control of others. It's where I seek power. I don't know how people perceive me, but I imagine it's like that. I think I'm perceived as the person in power, like JFK, but the person attracted to me is JFK junior. I'm not talking about physical looks. Because of my size, I'm initially perceived as a top, and on the prowl, I deliberately project this. The result is my taking on that role in sex. However, for sex, I seek a top. My most exciting sexual trysts are top to top, in a successive reversal of roles where both fit the top image. Neither person is real, however. This doesn't diminish the pleasure, but precludes a sense of fulfillment. "Love" is not expressed or sought in these encounters. When I've fallen in "love" it's always been with a "top" image, but not necessarily a top mind-set. I'm cloudy on this particular point.

Some opposites identified with tops and bottoms are: Big dicks, little dicks. Big balls, little balls. Tall, short; muscular, frail. Boisterous, rowdy, and pushy as opposed to modest, quiet, and timid. Self assured, uncertain. Decisive, wishy-washy. Outdoorsy, athletic as opposed to bookish and cerebral. Impregnable, vulnerable. [Laughs] It's very complex, I know.

[He's finished reading now.]

I never wanted to be identified as homosexual in the past. I still don't like it in certain ways. I don't like women to perceive me as being gay. I just love to be in a room with women and feel that the male-female interaction is there for me as an option. I don't want to be shut down. I'm much more relaxed about it now. I had two kids and that wasn't what I wanted to be perceived as.

I sit here in this chair and these guys get on their knees and service me. They love my boots and things and they like to get on the bike with me. It's like I'm their image of whatever. But there's no such person! It's a fantasy thing. A fantasy that's been painted before our eyes as kids in so many different forms. We've seen it in films. Some fag set designer spent hours making it look sexy and we think this is what men are! Actually, it's a little thirty-second ad or stage play that was made by some guys on Madison Avenue who know how to make hot numbers. They're always doing things we all find sexually attractive.

I can get very turned on by someone getting on me and groaning and moaning and looking up at me with this incredible look of fulfillment. That just turns me on like wild. But it's not because I'm a person who needs that kind of adoration, who seeks it out like food. I get turned on because I know how he's feeling. Because I would feel exactly the same way if I were in his situation, if I were with some guy who turned me on that much. So there's an edge that's going back and forth and it's crazy because with male and female, you can't have that. There's no way that you can be the female in your head and know how she feels because you never would. Which is sort of unique about male-male sex. That's why some men think that it's so much better than male-female sex. Which, of course, is kinda crazy. I mean the Shakers say, "We can't fuck," and so, as a result, there are no Shakers left! I can't say hurrah for homosexual sex because it doesn't produce a damn thing except for a mess on the carpet.

When someone's blowing me like that, something else happens in me which makes it more intense. I feel like I'm no longer me. I'm this animal, I'm going to this primeval state of being, which is me, of course, but it's not me as I'm consciously acting in the world. It's me as I am when I'm producing an orgasm. It's a kind of thunderous engagement of everything in my physical body along with my mind. It's a rare situation in life. It doesn't happen every minute, it only happens when you're preparing to have an orgasm. So in that time that I'm building up to that orgasm, the rhythm, the drum that brings it about is this basic sexual state. No longer being me as an individual, but being the basic male engaged in having an orgasm. It's a relationship that goes back with every male, to the time we were amoebas. There's a sense of being very much real in that moment. Not just real as myself, but taking part in some kind of instinctive, basic activity. It's so simple that it's hard to explain. No matter what else is going on, the body is saying I'm having an orgasm. It doesn't know whether it's having an orgasm to produce a baby or just, you know, to mess up the floor. The body doesn't know that, and the mind will submit itself. When you're having an orgasm, you cannot think voluntarily. You're no longer able to even stop. You can't even move. If a gun were pointed at me in the middle of an orgasm, I could not stop having the orgasm. We're no longer in control. I like that way of losing control in a totally masculine river. That is where I, despite everything in my life telling me otherwise, can sense myself, my manhood. It doesn't matter if I had any doubts about it. The thoughts of being a sissy, or a loser, all those deprecating thoughts that we carry around as homosexuals are washed away in that moment.

I don't know what it's like now, but when I was in my twenties there was a universal abhorrence of homosexuality. Now, it's different. Now, it's not universal and maybe it's gone from abhorrence to simply intolerance. Guys can now come out and not fear a whole bunch of stuff that was feared back then. Being so ashamed, one also had an enormous complex baggage of inadequacies.

My attitude toward homosexuality is so different from what's currently popular. I feel that it's, to a great extent, an emotional arrest situation. It's not as much a choice of lifestyle as an aberration. I'm much more open to debating it now. I'm not defending this position. I'd like to not have to maintain it, but I haven't had much proof to the contrary. I still see too many things that are common to homosexuals:

self-indulgence; a tremendous amount of vanity (and insecurity and vanity somehow go hand in hand). A great concern for frivolity; shallow distractions. I mean I've been in this town for so long. As a result, I've been very defensive of being called homosexual, bundled in with a bunch of people I don't particularly like. Just like I don't like the nouveaux riches, or a bunch of people I find obnoxious. I don't really think it's abhorrent. I don't put a judgment on it like that. I just think that maybe it's immature. [Laughs] They're sort of stuck, you know?

I do consider the possibility that it may be biological, but I haven't seen enough evidence to prove it. Even if it is biological, so is mental retardation. It's not like because it's biological, it's necessarily good. It's not necessarily a nonimpairing thing. I think homosexuals are impaired just like a retarded person is impaired, like a crippled person is impaired. There's a certain limitation to their life. To our life. You're never going to get married, you're never going to have children, you'll never have grandchildren, you'll never have an extended family except for your friends who will desperately have a much larger role in your life than normal friends do. Do you know what I'm saying? It's not just that we can't have children, it's that we can't feel we're a part of a family, which is a big thing in life as you go through it. If you're not part of a family from the very beginning of your adulthood, then you're only going to be a part of a homosexual family, and this gets to be, what's the word? . . . Incestuous.

I've had these conflicting thoughts since I was eighteen. Maybe even earlier. I was eighteen when I first went to see a psychiatrist because I didn't want to be this. I said, "God, I want to want what I don't want." Like DaVinci who said, "The desire to desire is the desire you don't desire." I thought it was interesting because I'd said the same thing. Of course, I knew even before that. You might say I had a history. My brother used to make me jerk him off and things like that. Things that may have pushed me in that direction. Also, as a kid I was not athletic. I was considered to be a sissy, I was always drawing pictures and I was very sensitive and very responsive to things that boys weren't supposed to be. I was a mess by the time I was twelve.

The basketball coach made fun of me in front of the whole gym class because I couldn't play basketball at all. That was supposed to be his way of toughening me up, but it just destroyed me. I ended up seeing the school nurse and then the school guidance counselor and she went to the gym teacher, in front of the whole class, and chewed him out. Which only made things worse. I was already going through this type of anguish at the age of twelve.

I also had this friend that I loved, a boy, and I couldn't stand the fact that I loved this boy. I'd been very close to my grandmother and she'd died two years before. I had no other intimacies in my life and this boy came and befriended me, this nice, athletic, good looking guy, who was the same age as me. He wanted to be my friend. And it was a warmth, a friendship, that I embraced entirely. Then, we started jerking off together and stuff like that. And then, for some reason or other he rejected me and I had this breakdown at the age of thirteen. I'm sure he went on to have a heterosexual life—but I kept seeking him.

When I was fourteen, my family moved from Long Island to Rochester, New York, and that's when I decided no one was going to call me a sissy again. I mean, you can't change what people think of you in the school you've been in; but this was a new school so I'd practice, you know, walking like a boy, and be tough and everything else. I was trying to be like my friend. So by the time I got to that school in Rochester, I had completely reinvented myself. But I couldn't keep it up. The inside was saying one thing and the outside was saying another. I had a Long Island accent and [speaking with a Long Island accent] I'd talk like this and it sounded tough anyway. They asked me what I was going to major in and I said, "aht." And they said, "What's aht?" and I said, "ahht!" and they said, "Oh, art!" [Laughs]

Reinventing myself was the natural way out. Instead of being intimidated and being the victim to all these people who were "tops," the thing for me to do was to be a top too. To learn how to be one. No one ever taught me. My father never taught me, my grandmother never taught me. So I put myself through a crash course of being a boy.

I had to do this several times in my life. I felt inferior again when I was eighteen, I decided I would hitchhike across the country all by myself. I was again doing all the things that would make me into a boy, or into a man at this point. It wasn't the easiest thing to maintain going across the country. I got into some sexual situations. If it didn't make me into a boy, or a man, it certainly made me more of an individual. I realized later that I had much more balls, more dare, more courage, whatever, than my peers. So this effort to overcome this fear of inferiority certainly paid off. When it happened again in 1980, I took a job on a freighter and became a merchant seaman. And then I got the motorcycle. So I always found a way to become centered again, as a man, in order to rebuild myself because I'd be so destroyed by these relationships with these guys. I'd get out of hand, where I'd become so much the bottom that I couldn't function anymore.

Being real, being centered, gave me more control. If you're centered, you can be a top or a bottom and it won't matter; but you can't be centered if you're emotionally weak or if you've been fed an emotional diet that's made you falsely strong. You can become a top to the extent that you start beating people up and it can all get out of hand.

People want me to fuck them like crazy because of the way I come across. But I don't like fucking people. The reason I come across that way is because I want to attract people. Let's face it, there's no way I can present myself as a bottom without looking dumb and ridiculous. I mean what person's going to want a big tall bottom, except for some kind of a sickie? I've had too many Napoleons trying to knock me down as it is, people into destroying a big guy sort of thing. Some people have that need, especially short people. I don't like fucking in the ass, but throwing someone on that couch and fucking their face is such a great time. And on the motorcycle I get them on the gas tank and put my hands on the handlebars and I just go in and out of their faces and in and out of their mouths like fucking a wonderful cunt. While doing that, I feel like I'm everything in the world. It has to do with being a man. That's what you're getting, it's this back and forth interaction of wild, basic, animal, male-like control.

I've only been fucked about six times in the last ten years. I don't mind being face fucked. I discovered about myself that I like to be in control. I tried being in an S&M situation and I tried to be passive, but I cannot be dealt with harshly. I just respond with violence. People have tried inflicting degrees of pain on me and I just respond by giving it right back, which is of course not what they're after so it's not a successful thing. But when it comes to dicks, boy, my fantasies are always the same. I always have this fantasy for big dick. Thick. Big tip on the end. Cut. Hefty. And when I get one, I just suck on that dick. I don't care about anything else, that's all I want. Just to suck on that cock.

I met this guy in London and I got totally undone. I was destroyed by this person. I lost control of myself. I could no longer control my emotions. We had a wonderful date, but we had a lot of friction between us most of the time, not antagonism, but a great deal of friction. It was energizing, but also perplexing. He was so weary of me, so full of skepticism. He was tempted to engage himself with me, but he was skeptical. "Is this real? Are you real? Is it true?" I found myself sort of having to prove myself, but the burden of proof should have been on him. That's my style. But all of a sudden I'm on the defensive. So after this date I left, and I was going to meet this other guy who I'd met through a dirty chat line and he turned out to be a London cop. The fantasy he and I had on the Internet was that we'd get on a motorcycle—and he was doing all the talking—he'd tie me up on the handlebars and fuck me. So I'd made this date to meet this guy on Tuesday. I met another fellow on Saturday in some bar and he and I spent all of Sunday together. We parted on Sunday night and I was going to call him or he was going to call me, I don't remember.

The next night I had this date with the cop. He lived in the suburbs so I took the train out there, but it didn't work out. I was supposed to meet him at a station and he didn't show up and the next day I called to find out what happened and he gave me some excuse. The reason we were going to get together that night was because his wife was away and we could have a couple of hours alone. That's why I'd agreed to go. I figured I'm going to be in his wife's house and he's not going to tie me up for the rest of my life and leave me. I mean who goes to a London cop's house and gets tied up? Of course, it all could've been a lie. I mean what was I doing?

In a way I was relieved, but I felt so empty. Having gone all the way out there. I returned to London on the train, this half-hour ride, and I'm at the station and I'm sitting at McDonald's and I'm looking at these bums, and I'm looking at these people and I thought, "Oh, God, I feel so desolate!" So far away from home. I'd gone there for the purpose of creating a Web site, to get into the millennium thing. I'd indulged myself in this purpose, but I was being diverted from this purpose and I was despairing. I was feeling my life was falling apart, it was coming undone at the seams.

This whole thing opened up like a blossom. I was on the lookout for something in my life, something exciting. I had everything in the world except for a nice relationship with a really hot man. And I'm ready for it. [Laughs] Not only that, but I'm perfectly eligible and I have everything going for me and I'm supposed to get the creme de la creme. That's not deluding myself, I really felt that way.

So I was in this station and I was feeling desolate, and I thought of the guy I'd been with on Sunday, but I didn't have his phone number. He'd given it to me, but I didn't know what I'd done with it. I knew where he lived. So I bought a card, a picture of a bunch of trees in the woods, a greeting card, and I went to his place. He wasn't there so I sat on the steps and I wrote to him. I don't remember what I wrote, but I pursued him. I said you're the kind of guy, blah, blah, blah, who's wonderful because of this that and the other thing, and that it would be unfortunate if we'd let this go to waste, and why don't we go somewhere, let me take you somewhere and so on. I wrote down my phone number and told him to call me. So he called and we had a long conversation, which was nice. We decided to meet for lunch the following day, and then we said, we'd rent a car and go to the Isle of Wight together. I'd been there before and it was such a wonderful, romantic place, a glorious place with cliffs. I was going to pay, and he said, no, he'd pay for half, and all I wanted to do was go there with him. With a guy like that, and play, have a wonderful time, and say goodbye, and go back to London. That was the plan and he agreed to do it. He said he had some company who was going to leave and he'd call me the next day.

Okay, so I waited, the next day came, lunch time came and went. The whole day came and went. Every time I tried to call, there was no answer. I kept leaving messages. By that night, I was going crazy. More and more of myself was giving over to what was happening here. My plans to go on the trip and so on, which were so good, were being eroded by the minute. It got to the point until there was nothing but constant preoccupation with waiting for him. So I could do nothing else but that. I'd gone through that before, waiting for someone who said they were going to come and didn't, and I knew how I'd go crazy. It doesn't take much for me to go to that state from being a perfectly sane person.

So after two days of this, and realizing it's not going to happen, I'm leaving Friday or Monday or whatever, the chances of going on this trip are now perfectly nil. I wrote him another letter and selected a bunch of photographs and I was going to drop this letter off and see if he wrote back to me or something. So I got to the place and I was trying to figure out where to leave the letter and he showed up. With his friend. His friend left and I was out of my mind and I kept asking, why, why, why? We got out of the hallway and that same kiss, that same kiss went on for twenty minutes. His explanation was that he'd been scared. Because we argued a lot and he didn't know what to say to me and he didn't know how to say it, I don't know, I mean I couldn't figure it out. We spent the afternoon together, and the night. It was very tempestuous and so hot. So hot. Then I left and called him on Tuesday and he said, come on over, so I went over. We spent the afternoon. I cried. He put on a piece of music. And he said, "You're gonna love this." He put it on and within a minute I was in tears. He leaned down and licked the tears off my face. Which, to me, was almost like a religious experience in terms of expressing love. It was Sarah Brightman and that blind tenor. It's gorgeous.

Lust loses out to love and then you're prepared to make all kinds of amends to people, once you're, you know, you're willing to give in to anything. You just want this feeling to be sustained. So we both drowned in this. He was so wacky: there was no way of gauging it.

We went into town together on my last night in London and he was walking real fast and being gruff and not easy to be with and once in a while he'd say some really horrible thing. It was almost like he was fighting against I don't know what. But then he says, "I'll go out to the airport tomorrow to see you off." And we had the most lovely goodbye. And then three weeks later he came here.

One thing that happened that bothered me was on the first night we were together he told me he was HIV positive. He said he'd never had any manifestation of it. So I thought, as long as we used a condom, it would be fine. He looked around that night and he couldn't find a condom to fuck me. He had a big dick and the only condom he had was a Japanese condom or something. It was not a success. That was tough for me because I wanted to get fucked, but I wouldn't do it without a condom because the guy was HIV positive. So there was a little bit of penetration, but it didn't work. Anyway, so I was looking forward to it happening sometime in the future. But when I was kissing him the last time, he said he couldn't kiss me because he had thrush and he had sores in his mouth. He said you couldn't catch it that way, and he tried to reassure me and anyway, that was that. There was a limitation. Okay, so when I came back, I mentioned to someone the thrush thing and they said it was a symptom of full-blown AIDS. He hadn't told me that and all of a sudden I'm feeling betrayed. I feel maybe I've been infected by him because, I mean, I ate his ass and God knows what else. That was what he was into. So I didn't know what to do. He was coming and I felt weird. I said to my doctor, "Well look, if I were exposed, is there any kind of medication that I can take?" He tells me about this cocktail and I say, "Okay, is there any harm in my taking it if I haven't been exposed?" and he said no. "Is there any advantage to starting it, the sooner the better, rather than waiting for six weeks to find out if I've got AIDS?" and he said yes. I spent twelve hundred bucks and went out and got that goddamn medicine. I'm taking those pills and he's coming here, you know what I'm saying? I'm figuring that he's contagious at that point. So all of this just tore the beauty out of the whole thing. And when he got here he said he had a sore in his mouth and because of the way I felt, he couldn't even kiss me so it was like doomed. So we had an argument and he sort of got violent and I said, "Out!" I called a friend who has an inn and he put him up for the next few days. A few days later, I'm regretting that I sent him away and I'm pursuing him all over again. There was nothing else to think about. I was obsessed with him, morning, noon, and night. It wasn't just ordinary feelings, there were hundreds of conflicting emotions going on within me. Then it was Thanksgiving and he was here and my daughter came. And then I had a heart attack within two weeks. My other daughter comes and I end up telling her all about his guy. I was so done in that I couldn't even, you know, keep it from them. I mean I needed them for emotional support at this point. So sure enough my older daughter spends two weeks with me and I began seeing this psychotherapist. The main thing was to get myself over this guy. I was totally deluded by this guy. He was a jerk.

The whole thing's not even interesting now that I tell it.

20

Clayton and Leonard: More Versatile

Clayton: Top, Age 52;
Leonard: Bottom, Age 44

Leonard saw my sign at a gay bookstore in Boston. He and Clayton sent me an e-mail, signed by both, telling me they'd been together for seventeen years and still going strong. Although they were clearly interested in the subject, initially they seemed reluctant to be interviewed. I avoided putting any pressure on them and it took several weeks for me to gain their trust. Finally I received the following note:

> Dear Steven: We are interested in exploring this subject. In many ways, we're more interested and ready to discuss our sexual preferences this year than we might have been before. Over the years, we both have become more versatile and Clayton is bottoming more with me topping him. We are reading some books about the challenges facing gay men in mid life, since I am forty-four and Clayton is fifty-two. This has been a very volatile year and we are coming out of a very emotionally challenging period which began last fall. Anal sex has played a prominent role in this recent challenge to our relationship and we suspect will continue to be a point of discussion as we move forward. We do not have any more questions. We are ready to answer the questions you have for us.
> Leonard and Clayton

I don't know what I was expecting. Their e-mails suggested that they'd be a reserved, even an old-fashioned couple. I imagined they were a couple of college professors, polite, well educated, and overly concerned with their privacy. I guessed one would be an English professor (probably the younger one, Leonard), and the other a doctor of philosophy.

I was in for a surprise.

They walked up to my house on a sunny afternoon in May after they'd finished doing the rounds at that morning's yard sales. I'd suggested that I interview them at my home office since they were going to be spending that weekend in Provincetown.

Clayton's a chunky daddy type at five feet eleven inches, with a deep voice, intense brown eyes, and a bald head. At fifty-two, he's nearly a decade older than his partner. He's wearing a T-shirt and khaki shorts that show off his well-defined legs. He's assertive, masculine, extremely outspoken and rather loud. He worked for the State of Massachusetts for many years and currently works as a barber.

Leonard works for a software company as a quality assurance technician. He's thinner and taller than Clayton, and speaks in a gentle and quiet manner. He has a full head of thick brown hair and a carefully trimmed beard. He's the one that makes the initial introductions. I'd asked to interview them separately so Leonard leaves Clayton with me and goes for a stroll.

Clayton sprawls himself over my couch and declines my offer of something to drink. He's readily comfortable in talking about sex. He goes full blast into telling me that he's always been a top, but has recently started to enjoy getting fucked. He was the one who suggested a year ago that he and Lenny spice up their sex life. They've been attending a leather "play group" that meets once a week in Boston and have also had several three-way encounters. Throughout our talk, his tone of voice, his gaze, his approach to the subject all indicate to me that he's trying to interest me in a three-way with him and Lenny. I'm focused on the interview and show no interest and that seems fine with him. It's difficult to sort out how much of what he tells me is geared toward gauging my willingness and availability, but we still have an interesting and revealing chat. Before he leaves, he gives me a kiss on the lips and suggests that I give them a call if I ever want to play.

My talk with Leonard is free of sexual tension and much more relaxed. He sits upright on the couch the whole time, and is very attentive. He considers each question carefully and makes an effort to give an honest answer. I feel a great deal more at ease with him.

*   *   *

Clayton

All my life I've basically been a top. I like to fuck, but I also don't mind getting fucked once in a while. I love to get fucked, but when I become sexually aroused, that only leads to me wanting to fuck. It's the way I am, I don't know why. I haven't really given it much thought. Sometimes, if Lenny's playing with my ass and he goes, "Can I fuck you?" I'm like, "Yeah, fuck me." I love sex. I love sex with more than one person. My favorite thing in the whole world is to fuck and be fucked at the same time. I love being in the middle. I love it more than anything in the whole world.

My best sexual encounter was with Lenny and another guy and me in the middle. We did that with my friend from San Francisco. I fucked Lenny and my friend fucked me, and then Lenny fucked me and I fucked my friend. Ahh, it was just so good. I'm getting a load shot up my ass and I'm shooting a load, ahh! It was unbelievable.

I met Leonard seventeen years ago in the men's room at Northeastern University. Usually, we don't tell people that we met in a men's room. We were both in relationships at the time. After playing with his dick and so forth, I went over to the stall to suck him off and he got so hot that he blew his load. So we went somewhere on Mass Avenue and got ice cream cones and I fell in love with him. Just like that. It was his eyes, his smell, just the way he made me feel. I was walking him back to work and I looked at him and I said, "You can't just walk away, you have to give me a number." And he said, "I have a lover." I said, "I have a lover too. Can I give you my number at work?" He wrote it on a piece of paper seventeen years ago and I still have that paper.

People say you can't fall in love with somebody at the tubs. I'd met my previous lover at the Club Baths. You can meet anybody anywhere.

The relationship I was in at the time had been going on for about five years. Andy was much older than I was. He was a college professor. Our relationship was falling apart. We owned a house and some property so we were trying to stay together because of that.

Leonard

I was twenty-seven when I met Clayton in a men's room. I was involved with Bill at the time. I was working and going to school at night and he was struggling to become a cartoonist. We didn't have much time, money, or whatever to have any other social contacts. Our relationship was falling apart. We'd separated for a year and gotten back together about eight months before I met Clayton to try to salvage the relationship. I felt all this stress and pressure. Bill was my first relationship and it was how I understood relationships and commitments to be. We were gonna work it out, he was going to have his success and I was going to have been there through it all. I enjoyed all that, I really did feel he was very talented. It was all going to be great. My relationship with him was monogamous, although obviously I was playing around and that's how I met Clayton. I would venture out at times. No anal sex. Just mostly oral sex. In the woods or men's rooms. I don't know if Bill played around or not.

One of the things that disturbed me was that I was so committed to Bill and all of a sudden, because of Clayton, I saw my situation with Bill completely differently. All the pressure disappeared very abruptly when I was with Clayton. How could I change my view so quickly? That bothered me a lot. You start mistrusting what you think about many things.

Clayton had several social circles and he was gonna introduce both Bill and I. We were going to become two couples and get invited to these things. It didn't work out. It went very, very quickly.

Clayton and I spent a weekend here in Provincetown together and I told Bill I was going to be at my folks'. Bill had a sixth sense about everything and I'm a terrible poker player so I couldn't pull anything off. He knew something was up. He called my parents on Friday night and found out that I wasn't there. Anyways, when I got home Sunday night it was hell. I couldn't even stay there that night, I had to leave. That's when I met Clayton's partner Andy.

Clayton

I told Andy that my new lover was going to have to move in with us. Andy was very easy going. He knew we were falling apart. He said, "Go ahead, if that's what you want. Why don't you guys live upstairs?" We had just put in a dormer with two bedrooms and a bathroom so Leonard and I went upstairs and he stayed downstairs. After a few weeks, it was a little bit too much for him so he asked us to move out. A good friend of mine owned a house in the South End and he's very wealthy and he needed a cook. He told us if we could fix lunch and dinner for him we could stay there for free. We had a bedroom and our own private bath. Then Lenny and I made arrangements to buy my lover's share of the house out.

Leonard

I think I've always known I was gay. I don't know how this is going to slant things but when I was very young I was assaulted anally. I've looked at it over the years in relationship with everything else and I've talked with a therapist about it. I was four. It was stupid. My memory is that it was a woman and it was a finger, not a penis. She had done it with other kids in the neighborhood and they're the ones that got me there. They took me down to her place and told me to go in there and she'd give me candy. So I did. It was a hair salon. I was sitting in one of those black leather chairs and she had my pants down and she was playing with me. What I think happened was that someone looked into the window and saw her. It was one of the boys in the neighborhood who was kind of protective of me and I think he saw what was going on. She abruptly stopped and started screaming, and that, to me, was the most upsetting thing. I was eating the candy, I didn't care what she was doing. She was just going at it. It was the screaming that actually caused me to cry. I left there crying, upset. I didn't really remember it for quite a while after that. Clayton's uncomfortable about me talking about it because that was the past.

Clayton

I played around with my friends when I was an adolescent, but we never fucked each other. We just usually jerked off, the boys. When I was about twelve years old, my best friend Buck and I used to give each other massages. He had a big old dick. We would get stiff dicks and beat on each other for the longest time, but neither one of us had shot a load. We had heard other guys talk about shooting their load, but we didn't really know what it was. We were in the hallway on a hot summer day giving each other massages and he was playing with

his cock. I started to jerk him off and then he started moaning and getting crazy and he kept saying, "No, don't stop, don't stop!" He blew
his load and splashed it all over me and it scared the shit out of us.
Then we realized this is what guys meant when they said shooting
their load. We didn't know what the fuck it was. Then it became a regular thing. There was no kissing or anything. I kinda wanted to do
more, but I didn't think he would want to. I didn't want to cross that
line and he probably didn't either. I've often wondered what happened to him. I don't even know if he's gay today. We moved away
and lost contact.

After that I got a job on the Cape, near Hyannis. I became good
friends with this other kid and we fooled around the whole summer.
I'd sleep over at his place. We had twin beds and he'd say, "Clayton,
why don't you get in my bed?" We basically got on top of each other
and just grinded on each other. I was about sixteen and it was the
same kind of thing with him. I wanted to do more, but I didn't try. I'd
heard other guys say that you could stick your dick up his ass. I didn't
want to ask him because if I did he's going to say he wants to stick his
dick up my ass too—and if he says no, then I'm gonna say no. I didn't
know if guys really did that. We just never went there. We'd just get
on top of each other and rub. His mother was downstairs and we made
so much noise that she'd yell, "You guys go to sleep up there!"

After that I went with girls. Girls let you fuck them. The girls I
went with never really sucked. They'd put their mouth on it, but that
was about all they ever did. Then my girlfriend got pregnant and I got
married and had a kid.

When I was married, I never thought about whether I was gay or
straight. Sex with men never caused me any feelings of shame or
guilt. People always say to me, "You can talk about sex so freely,
most people are a little nervous." I never had a problem with sex. I
just like doing it.

Leonard

My first sexual experience with a boy was during my teenage
years. Up until after high school that was all excused as just playing
around. No one put any labels on each other, we were just playing
around and I did a lot of that with the neighborhood kids. My parents
had a summer place on a lake in New Hampshire and I got together

with other guys up there. So I was probably twelve the first time I played around with someone. This other boy and I did it for four or five years. In the winters I wouldn't see him, but in the summers we'd connect again. We became sixteen, seventeen, and there was friction. We couldn't play around anymore because that was going to mean putting labels on each other. He was uncomfortable with that, I was fine with it. I always knew I had that attraction to him and he just passed it off as just being a game. When I was seventeen or eighteen, I sucked him off one last time. He didn't reciprocate and it was fine, but I knew it was the end of it. We didn't have sex again after that. I knew if I was going to make a connection with men from then on it was going to be defined as gay.

I had a high school sweetheart for a while and sex with her was satisfying, but I always had men on my mind.

I definitely think being gay is in the genes. In both sides of my family there were gay people. I'm positive we're born that way. I had no choice at all. I did everything to avoid making the decision to live my life as a gay person. I think if you talked to my parents or to my grandparents, they'd all tell you that there was something about me. They all know now. One of the most powerful experiences was when my mother told me that she wanted to tell her parents that I was gay—and the moment my grandparents affirmed their love for me, and acknowledged who I was, was extremely powerful for me. I never thought I'd feel that way.

Clayton

After I got married, I got a job at a department store in downtown Boston. This guy Walter was head of the tailor shop and he was the nastiest guy. He worked with a lot of Italian ladies. They would always talk sex. I was working in men's clothes and I would come up to have the bottom of the pants cut. As soon as I went up, Walter would come over to me and say, in front of all these ladies, "I would love to suck your dick. I would just love to suck you off." I would turn red, green, purple, I mean everybody could hear him. The ladies would say, "He's just a nasty pig, he's like that all the time." "I'd love to suck your dick." Oh my God, in front of all these ladies? I'd be so embarrassed that I wouldn't know what to do. He was married and had kids. Him and a lot of these guys who worked there, they'd play cards on

Beacon Hill at this guy's house once a week. I heard people say that they fooled around at those parties and I always wanted to go. They took me to a strip club, then they took me to one of these card parties. When I got there they just got all naked and started fucking and sucking each othe and I'm just standing there with a roaring hard on. Walter took me to the bathroom and just sucked me off until I practically passed out. He sucked my dick like it had never been sucked before. So after that, every time I went into the tailor shop, he was always pushing me in a hallway somewhere sucking my dick. He just loved it. But he didn't only suck *my* dick, he sucked everybody. That's all he did, was suck dick.

I made a mistake. I knew he was a whore and he told me he was a whore, but I was just really taken by him. I don't know if I was in love. Since he and I had become best friends, he wanted my wife and his wife to become best friends too: my wife loved to sew and so did his wife; they would talk on the phone; he had a son, I had a daughter, blah, blah, blah. Walter tried to convince me that we should buy a two family house and move in together and we could fuck around in the cellar all the time. All my friends who knew we were fucking around said, "Don't do that. If anything happens, what the hell are you gonna do?"

Then one night we went out drinking and he brought me back home. My wife was asleep in the back and we were in the TV room in the front. She got up to go to the bathroom or something and she came into the TV room and she saw us. I don't even know how long she was there. I was on the sofa and he was naked, sucking my dick. She went and called his wife and said, "Jan, I want you to come over here immediately. I just caught your husband sucking my husband's dick." His wife comes over and she goes, "Now what's going on here?" Walter goes, "Well, you know, just what she told you." She goes, "I want *you* to tell me." He says, "I was sucking on his dick and his wife came in and caught me sucking his dick." She goes, "Well, I want a divorce." She kicked him out and he and I moved in together.

Walter and I got divorced a week apart. It was a horrible, horrible relationship. I was used to being married to a woman. You sorta own your wife. Your wife doesn't fuck around with anyone and nobody fucks your wife. It just doesn't happen. Now that Walter was living with a man, he's fucking around with everybody in sight. When the people at work heard that I got divorced and got my own apartment, some of the guys came over, brought me gifts and everything and we had a party. One of the guys had never been to my house before. Walter got him and he was raping him in my bathroom. So this guy comes out and he goes, "Clayton, I was just trying to take a piss and your friend followed me in there and tried to suck my dick and he was raping me. I'm leaving." So I go, "Walter, is this true?" We got into a fight, him and I. And when I say we got into a fight, when we fought, he would pick up the TV and try to bash my head with it. We fought like crazy and we were together for two or three years. So we were fighting and he tried to choke me and I picked up a knife and I slit his throat. He ran out of the house, all bloody. Thank God it didn't go deep. I had to sit there and wait for the police to come and get me because once he goes to the hospital, they're going to say, "Well, who did this to you?" Well, I don't know how he did it, but he lied his way out of it. He came back with his throat all bandaged and apologized. It was horrible. We fought at least twice or three times a month. And I loved him. Seriously. We'd fight and be all bloody and bandaged and we'd go to bed and have the best sex. It was a very sick relationship. I mean, just before I left him, he threw the refrigerator on me. I was passed out on the floor and he threw the refrigerator on me. I couldn't go to work because I was so beat up. I couldn't tell people that I walked into a door every time. So I got out of that relationship. That was the only abusive relationship I was ever in my whole life.

Leonard

As long as I've been gay I've known that I was anal. I don't know if it's because of that first experience when I was small, but I've always been sensitive to being aroused in that area.

I'm not religious. I'm spiritual, but antireligion. When I was young, I'd be talking to the Creator, saying, "Why did you make me desire and get so much pleasure from anal sex if it's not what I'm supposed to be doing? I don't understand. What's the joke? It's a *horrible* joke." So I definitely believe that the Creator created the male body to have anal sex.

My first anal intercourse was with this guy I met at Sporters. I lived in the South Shore and I'd come to Boston when I was extremely horny. He told me I'd never forget his name, but of course I've forgotten it by now. When I met him I was still dating my high school sweetheart. We got together and he was very rough. He was getting off on

this trip thing and I didn't even know how to tell him to stop. I had no
sense of any of that at that point. That experience made me feel like I
didn't want to be gay. There was no tenderness at all. No foreplay, no
kissing. I don't know what was going on in his life, but he was just
taking something out on me.

Then, in my early twenties I met this other guy, Todd, and that was
very different. I was standing next to the dance floor at a bar and Todd
sent me over a vodka gimlet. We danced and I went home with him.
He had a water bed, nice music, dim lighting. It was just very romantic. Actually, I topped him the first night we were together. It was either the next time or the third time we were together that he asked if
he could top me. It was great. No pain, all pleasure. He was an older
guy in his thirties. He would take me out to dinner. I saw him maybe a
half a dozen times. He showed me some of the ways of having anal
sex. And then I think he realized that I was kind of falling for him and
he wasn't interested in that. There was too much of an age difference.

Shortly after that I found out about the movie theaters and videos.
It was through porn that I learned all the different ways that you can
have sex.

When I met Clayton, he was always the top and I was the bottom.
He orchestrated, he directed, but in a very loving way. I felt comfortable. The first time we had anal sex was at the apartment of a friend of
ours. Then I realized I really cared a lot for him. I realized I loved
him. A lot of it was his personality, his character, his ease and com-
fort; I just felt so comfortable and safe with him.

Clayton

After I left Walter I got an apartment directly across the street from
The Fenway* and I could have all the sex that I wanted. There were a
lot of gay bars in that area and one of them had a big sex room in the
back. If you couldn't pick anybody up in all those places, you could
go to an all-night restaurant in that area and pick someone up there.
This is in the late seventies, before AIDS. Quite a different time. It
was a lot of sex.

When Lenny and I first got together, we had a monogamous relationship. It was fine, there were no problems. After we were together
for five years, we took a month off and went to Hawaii. There were

_____

*A cruisy park in Boston.

beautiful nude beaches there and everybody was running around naked, even the straight guys. We met someone and that's when we had
our first three-way. It wasn't a regular thing. It would happen if we
were on vacation or something. It was always the two of us and we'd
bring a third person in. We wouldn't go out and get sex outside of the
relationship. Lenny would never accept that. He's my baby. Even if
he wanted to suck someone's dick, he'd ask me, "Can I suck his
dick?" He wouldn't just go and suck his dick. Well, I'm a daddy and
he likes that, and it's fine with me. I like to be in control and that definitely has something to do with being a top. It's not associated with
masculinity or anything, it's just about having control. In sex I'm usually the one who's the aggressor. He sees what I'm gonna do and he
follows through. He's an easygoing guy and very much a bottom. He
goes with the flow.

Leonard

What interested me about this interview is all those personality traits
and the way they reflect on whether someone is a top or a bottom. Like
Clayton being the protective guy who leads and directs, is more in control and I'm not. I'm not a passive bottom. I can initiate and direct the
entire thing and he's at my mercy in a sense. I do what I want. We both
experience pleasure from it. He loves it when I'm on top, his cock is in
my ass, and I've got his arms pinned to the bed. That really does something to him, he really loves it and I love it too. We're both aware of
each other during sex. If we're not verbal, we make sounds so we both
know what we're enjoying, what we're not enjoying. Yes, there are personality traits, but I don't know how they play out and how men experience anal sex. That whole subject intrigues me.

This friend of ours, Joe, lived in LA and he was heavy into the sex
scene out there. He wanted to be a bottom, but because of his physical
attributes, particularly because he was well endowed, he came into
this sex stuff defined as a top. Everyone defined him as a top just because of his cock. But as he got older he wasn't just a top. He liked to
bottom, but he certainly could put forward the whole image and the
voice, he could capture the whole top thing and make a very satisfying scene for whoever the bottom was.

Clayton

Our sex life has always been good. But I mean you fuck and you suck and it gets routine. We both work hard, we're buying a house, blah, blah, blah. On Saturday mornings you start to suck and fiddling and diddling and you fuck him or he sucks you off or whatever and it got to be a routine. So we said let's do something a little different. Nowadays, we go to these leather play parties and so forth. We've been doing that for about a year. If you don't know much about leather, and you want to learn, you can come to a play party. You don't have to wear leather. You can wear a jock strap or your underwear. Some guys go naked. You don't have to play. You can watch what the other guys are doing, see what turns you on. It costs five dollars but they give you plenty of food and they have the best pretzels in the whole world.

We've been to leather conferences where there was straight couples as well as gay and I was surprised that the women were usually the tops. The men were on leashes and so forth. It was kinda nice to talk to them. They were businessmen and executives and that's what they're into. It's giving up control.

Leonard

So now we're becoming more versatile. Clayton's more versatile than I am and that's one of the reasons I was intrigued by this interview. Clayton likes to be the bottom sometimes and I'm trying to explore the top side of me. I would like to be more versatile. I'm trying to tap into what excites me and what would keep me motivated to be a top. When I was younger it was no problem, you got an erection just by walking down the street.

Clayton has no trouble staying hard. He's not as hard as he used to be sometimes because of his age and his medications. He says that sometimes he gets so excited and he holds back and then he can't cum. I'm usually erect when I'm getting fucked. I can cum without even touching myself. I get very excited.

But if I'm not into what's going on, I can't always stay erect. So there's something there that I'm trying to figure out 'cause I'm definitely a bottom and I tend to naturally be a bottom. I believe it's always been that way for me. We can play with toys and whatever, but it's not the same. He wants me to fuck him and I want to be able to do it. He's not putting any pressure on it right now, but it's something I'd like to be able to do.

Clayton

I definitely believe that the male body was built to be fucked and the asshole was made to be fucked because I've fucked straight guys too. Straight guys become my friends and they're married and everything and eventually they'll ask me to fuck them. Like this friend of mine, Jack. Lenny doesn't know about this. Jack and I became very close in Barber's school. He told Leonard and me that he loved us, but not in a sexual way. He's a licensed electrician and he's also my plumber. He loves to do things. The dishwasher broke a few weeks ago and I called Jack. He goes, "Oh yeah, I got Mondays off, I'll come over."

So he came over and started messing with the dishwasher. Lenny was at work. Jack said, "Clayton, just dump this thing and get a new dishwasher, blah, blah, blah." So then I fixed him breakfast and he's hanging out and he goes, "Uhm, do you have any gay movies? I was just wondering what guys do."

I mean what gay person doesn't have gay movies? So I show him the gay movies and he and I watch it together, and he goes, "Do you have a hard on?"

I go, "No," and he goes, "I do!"

He starts taking off his clothes and he goes, "Why don't you fuck me?"

I said, "Jack, you're married, do you want this?"

He goes, "Well, I've never been fucked, and I'm watching these guys doing it and I want you to fuck me."

"Jack, you sure you want this?"

He goes, "I've been wanting this every since I knew you were gay and I want you to be the one to fuck me. Just fuck me. Fuck me, fuck me right now."

Jesus Christ!

So I'm like, "Let me get a condom."

He says, "Oh, no, you don't need that."

I said, "Oh, yes I do."

So I fucked him.

Afterward he asks, "Is it all right to talk about it now?" I said, "Sure." He goes, "I don't think I'm gay." I said, "Well, did you like it?" He goes, "Yeah but we shouldn't do it again."

I said, "That's fine."

I didn't tell Leonard I fucked him because I didn't even want to do it in the first place. I'm not even attracted to Jack. He's a good person. I'm gonna give him a call when we get back because I don't want him to feel guilty.

Leonard

We consciously decided to open the relationship to outside experiences about a year ago. I don't seem to have any control over that. I don't mean that Clayton's forcing it on me. I described it to him the other day like this: I go into these situations and half of me is there, but the other half of me is struggling with it. But the half that's there is winning out. Clayton says, "We can stop doing this if you want." And I say no.

This seems to be part of what we're experiencing right now. I think it's age related. I think it's this phase we're going through. Maybe we've been watching too many videos. We've had many, many years of just the two of us and it's been wonderful.

I don't know what Clayton told you, but one of the most exciting experiences we've had was when Clayton was fucking and being fucked at the same time. He loved that. I'm more oral than that. My hottest time was when I was being fucked and I was sucking him off. And you need at least one other person there to do that.

The last time we had hot sex was earlier this week. I was tired, but he was horny and he kept playing with me and he got me really hot. One minute I was falling asleep, but he was playing and all of a sudden, boom, I was there. We tried to please each other anally, orally, everything. But a third person would've made it much easier. We were doing contortions to try to do it all. It was great sex, but something was missing. And it's not like we're trying to spice up our life. It really is a dimension, when you add a third person on, in a group scene, it's a different experience.

There are certain things I'm finding out now. Clayton's become more aware that he has a raunchier side. If I was younger, I'd have been uncomfortable hearing that. It would've been a threat. My theory is that it's kind of like when men first discover their nipples. Something like that happens with older men when they discover their raunchier side. When he sees guys and he points them out and says that he's hot, this guy doesn't have a haircut that looks anything like mine. There are some physical characteristics that resemble me, but I couldn't wear one of these flat top kind of haircuts buzzed on the side.

We're both mostly attracted to the same type of guys. Guys who are definitely more athletic than the two of us. Bald, less hair on the head the better. Facial goatee maybe or some kind of facial shadow kind of thing. Someone who spends more time at the gym. And maybe we should spend more time at the gym ourselves. Clayton likes a nice butt and I like a nice cock. It doesn't have to be huge, but, you know, nice lookin'.

Just today we saw a guy walking down the street and we could definitely see through his jeans that he had this enormous cock. I told Clayton I'd love to see it, but I really wouldn't want to have to handle that. I don't think I'd want to fall in love with someone who had that much of a cock. My first lover did not have a large cock and anal sex was not as pleasurable. Clayton has the size and shape that's just right for me. He's put together just right and we fit together very nicely. I did have anal sex recently with another man and that hadn't happened in all our years together. Clayton was there. I've had oral sex with other men, but never anal sex. His cock was a little smaller and it was more stiff because he was a younger man, but it wasn't the same. I didn't have as much pleasure. Dick size definitely does play into it.

Clayton

Lenny thinks I have a big dick. His dick is not as big as mine and he's always had a problem with that. I have no problem with it whatsoever. I like a big dick, I mean they look good. Walter's dick was so big that I couldn't suck it. He would always get me to puke. He'd ram his fucking big dick down my throat and I'd puke all over him.

When Lenny sits on my big dick, I can make him cum without him touching himself. He rides my dick and shoots all over my face and everything and I love that.

Leonard

We met this guy Dennis recently. We were both intrigued by him because he's verbal. He also seems to be aware of things that I'm not. I think I could learn from this guy Dennis. He's really a bottom, but he can top. We met him at one of these group things and we're probably going to meet him there again. We both want to talk to him more and find out his perspective. When I was servicing Clayton, Dennis was whispering to him and saying all this top stuff. Like an appreciation for someone who can suck cock like that, that kind of thing. Then Clayton basically told me to go and suck him. I enjoy that. So I'm servicing Dennis and he's being verbal again. When I hear the guy talking, it gets me hot. But as the night went on it became clear that Dennis probably has more in common with me than he does with Clayton. I thought he was a top, but he can switch. Later in the night, he's on his knees and he's sucking someone off and getting off. I think he has to be a bottom to get off like that although he can play the role of top. He had a short hair cut, he was kind of chunky, but he had some definition. Nice butt and a nice cock that curved one way. So it was interesting looking. [Laughs]

We haven't had anal sex at this place yet. I don't feel comfortable enough to do that there. So it's all oral and masturbating. But if we got Dennis and it was just the three of us, there would be some of that, possibly. Although we've always had bareback sex with each other, we always have safe sex when other people are involved.

I feel this pressure a little bit now to be versatile. I think people say they're versatile too, but I don't think most people are. I try to think of myself as being versatile, but no, I'm a bottom, basically. If you're versatile, I guess you're more talented, more gifted, or whatever. Years ago, like twenty years ago, a top was a top and a bottom was a bottom. When I first came into the gay world, that's the way it was. Clayton enjoys both, but mostly topping, and I enjoy both, but mostly bottoming. So we've been very compatible in that area.

I think there is some shame and guilt associated with being a bottom because of what people say. There is a connotation of that. Like for instance, if you're a bottom and you're having sex with other men all the time, you're the pig; but if you're the top and you're topping other men, you're just being a man. It's the same in the straight world. A woman who fools around with other men, she's a slut, but a guy that does is just a guy. I don't know. I don't think I feel shame about it although there is this negative connotation about it. You're not less of a man just because you get fucked. Clayton and I have talked about that. I'm wondering if maybe he had some issues about that. He used to bottom very rarely and maybe he's resolved those issues and is able to do it more often now. Like he thought getting fucked would take away from his status as a top. I'll have to ask him about that.

Clayton

Now Lenny fucks me whenever I tell him to, every two weeks or so. We had a threesome with this guy Carlo and I wanted him to fuck Carlo, but he wouldn't do it. He won't fuck anyone but me. Carlo is Italian, much darker than I am and very macho looking. Lenny's a pretty good size, but Carlo is even smaller. When you look at him, he's so male that you think he must have a big dick, but when he takes his pants off, he doesn't.

We met Carlo at a play party. We came late and there were about forty to fifty people there. I made eye contact with him as we walked in. Leonard and I went upstairs to change and Lenny goes, "Did you see that guy?" I said, "Oh yeah, I saw him when we came in." We went downstairs and Carlo had already connected with some guy that wanted to get whipped. We're into play and stuff, but we're not into getting beat up or anything. I'm not putting it down because some people get off on it. But he was whipping this guy, and I mean really whipping him. The guy had these weights on his balls and Carlo was whipping him and he was really getting off on it. That just turned Lenny off. Carlo was looking over to me for permission, which I was really getting off on. I was getting off on him, not on what he was doing to the guy.

When it was time for us to leave, Carlo comes over and he goes, "I think you guys are hot. I'd really like to play with you guys sometime." I told Leonard, "I'm going to give him our number. He's not gonna whip you and he's not gonna whip me. I'm gonna fuck him." Leonard says, "Well, you tell him that." So I go, "Carlo come here." And I say, "If you wanna play with us, I'm gonna fuck you." He goes, "Oh, I don't get fucked." I said, "Here, take the number and when you want to get fucked, you give me a call." And he gave me his number too.

So the following Sunday Lenny and I were driving back from his parents' house and I gave Carlo a call to see if he was still interested in us. He goes, "Why don't you guys come over to my place in Brookline and have a drink?" So we went over and he tried to get us drunk. We had wine and cheese and he brings out the Jack Daniel's. Leonard's getting drunk and he and Carlo are kissing and fooling around. Carlo says, "Why don't we go upstairs and fool around?" I said, "No. You invited us over here for a drink, you didn't invite us over to fool around." He goes, "What's your problem?" I said, "What did I ask you at the party?" "Oh, I don't know, I don't remember." I said, "Well, when you remember you let me know." Leonard's going, "Shouldn't we go upstairs and play with him?" He's the one who didn't want to play with him in the first place, but now he's getting undressed. I said no. So I got total control. It was getting late. We both had to work the next the day, anyway, so we left.

The following week Carlo called and came over to have dinner with us. He goes, "Can we all get naked and have a naked dinner?" I said, "Well, sure!" So we got naked and had a naked dinner in the dining room. Then he goes, "Are we gonna go upstairs?" and I go, "To do what?" He asks, very timidly, "Are you gonna fuck me?" I said, "Okay." But when we got upstairs, Lenny was sucking Carlo's dick and Carlo wanted me to suck his tits. He was just laying there. I was telling him to suck my dick, but he was, "Oh, no, I don't suck dick." I said, "Lenny wait a minute, that's it, that's it!" I said, "Carlo, what are you gonna do? I told you what I wanted to do—what are you gonna do?" He goes, "I don't do much." So I go, "Well then get out!" I said, "This is bullshit. I'm letting you know what's going to happen. I'm gonna fuck you up the ass—if that's what you want, then fine." He goes, "All right, go ahead, fuck me up the ass if you want to." And then I fucked him and it turned out fine.

Afterward they both fucked me. Carlo's very rough. He was trying to hurt me, which I was getting off on. He was just trying to fuck the shit out of me. He was being as rough as he could and Leonard didn't like that. He doesn't want to see Carlo again.

21

Payne and Stanley:
An Equal Sense of Power

Payne: Versatile Top, Age 45;
Stanley: Bottom, Age 26

"My boyfriend and I are totally open about the top and bottom issue," Payne tells me at a party where we've met only minutes ago. He sets down his martini and sits back, grabs the back of the couch with both arms, spreads his legs and fixes his gaze directly on me. I don't think he's exactly flirting, although he seems acutely aware of his own sex appeal and only diverts his gaze after I stare back, calling his bluff. At forty-five, he has salt and pepper hair, a compact, athletic build and a self-assured, relaxed disposition. He was a star athlete in high school, captain of the football, swimming, and soccer teams, and he speaks with an unaffected, deep, masculine voice. He tells me his boyfriend Stanley (who's away on business that night) works as a counselor for an AIDS prevention organization where he runs an outreach program for gay men. "He talks about this stuff with his clients all the time," Payne says. "We'd be more than willing to be interviewed for your book."

A week later Payne and his Jack Russell terrier greet me at their new house in a working-class now-turning-upscale suburb of Boston. The dog barks and circles me hysterically while Payne calls upstairs to let Stanley know I've arrived. He's recently started renovating the house and apologizes for the sparse condition of their living room. There is no furniture except for a saw horse, a drafting table, and a couple of stools for us to perch on. Dressed in a flannel shirt and faded jeans, Payne is snugly in his element in the midst of blueprints, carpentry tools, and freshly cut wood.

When Stanley comes downstairs, I'm so immediately struck by his boyish looks that all I can do is mumble an unintelligible greeting and make the bravest effort to conceal my surprise. It turns out he's really twenty-six, but doesn't look a day older than sixteen. His face is freckled and round, and a tight T-shirt shows off his gym-built pecs.

I ask them if it would be all right if I interviewed them separately. I tell them it's mostly for editing purposes, which is a lie. The real reason is that I don't want either one to censure himself for fear of what his partner might think of his replies. Payne initially seems fine with the idea, but Stanley is clearly not comfortable with it. "We're totally honest with each other, we have nothing to hide," he tells me quickly, glancing at Payne. Payne nods obediently and it's clear that I have no recourse. I don't regret it at the end since watching them interact gives me deeper insights into their relationship.

For Stanley, life is full of beginnings. His relationship, his career, the new house, his life as a recently out gay man, all hold the promise of a bright future. He reminds me of Caravaggio's sensuous Bacchus: smug at being the object of desire, especially Payne's. He smiles generously when Payne touches him lightly on the leg. He's smart and intellectually engaged. Like most men his age, he's immortal, invincible, and ready to take on the world. What's there to worry? He's got it all figured out.

Payne, on the other hand, has been here a few times before. He's had three previous long-term relationships (the first lasting four years, the second and third eight years each), and the struggle to come to terms with his sexuality has not been as clear-cut as Stanley's. Although he seems very much infatuated with his current partner, he's clearly more cautious, acutely aware of the possibility—perhaps, even, the inevitability—of things going wrong. Instead of shielding him though, this discretion rather makes him more vulnerable. He smiles guardedly and less often than Stanley, but when he does, the room seems to light up. His answers are tenuous, not as easily accessible as Stanley's. He considers his words carefully and articulates his thoughts precisely. Stanley, bubbly and impatient, sometimes jumps in to complete Payne's line of thought for him, but Payne clearly has the upper hand. He takes these things in stride, like a patient parent. Both men treat each other with the utmost respect and consideration. Together less than two years, they still dwell in blissful harmony.

Fresh out of the shower, Stanley's skin glistens with moisture. It occurs to me that he has that special glow: the one that men often get soon after they've been fucked in that most gratifying, wonderful, and loving way.

*   *   *

Stanley

I became aware of my homosexual feelings around puberty. I was scrutinized and teased at school for being effeminate. I think I was a lot more effeminate when I was in junior high. When I came out in college, everything was about coming out and "let's be more flamboyant." I didn't know who I was yet. I was following other people. I think I've developed a deeper sense of what I stand for since then.

I had my first sexual experience when I was nineteen, after I came out to some friends. It was with this guy who was really interested in me. I wasn't really sexually attracted to him, but I was eager to have a first experience. We got together in his room, but it was kind of a flop because I didn't even get hard. I was uncomfortable because I knew he had strong feelings for me and I wasn't attracted to him.

A couple of weeks after that I met a guy at a support group for gay college students. He was going through the exact same thing that I was. He'd just come out to a couple of his close friends. We were in the same place and we connected on that level. I really consider that to be my first sexual experience. There was hugging and kissing and it was the first time someone performed oral sex on me. It was pretty amazing, except he would go down on me, but he wouldn't let me go down on him. I don't know why that was. He made a lot of excuses. I suspect it was because although we were together for the next few months, we had to pretend we weren't together at all around friends. I was moving really fast, I was like flying out of the closet. He got really scared and withdrew back into the closet. I think that was part of it.

Payne

This is going to be a little more difficult for me because the whole coming out thing was not as black and white in my case. I remember having feelings for another guy really early, as early as kindergarten. I'm not sure if it was something I was born with or if it was socially induced or if it was a combination, but it happened at a very early age, as early as I can remember. I've always had best friends. I fell in love with a series of boys who were my best friends. I was the captain of the swim team, captain of the football and soccer teams. It was all about my parents' expectations and the way I was raised. My teen years were really miserable. I was so confused about the feelings I was having. It was so sublimated that I had no idea what was going on with me. My expectations of myself weren't that I was supposed to be gay. I dated women and actually had intercourse with them before I had my first real serious sexual experience with a guy.

My first gay sex was with my foster brother who was two years younger than me. My parents brought in this kid and he lived with us for a couple of years before he was adopted by another family across town. He and I didn't get along that well because he wasn't good at sports and all the things I was good at. There was a lot of tension between us. We had some childhood exploratory stuff together while he lived with us, but it never went to the point of orgasm.

Some time after he was adopted by the other family he showed up one night and climbed in my window. We were both older by now. He started to give me a blow job. I was completely excited about the whole thing, but I pretended to be asleep. There was no way that I was going to wake up and admit to the fact that it was happening. Afterward he crawled out the window and left. I was racked with guilt. He came back on a series of nights after that and did the same thing. I always pretended to be asleep. I wasn't sure why he kept coming back. Then the guilt got the best of me and I chased him out one night. It was kind of horrible on my part. I've often thought about him since then. I heard that he moved to Florida and I tried to find him online once, but couldn't. I wouldn't be surprised if he's dead. We both came of age at exactly the wrong time to be experimenting around. So that was my first gay sex, but it wasn't reciprocal.

The next time was with a gas station attendant that I met when I was nineteen. My memory is a little vague on it, but I remember it was very hot. My parents had recently divorced and I was living in a little trailer on my father's property. I had a lot of privacy. This guy worked at a Gulf station back when they had to wear uniforms and there was no such thing as self-service. He would come over before work in the morning and climb in my window and have sex with me. We had like a three-month thing. It was all very secretive. I can't remember if we had anal sex or not, but my guess is that we did, except it was probably not very successful. The concept of lube didn't even exist in our minds. So my guess is that they were very futile attempts at it. It was a guilt-ridden situation and it ended when I went away for college.

Stanley

The first time I tried anal sex it didn't really work. I'd just discovered my ass as an erogenous zone and that got me kind of curious. If I put my finger up my ass when I was masturbating it felt really good. I wanted to try it and see what it was like. It was with a guy I met in college and I was the bottom. I didn't know what it was supposed to be like the first time. I didn't know anything about bearing down or relaxing or any of those things. So when he went inside of me it was very, very painful. I was like, "Get out!" And that was that.

My senior year, I dated this guy who I was really in love with for five or six months. He wanted me to fuck him so we did it and it was great. That was the first time I had a satisfying anal sex experience and I was the top. I was in Australia during graduate school and this other guy I met there wanted me to fuck him too. So my first two anal experiences were as a top.

Payne

In college I sought some counseling and had the misfortune to hook up with this straight counselor who tried, basically, in his words, to "reinforce all my heterosexual leanings." It was exactly the wrong thing for me and set me back a few years. I continued to have best friends through college and I'd develop these feelings for them. I was best friends with this guy who I think was also gay, but wasn't out and I was too afraid to pursue it sexually.

I got drunk at a party with my second best friend and we went to my place. One thing led to the next and we had sex—but it was horrible because afterward he didn't want anything to do with me. He didn't call me for the next three weeks. This was the end of the year so I went home feeling desperate. Eventually, we hooked up over the summer and fell in love. He became my lover and we were together for four years. It was a very stormy relationship. It was with him that I had anal sex for the first time in a successful way. I was about twenty-four. We were fairly versatile, but I was mostly the top. I was the bottom probably one out of three times. I definitely felt more comfortable being a top with him. It was more satisfying for me.

Stanley

At this point, I consider myself mostly a bottom. I'd say ninety-five percent of the time I'm the bottom and it's great. [He smiles at Payne.] In fact, it's fantastic! It's sensual and gratifying. The fact that it's with Payne makes it even greater. I have a very strong sense of intimacy with him and I guess he's a very good top. Trust is a really big thing and I have that with Payne. It's really good. I feel really, really comfortable with him.

Payne

I had three long-term relationships before I met Stanley. After that first four-year one, I had two eight-year relationships back to back. I never really enjoyed being a bottom with the first two boyfriends. It never did much for me. It was probably because of power issues. My first two boyfriends definitely had more power in the relationship. Or at least I allowed them more power. I'm not sure why it ended up being that way. Being a top was my way of balancing things off, I think, because I didn't have control socially and in many other areas of the relationship. It was easier to reconcile my view of myself as a top. It's just uncomplicated for me. It's more complicated to view myself as a bottom, especially strictly as a bottom. I'm not really sure why that is. I fall prey to all that stuff. I think about it a lot. Stanley is younger and has less baggage about those things.

Stanley

There are a lot of constructs about sex, and especially about anal sex. Femininity and all that stuff. I've thought a lot about them and I don't necessarily subscribe to those stereotypes and categories. Part of me enjoys taking the submissive role in anal sex. A lot of people have shame or guilt around that, but I just don't. For me, it's fine and very natural. I think as long as the other guy respects my boundaries and respects what I want, it's good. I also don't believe in the construct that submissive means feminine. The notion that you're feminine if you're submissive is a sexist part of our society and that's why I don't subscribe to that.

I don't even exactly label myself as submissive. It's just something I get pleasure from. It's a feeling like you're kind of losing yourself in somebody else. Other people have told me that too. Giving yourself up and losing yourself in the moment. That's a really exciting turn-on.

Payne

In my third relationship, I relaxed a lot more into it. I was mostly the top the first year we were together, but then he decided he wanted to change that. He basically insisted that we do it evenly, fuck each other every other time. In fact, I think he kept a calendar. [All laugh.] "Whose turn is it now," you know? I was fine with that. I actually did pretty well with it. We learned how to make it work together. That was the first time I really learned to enjoy being a bottom. It turned out both of us had leanings toward being tops, once we figured things out. We just sort of did the other to accommodate each other. It was a fucked-up relationship, fraught with all kinds of difficulties. Power-wise, it was more balanced than my two previous relationships. We both held this weird power over each other. We used sex to work out all our troubles. We'd have huge fights and then we'd have sex. That was how we kept some kind of equilibrium.

In any relationship there's an arc. There are ups and downs, cycles to what happens sexually. Sex can be used for different purposes. It's all very mysterious. Although today I consider myself a top, I did have that eight-year thing where I was versatile so I don't rule it out. But given a choice, my inclination is to fall into the role of being a top. It's hard to say how much of that inclination is based on my view of myself versus what my real desire is. It's hard to figure that out. It's a fuzzy issue.

I think if you fall in love and the other guy wants you to compromise by trying out a role you're not comfortable with immediately, you should give it a crack. You might find that you can ease into it. I was surprised, but happy about the fact that I enjoyed it.

Stanley

I question it when people are rigidly locked into categories. Payne isn't and that's kind of important to me. He can bottom sometimes. Every once in a while I like to switch because I'm in the mood or whatever and Payne is like, "okay." If people are really rigid in these roles, it raises a red flag for me. Why are they so rigid?

I feel that Payne and I have a very equal sense of power. It doesn't bother me that in bed, and sexually, we push the boundaries of power. In day-to-day decision making we can get very indecisive together. "What do you want to do?" "I don't know, what do you want to do?" We were doing that about going dancing last night. It was like, "I don't know. I could be convinced." "Well, do you want to go or not?" Payne is very easygoing, but up to a point.

Payne

My history about decision making is that I go with the flow. As I look back on my past and try to define what my issues are, I see that I always had a difficulty setting my boundaries. I'd often let other people make the decisions and I'd go with the flow, and then I'd resent it. [Laughs] That's not always the case with Stanley and me.

It's rare that you mesh with someone on a social level as well as on a sexual level. I had an ideal in my mind for the kind of relationship that I wanted when I was younger and for some reason that hasn't shifted as I've grown older. I'm still attracted to guys in their twenties. I get all kinds of grief about that, even in the gay world. When I became sexually aware, those were the guys that I liked and it never changed. Once in a while I see a guy in his thirties that I find attractive, but I'm rarely attracted to guys in their forties. I don't necessarily view that as healthy in myself. I just have to live with it.

Stanley

I got grief for the age difference at the beginning too. I got shocked sorts of reactions. I could tell that people thought that it wasn't going to work or that it wasn't good. I've dated guys who were younger than me or my age or older. I definitely have a leaning toward older men, though. I think it's a kind of hard wiring. I think there's something in your brain that makes you attracted to certain types of people. There's something very instinctual, kind of gut and visceral about older men for me. I wasn't abused by an older guy when I was a kid or anything. I think it's the kind of biological hard wiring and that's why certain people have certain fetishes. I'm sure there's a small part that's social or environmental, but for me I think it's overwhelmingly biological.

Similarly, my desire innately centers around being a bottom. I'm very in tune with other people's feelings so if someone wants me to top them I can do it. I can go outside of it, depending on the circumstances, but I always come back to being a bottom. Being a bottom is a kind of hard-wired biological thing for me too, although it could be a lot of things I'm not aware of. It could be the fact that when I was small, all my friends were girls. That's who I identified with. Girls are socialized in certain ways to play certain roles and do certain things. If the fact that I was around so many girls plays into my being gay or being a bottom, I'm okay with that—but I feel like I'd have some sort of awareness of it if that were the case. I don't connect that with my sexual experience.

I feel it's natural for men to be intimate with each other. That includes anal sex. We're sexual beings and that's a way for us to be connected physically. It's part of exploring each other's bodies.

Payne

I'm not sure I want to put those kinds of values on sex: whether anal sex is natural or not. There's clearly no scientific evidence that any harm is being done. Whether it's natural or unnatural seems irrelevant. To me, nothing can feel more natural. The sex Stanley and I have is mostly anal sex and it's great. There's a sense of intimacy I feel with anal sex that I don't feel with any other kind of sex. I believe it has to do with the amount of trust it takes to be in that way with someone. It's hard to articulate this, but it feels like when I'm having anal sex is the closest that I ever get with someone. Something about oral sex feels almost like someone is doing *to you* or you're doing it *to them,* you're not really doing it together. Anal sex is much more pleasurable.

There are certain things that lead me in certain directions that I may not want to explore initially, but eventually I end up there and I have to accept that about myself. It's just another form of coming out. In the early stages, I may have felt guilt about anal sex and thought it was the wrong thing to do—but I've long since forgotten about that. I've dismissed that construct as incorrect. There are all kinds of things like that that I still feel influenced by.

I view relationships as a sort of sexual exploration you go on with someone. Where you end up is always a mystery and a surprise. I think it's easier with anal sex to get into exploring some of the darker sides of desire. I'm not particularly into S&M; that whole movement doesn't have a huge fascination for me. But there are times when things have gotten rough between us and it's been fun. Something you would characterize as aggressive.

Stanley

[Delightedly] Yeah! *Very* aggressive. Sometimes, we've played around with the belt. Tied up my hands. It's always Payne who gets more aggressive. I've never gotten into that role. I've been a top, but not aggressive like that and I haven't been aggressive as a bottom. I've been vocal about what I wanted to be done to me, but not aggressive like Payne has.

We complement each other really well in terms of what our desires are. At the beginning Payne was worried about getting involved with another young thing. [They both laugh.] He's been involved with other young men in tumultuous and difficult situations. I was the one who pushed for monogamy and he was reluctant at first.

Payne

I'm fine with it now. In the beginning I was a lot less willing to commit to the relationship because it was too early. It wasn't about having sex with anybody else. It wasn't about that.

Stanley

I said, "How are we going to figure this thing out if we're not really doing it all the way? I can't invest in it otherwise." We talked about it a lot. Payne's very serious about the relationships he goes into. He wanted to make sure this was really something that was going to work before he made that kind of commitment.

I think what's good about our relationship is that he's pretty much a top and I'm pretty much a bottom. I see in the work that I do in the public health field that there's this pressure to be versatile because it's thought to be more healthy. There's a notion out there that if you're versatile you're more balanced and the power dynamic is more normal. There's a whole range of ways for people to exist. There are tops and bottoms and everything in between. They're all fine. The important thing is to do some exploring around your desire. Why you like a certain thing. What you get out of it. How that relates to the people you're with. People may view my relationship as being unbalanced, but it's not.